SIGNATURES

Rare Finds

Senior Authors

Roger C. Farr

Dorothy S. Strickland

Authors

Richard F. Abrahamson ◆ Alma Flor Ada ◆ Barbara Bowen Coulter

Bernice E. Cullinan ◆ Margaret A. Gallego

W. Dorsey Hammond

Nancy Roser ◆ Junko Yokota ◆ Hallie Kay Yopp

Senior Consultant

Asa G. Hillard III

Consultants

V. Kanani Choy ◆ Lee Bennett Hopkins ◆ Stephen Krashen ◆ Rosalia Salinas

Harcourt Brace & Company

Orlando Atlanta Austin Boston San Francisco Chicago Dallas New York Toronto London

Requests for permission to make copies of any part of the work should be mailed to: Permissions Department, Harcourt Brace & Company, 6277 Sea Harbor Drive, Orlando, Florida 32887-6777.

HARCOURT BRACE and Quill Design is a registered trademark of Harcourt Brace & Company.

Acknowledgments appear in the back of this work.

Printed in the United States of America

ISBN 0-15-306403-X

6 7 8 9 10   048   99 98

Dear Reader,

Have you ever had the experience of finding something rare? You may not have dug up buried treasure or come face to face with a cheetah. However, you may have discovered a beautiful wildflower, met a special person, or found an important message in a book. If so, you know that while you may search for things like these, often you come upon them unexpectedly.

In **Rare Finds**, you will meet many people who have made rare finds. You will share the experiences of a young girl from El Salvador as she finds a loving home and learns to communicate. You will find out how some African American inventors made valuable discoveries and how the young Chinese artist Wang Yani puts her discoveries about the world into her paintings. As you read **Rare Finds**, you may also make some rare finds of your own. You may find a character you can relate to and learn from, or some information that starts you on a process of discovery. Along the way, you may discover something important about yourself.

So look closely, and find something that is special to you! We hope you enjoy this book as much as we do.

Sincerely,

The Authors   The Authors

Guiding

Your Way

Contents

Contents

WORKING IT OUT

NATURAL CHANGES

CONTENTS

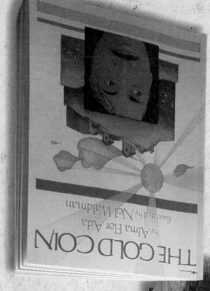

THE GOLD COIN
by Alma Flor Ada
illustrated by Neil Waldman

BY THE GREAT
HORN SPOON!
SID FLEISCHMAN

THE CALIFORNIA
GOLD RUSH

Blue Willow
DORIS GATES

Little House
on the Prairie
LAURA INGALLS WILDER

PIONEERS

A LIBRARY OF CONGRESS BOOK

MARTIN W. SANDLER

IN SEARCH OF A DREAM

Contents

EXTRAORDINARY
BLACK AMERICANS
FROM COLONIAL TO CONTEMPORARY TIMES

BE KIND
TO YOUR
MOTHER
(EARTH)
and
BLAME IT ON
THE WOLF
Two Original Plays
by Douglas Love

A RIVER
RAN WILD
Lynne Cherry

THE BIG BOOK FOR OUR
PLANET

The Almond Orchard
Laura Jane Coats

MAKING PROGRESS

CONTENTS

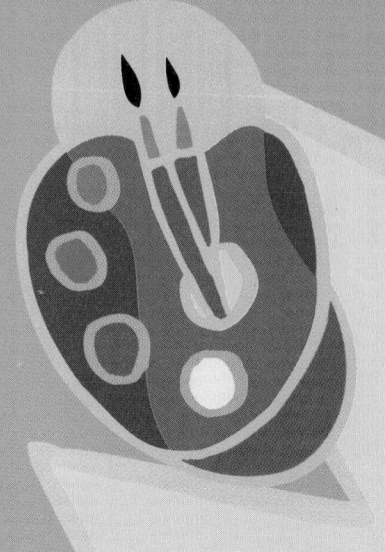

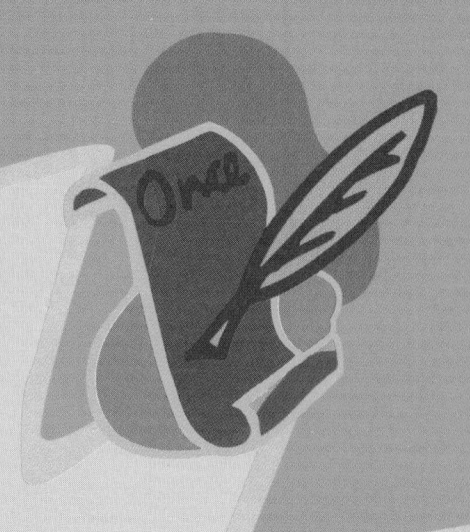

GARY SOTO

THE SKIRT

illustrated by Eric Velasquez

ALVIN AILEY
Andrea Davis Pinkney
illustrated by
Brian Pinkney

The
NIGHTINGALE

A
Young
Painter

PUEBLO STORYTELLER

BY DIANE HOYT-GOLDSMITH
PHOTOGRAPHS BY LAWRENCE MIGDALE

GREAT INSPIRATIONS

Contents

Guiding Your Way

Has anyone ever helped
you learn something
important about yourself?
Some of the characters
in the selections in this
theme are helped by the
guidance of others.
Other characters learn from
their own experiences.

CONTENTS

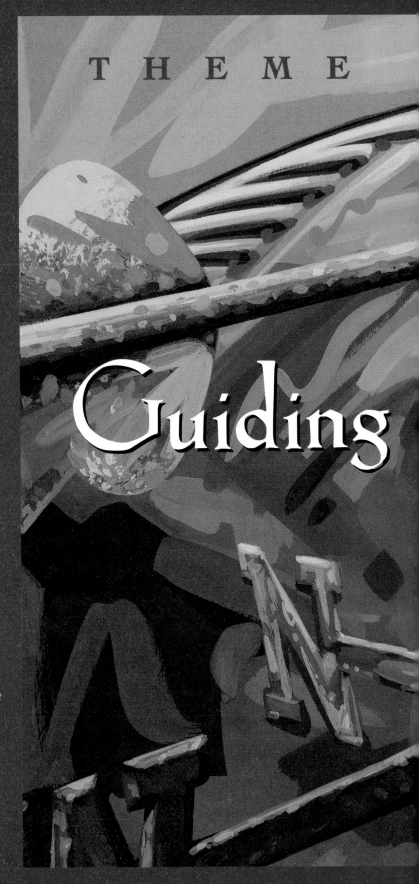

THEME

Guiding

Your Way

Bookshelf

The Canada Geese Quilt
by Natalie Kinsey-Warnock
illustrated by Leslie W. Bowman

A special gift from her grand-mother helps Ariel adjust to the changes all around her.

ALA Notable Book,
Notable Book in the Field of Social Studies
Signatures Library

Stealing Home
by Mary Stolz

When Great-Aunt Linzy comes for a visit, Thomas and Grand-father find their lives changed.

Children's Choice
Signatures Library

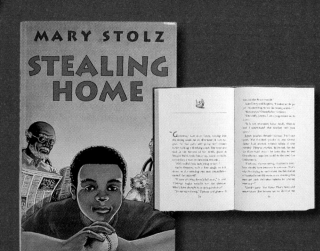

The King's Equal
by Katherine Paterson
illustrated by Vladimir Vagin

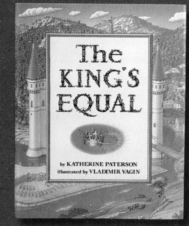

Prince Raphael learns a lesson in self-discovery as he sets out to meet a royal challenge.

Award-Winning Author

Finding the Green Stone
by Alice Walker
illustrated by
Catherine Deeter

A young boy's family and community help him find his lost treasure.

Award-Winning Author

The Woman Who Outshone the Sun
by Alejandro Cruz Martinez
illustrated by Fernando Olivera

A village is struck by the beauty within Lucia, which shines as brightly as her hair.

ALA Notable Book

Mandy

By Roberta Karim
Illustrated by Karen Ritz

Morning wind tickles my ear.
My eyes blink open.
Down in the cornfield, crows caw
    and caw.
I sing along:
    Today's the day
    Yahoo Hooray
    Mandy Sue Day today!

Harvesting's hard work here
    on Amos Acres.
A mama and a papa and
five brothers and sisters
all bringing in the bounty.
Combines and calluses.
Pressing cider and
putting up pumpkins.

But I remember Papa's promise:
"A week's worth of Indian
summer is dropping by!" he said.
"One day off to each of you
children for good behavior."
And today is MY day!

Sue Day

Mandy Sue Day

By Roberta Karim   Illustrated by Karen Ritz

Bacon for breakfast
and no schoolin' after lunch.
Yahoo Hooray for Mandy Sue Day!

"Will Ben take good care of you?"
asks Papa.
"Best friends always do,"
says Mama. *"Shoo!"*

I'm out the screen door. *Slam.*
Squeak goes the third step.
I canter to the barn,
fingers ticking off the fence posts.
Twenty-four to the old barn door.

Ben whinnies low. I whinny back.
Nineteen steps, or eight bunny hops,
to Ben's Dutch door.
Today I hop.
Impatient, Ben snuffs my hand.
He noses up my arm, my neck,
blows windily in my ear.
"No carrot there, Ben.
You lose.
Today it's hiding in my boot."

Ben grumbles with delight.
I squeeze the fat carrot top.
Strong teeth tug the bottom.
Closer and closer
comes the chomping.
At the last second, I make a palm.
Ben gulps down the carrot top.

For dessert,
he polishes my hand
with his tongue.
"What do I look like?" I ask him.
"A salt block?"

Halter click-clacking.
Ben's deep in his bucket.
Slurp of water. Slurp of air.
"Time for a refill, Ben?"

My fingers brush along rough wood,
out to the smooth pump handle.
Water gurgles up from the earth,
whooshes down to the bucket.
Metal handle digs deep in my hand.

On Tuesday, Mama taught us
centrifugal force.
Will it hold true on Wednesday?
I start to spin.

Soon the pail is flying sideways,
but not a drop of water spills.
Must be mashed to the sides,
like Little Jeremy and me
on the fair's Whirly-Gig.

Ben snorts a "where-have-you-been?"
"Here's your water, Carrot Breath."
Noisy gulps slow to splashes
and I know he's playing in his water.
"Sillier than Baby May
in the kitchen sink,"
I tell him.

"Grooming time, Ben. Curry first."
Round rows of metal teeth
circle and circle his coat,
    stirring up loose hairs,
    rubbing his tummy.
"You're one big dust cloud," I scold.
His withers twitch.

"Stiff brush, Ben.
Hold on to your skin."
Two hands for one brush,
and the hairs and dust fly.
AH-CHOO.

Soft brush last, silky coat.

Now the knotted mane.
I sigh like Mama.
"Been chewing gum
in your sleep again, Benjamin?"

Triple-knotted tail.
"You've tangled with every fly
in the county, Ben Boy."

Hoof pick's in my hand,
so Ben plants his foot.
I shove him off balance,
clean stones from the Vs.

Smooth out the wrinkles on the
Navajo blanket.
Fly the heavy saddle up and over,
stirrups swinging like a runaway.

Ben puffs up his belly,
all stubborn against the cinch,
but he's no match
for a bony kneecap.
I serve up his bridle
with a cube of sugar.
He falls for it, as usual.

Ben jangles his hardware
and paws the dirt.
"Hold your horses, Crazy One.
Let me get on."
At the stone wall
    I feel for footing,
    feel for a stirrup,
    fling myself up.

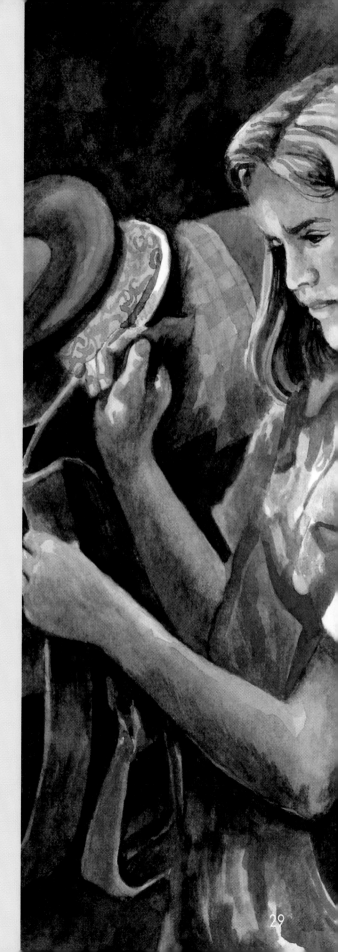

Out in the lane,
hooves clip-clopping,
crunching leaves.
I jump
as something brushes my cheek.
What was that?
　　I reach out—
　　it's raining leaves!

Slide into cool.
We're in the woods.
I hug Ben's neck.
No twigs stinging *my* face, no sirree.
I pat his shoulder,
hard muscles working
under soft skin.
He jumps.
"Rabbit cross your path, Ben?"

Burst into warm.
We're out of the woods.
Ben stops.
I stand in my stirrups
to touch his ears.
They're pricked forward,
listening to the meadow beyond.
"I love you, Ben."
His ears flick back to catch my voice.

One nudge and
we're off in a bouncy trot.
He gathers steam,
breaks into a rocking-horse canter
that takes my breath away.
I bend low.
My knees grip hard.
He hits a gallop, and I'm a Sioux,
racing across the plains.
We're one with the wind.
I'm one with him
or I'd fall to the herd
of trampling buffalo.

Whiffs of wood smoke
and Concord grapes.
We're almost home.
Ben slows to a walk.
Clatter clatter up the stone path.
"I smell donuts!"
Ben's already busy
untying my half hitch.
He *does* love a kettle-fried donut.
Mama brings out cider for me.
Melted apples slidin' down slow.
"Need any help, Mama?"
"No child, you frolic.
This is Mandy Sue Day all day,
remember?"

I land on Ben.
"Drive me to the barn, taxi."
He pulls up at the trough
to wash down his donut.

Off with the bridle.
Off with the saddle
and Navajo blanket.
Pick off the burrs.
"Post time, Ben."
Barn door bangs open and he's off,
pounding the path.
I straddle the top rail and wait.
Soon he's back to nuzzle my knee.
I slide on.
He wanders and I weave my fingers
through his mane.
He bends to graze
and I lie back on his rump.
The wind blows full of wild roses and
warm horse.

BONG BONG BONG.
The dinner bell calls
all hands from the fields.
One scoop of oats,
one scoop of sweet feed,
half bale of hay.
Evening water weighs way too much
to measure centrifugal force.
"Gate's open," calls my brother.

"You've outdone yourself, Ma,"
say my brothers.
Food swirls by.
Fried chicken, mashed potatoes,
biscuits and gravy,
tomato-and-cuke salad,
sweet corn by the bushel.
"And for dessert?" they hint.
"Peach pie with a candle," she says.
They sing in three keys:
"Happy Mandy Sue Day to you."
"Mama and Papa," I say,
"since it's still my day,
could I sleep in the loft tonight?"

"Well." I hear their smiles meet.
"Ben will take care of her," says Papa.
"That's what best friends are for,"
says Mama.

Soon she says, her voice muffled,
"Here's your pillow, sheets, and quilt.
Let's carry these out to the basket, Pa."
His chair scrapes back.

Mama, Papa, and I
step through the crisp evening.
The screen door bangs.
Papa turns.

"Whatcha got there, Little Jeremy?"
"Flashlight for Mandy Sue."
"Oh." Papa's voice smiles.
I answer, "I don't need one, Little J.
    Remember?
    I can't see."

"Oh." Jeremy's voice thinks.
"Well, how about a peppermint stick?"
"Thanks, Jeremy."
"Sweet dreams, Mandy Sue."

Papa's arm around me,
no need to count fence posts.

Hand over hand,
I climb the loft ladder.
Hand over hand,
I draw up the basket of bedding.

Soon, snug in the straw,
my hand burrows
down to the floorboard crack.
"I love you, Ben," I call down.
"Sweet dreams."

And in the darkness,
I can see his ears flick
to catch my voice.

ABOUT THE AUTHOR

Roberta Karim

Roberta Karim's beautiful memories from childhood became the inspiration for this book. When she was six years old, she won her very own pony in a contest. She soon found out that having a pony was a lot of hard work. She had to clean out the stable every Saturday while her friends were free to go outside and play.

However, the work was worth it. When she wasn't working on her homework, she spent every moment with her pony. She rode it, brushed it, and even took naps on it.

When Karim became an adult, she studied writing at Ohio Wesleyan and Purdue universities. Later, thinking about her memories of the time she spent with her pony, she realized that they were more than just pictures in her mind. She could remember sounds, smells, feelings, and even special tastes. She turned her memories into words by writing about them.

Today Roberta Karim lives in Bay Village, Ohio, with her husband and two sons.

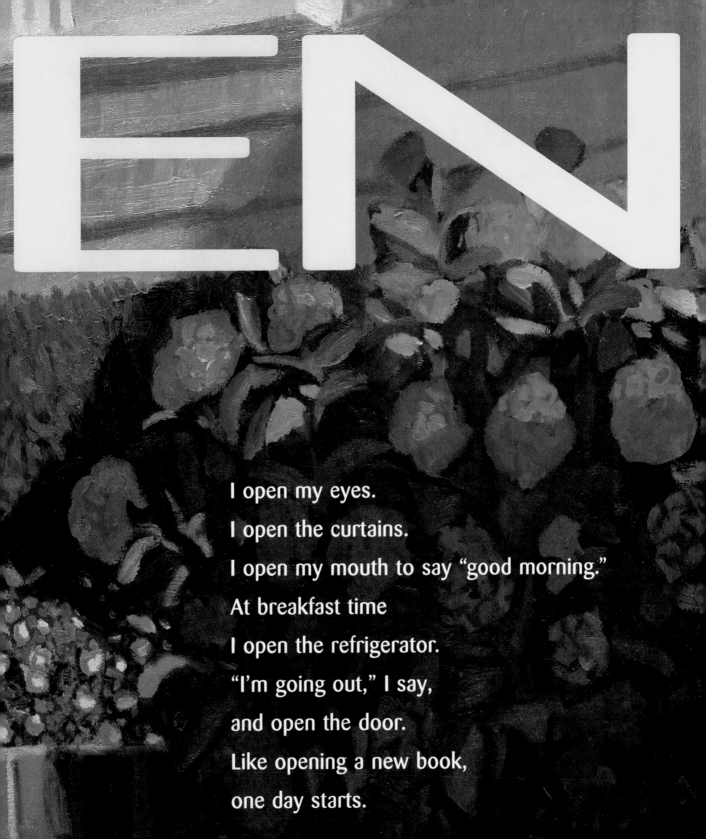

EN

I open my eyes.

I open the curtains.

I open my mouth to say "good morning."

At breakfast time

I open the refrigerator.

"I'm going out," I say,

and open the door.

Like opening a new book,

one day starts.

Chikaoka Saori, fourth grade

41

Response Corner

WRITE A SONG

Something to Sing About

A day like Mandy Sue Day is something to sing about! Write a song that tells how the story made you feel. Brainstorm some favorite tunes. Reread the poem "Open" for ideas. Then compose words for your song based on your feelings about "Mandy Sue Day." You may want to describe some of the things Mandy Sue did in the story or tell how it must feel to have a day off all for yourself.

PERFORM A SCENE

Mandy Sue Play

Work with a small group to write a short scene for a play based on "Mandy Sue Day." Use sound effects and small props where possible. Practice your parts. Then perform your scene for the class.

A Touching Story

Much of Mandy Sue's world comes to her through her sense of touch. Make a collage about Mandy Sue or about the things she does on her special day. First, cut out magazine pictures that remind you of "Mandy Sue Day." Combine these with scraps of materials that feel interesting. Then arrange and glue these materials on posterboard, and let them dry completely. Ask classmates to feel as well as view the collage to guess what you are trying to communicate.

What Do You Think?

- What things does Mandy Sue do that show she is independent?
- Were you surprised at the end of the story? Explain your response.
- How do you think the child in "Open" is feeling? How is this like the way Mandy Sue feels?

JUSTIN AND THE BEST BISCUITS IN THE WORLD

BY MILDRED PITTS WALTER

ILLUSTRATED BY BYRON GIN

Justin lives in the city with his mother and his sisters, Evelyn and Hadiya. After hearing many complaints about the way he does household chores, Justin becomes convinced he can't do anything right, at least not the things his friend Anthony calls "women's work." In fact, while his grandfather is visiting, Justin gets so upset that he starts to cry. When Grandpa invites him to come spend some time on his ranch, Justin is eager to go.

Grandpa's house sat about a mile in from the road. Between that road and the house lay a large meadow with a small stream. Everything seemed in order when Justin and Grandpa arrived.

Justin got out and opened the gate to the winding road that led toward the house. The meadow below shimmered in waves of tall green grass. The horses grazed calmly there. Justin was so excited to see them again that he waved his grandpa on. "I'll walk up, Grandpa." He ran down into the meadow.

Pink prairie roses blossomed near the fence. Goldenrod, sweet William, and black-eyed Susans added color here and there. Justin waded through the lush green grass.

The horses, drinking at the stream, paid no attention as he raced across the meadow toward them. *Cropper looks so old,* he thought as he came closer. But Black Lightning's coat shone, as beautiful as ever. Justin gave a familiar whistle. The horses lifted their heads and their ears went back, but only Black moved toward him on the run.

Justin reached up and Black lowered his head. Justin rubbed him behind the ear. Softly he said, "Good boy, Black. I've missed you. You glad to see me?"

Then Pal nosed in, wanting to be petted, too. Cropper didn't bother. Justin wondered if Cropper's eyesight was fading.

The sun had moved well toward the west. Long shadows from the rolling hills reached across the plains. "Want to take me home, boy?" Justin asked Black.

Black lowered his head and pawed with one foot as he shook his mane. Justin led him to a large rock. From

the rock, Justin straddled Black's back, without a saddle. Black walked him home.

Grandpa's house stood on a hill surrounded by plains, near the rolling hills. Over many years, trees standing close by the house had grown tall and strong. The house, more than a hundred years old, was made of logs. The sun and rain had turned the logs on the outside an iron gray. Flecks of green showed in some of the logs.

When Justin went inside, Grandpa had already changed his clothes. Now he busily measured food for the animals. While Grandpa was away, a neighbor had come to feed the pigs and chickens. The horses took care of themselves, eating and drinking in the meadow. Today the horses would have some oats, too.

"Let's feed the animals first," Grandpa said. "Then we'll cook those fish for dinner. You can clean them when we get back."

Justin sighed deeply. How could he tell Grandpa he didn't know how to clean fish? He was sure to make a mess of it. Worriedly, he helped Grandpa load the truck with the food and water for the chickens and pigs. They put in oats for the horses, too. Then they drove to the chicken yard.

As they rode along the dusty road, Justin remembered Grandpa telling him that long, long ago they had raised hundreds of cattle on Q–T Ranch. Then when Justin's mama was a little girl, they had raised only chickens on the ranch, selling many eggs to people in the cities. Now Grandpa had only a few chickens, three pigs, and three horses.

At the chicken yard, chickens rushed around to get the bright yellow corn that Justin threw to them. They fell over each other, fluttering and clucking. While Justin fed them, Grandpa gathered the eggs.

The pigs lazily dozed in their pens. They had been wallowing in the mud pond nearby. Now cakes of dried mud dotted their bodies. The floor where they slept had mud on it, too. Many flies buzzed around. *My room surely doesn't look like this,* Justin thought.

The pigs ran to the trough when Grandpa came with the pail of grain mixed with water. They grunted and snorted. The smallest one squealed with delight. *He's cute,* Justin thought.

By the time they had fed the horses oats and returned home, it was dark and cooler. Justin was glad it was so late. Maybe now Grandpa would clean the fish so that they could eat sooner. He was hungry.

Grandpa had not changed the plan. He gave Justin some old newspapers, a small sharp knife, and a bowl with clean water.

"Now," he said, handing Justin the pail that held the fish, "you can clean these."

Justin looked at the slimy fish in the water. How could he tell his grandpa that he didn't want to touch

those fish? He still didn't want Grandpa to know that he had never cleaned fish before. Evelyn's words crowded him: *Can't do anything right.* He dropped his shoulders and sighed. "Do I have to, Grandpa?"

"We have to eat, don't we?"

"But—but I don't know how," Justin cried.

"Oh, it's not hard. I'll show you." Grandpa placed a fish on the newspaper. "Be careful now and keep it on this paper. When you're all done, just fold the paper and all the mess is inside."

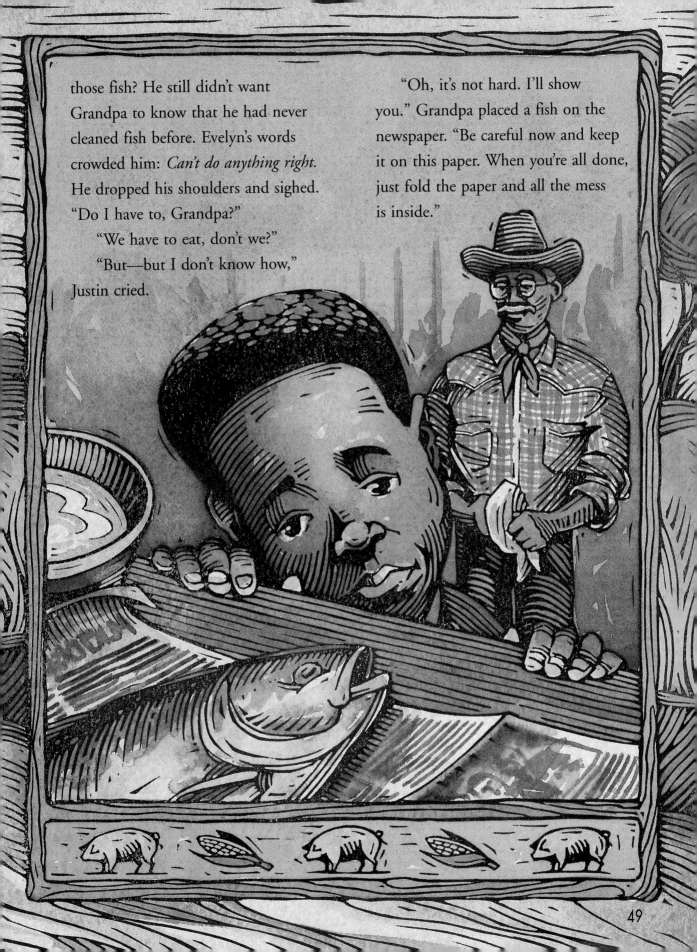

Justin watched Grandpa scrape the fish upward from the tail toward the head. Little shiny scales came off easily. Then he cut the fish's belly upward from a little vent hole and scraped all the stuff inside onto the paper. "Now see how easy that is. You try," Grandpa said. "Be very careful with the knife." He watched Justin to see if he knew what to do.

Justin scraped the tiny scales off confidently. Then he hesitated. Screwing up his face, he shuddered as he cut, then pulled the insides out. Finally he got the knack of it.

Grandpa, satisfied that Justin would do fine, went into the kitchen to make a fire in the big stove.

Later that evening, Justin felt proud when Grandpa let him put the fish on the table.

After dinner, they sat in the living room near the huge fireplace. Great-Great-Grandma Ward had used that same fireplace to cook her family's meals.

Justin looked at the fireplace, trying to imagine how it must have been then. *How did people cook without a stove?* He knew Grandpa's stove was nothing like his mama's. Once that big iron stove got hot there was no way to turn it off or to low or to simmer. You just set the pots in a cooler place on the back of Grandpa's stove.

"Grandpa, how did your grandma cook bread in this fireplace?" he asked.

"Cooking bread in this fireplace was easy for my grandma. She once had to bake her bread on a hoe."

"But a hoe is for making a garden, Grandpa."

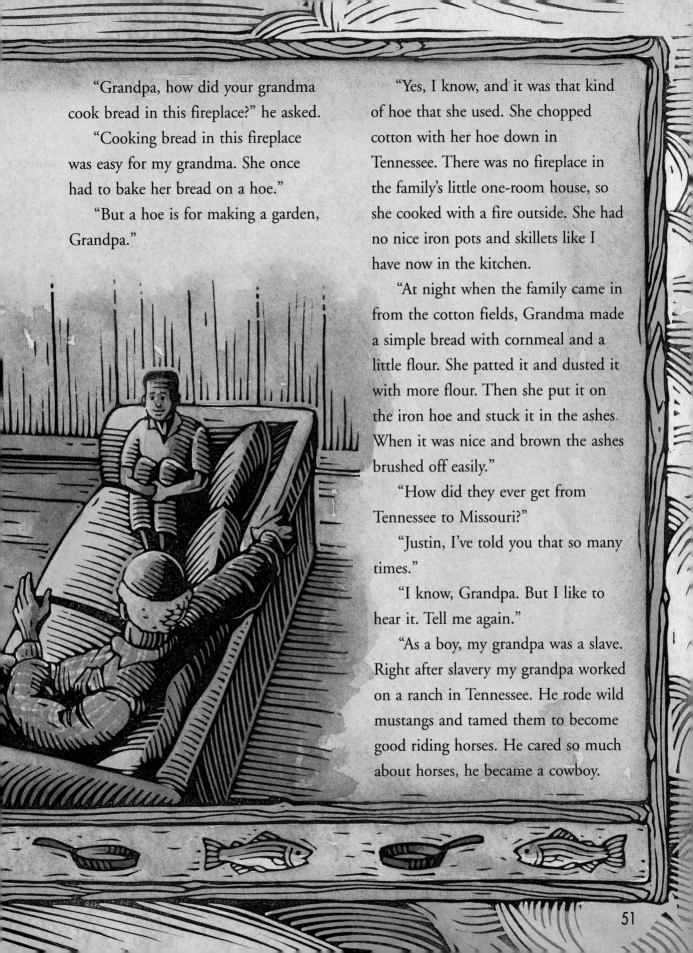

"Yes, I know, and it was that kind of hoe that she used. She chopped cotton with her hoe down in Tennessee. There was no fireplace in the family's little one-room house, so she cooked with a fire outside. She had no nice iron pots and skillets like I have now in the kitchen.

"At night when the family came in from the cotton fields, Grandma made a simple bread with cornmeal and a little flour. She patted it and dusted it with more flour. Then she put it on the iron hoe and stuck it in the ashes. When it was nice and brown the ashes brushed off easily."

"How did they ever get from Tennessee to Missouri?"

"Justin, I've told you that so many times."

"I know, Grandpa. But I like to hear it. Tell me again."

"As a boy, my grandpa was a slave. Right after slavery my grandpa worked on a ranch in Tennessee. He rode wild mustangs and tamed them to become good riding horses. He cared so much about horses, he became a cowboy.

"He got married and had a family. Still he left home for many weeks, sometimes months, driving thousands of cattle over long trails. Then he heard about the government giving away land in the West through the Homestead Act. You only had to build a house and live in it to keep the land."

"So my great-great-grandpa built this house." Justin stretched out on the floor. He looked around at the walls that were now dark brown from many years of smoke from the fireplace.

"Just the room we're in now," Grandpa said. "I guess every generation of Wards has added something. Now, my daddy, Phillip, added on the kitchen and the room right next to this one that is the dining room.

"I built the bathroom and the rooms upstairs. Once we had a high loft. I guess you'd call it an attic. I made that into those rooms upstairs. So you see, over the years this house has grown and grown. Maybe when you're a man, you'll bring your family here," Grandpa said.

"I don't know. Maybe. But I'd have to have an electric kitchen."

"As I had to have a bathroom with a shower. Guess that's progress," Grandpa said, and laughed.

"Go on, Grandpa. Tell me what it was like when Great-Great-Grandpa first came to Missouri."

"I think it's time for us to go to bed."

"It's not that late," Justin protested.

"For me it is. We'll have to get up early. I'll have to ride fence tomorrow. You know, in winter Q–T Ranch becomes a feeder ranch for other people's cattle. In spring, summer, and early fall cattle roam and graze in the high country. In winter when the heavy frosts come and it's bitter cold, they return to the plains. Many of those cattle feed at Q–T. I have to have my fences mended before fall so the cattle can't get out."

"Can I ride fence with you?" Justin asked.

"Sure you can. Maybe you'll like riding fence. That's a man's work." Grandpa laughed.

Justin remembered that conversation in his room about women's work, and the tears. He burned with shame. He didn't laugh.

Upstairs, Grandpa gave Justin sheets and a blanket for his bed. "It'll be cool before morning," he told Justin. "You'll need this blanket. Can you make your bed?"

Justin frowned. He hated making his bed. But he looked at Grandpa and said, "I'm no baby." Justin joined Grandpa in laughter.

Grandpa went to his room. When he was all ready for bed, he came and found Justin still struggling to make his bed. Those sheets had to be made nice and smooth to impress Grandpa, Justin thought, but it wasn't easy.

Grandpa watched. "Want to see how a man makes a bed?" Grandpa asked.

Justin didn't answer. Grandpa waited. Finally, Justin, giving up, said, "Well, all right."

"Let's do it together," Grandpa said. "You on the other side."

Grandpa helped him smooth the bottom sheet and tuck it under the mattress at the head and foot of the bed. Then he put on the top sheet and blanket and smoothed them carefully.

"Now, let's tuck those under the mattress only at the foot of the bed," he said.

"That's really neat, Grandpa," Justin said, impressed.

"That's not it, yet. We want it to stay neat, don't we? Now watch."

Grandpa carefully folded the covers in equal triangles and tucked them so that they made a neat corner at the end of the mattress. "Now do your side exactly the way I did mine."

Soon Justin was in bed. When Grandpa tucked him in, he asked, "How does it feel?"

Justin flexed his toes and ankles. "Nice. Snug."

"Like a bug in a rug?"

Justin laughed. Then Grandpa said, "That's how a *man* makes a bed."

Still laughing, Justin asked, "Who taught *you* how to make a bed? Your grandpa?"

"No. My grandma." Grandpa grinned and winked at Justin. "Good night."

Justin lay listening to the winds whispering in the trees. Out of his window in the darkness he saw lightning bugs flashing, heard crickets chirping. But before the first hoot of an owl, he was fast asleep.

The smell of coffee and home-smoked ham woke Justin. His grandpa was already up and downstairs cooking breakfast. Justin jumped out of bed and quickly put on his clothes.

Grandpa had hot pancakes, apple jelly, and ham all ready for the table. Justin ate two stacks of pancakes with two helpings of everything else.

After breakfast, Grandpa cleared the table, preparing to wash the dishes. "Would you rather wash or dry?" he asked Justin.

"Neither," Justin replied, quickly thinking how little success he had with dishes.

Grandpa said nothing as he removed the dishes from the table. He took his time, carefully measuring liquid soap and letting hot water run in the sink. Then he washed each dish and rinsed it with care, too. No water splashed or spilled. Soapsuds were not all over. How easy it looked, the way Grandpa did it.

After washing the dishes, Grandpa swept the floor and then went upstairs.

Justin stood around downstairs. He had a strange feeling of guilt and wished he had helped with the dishes. He heard Grandpa moving about, above in his room. Justin thought of going outside, down into the meadow, but he decided to see what was going on upstairs.

When he saw his grandpa busy making his own big bed, Justin went into his room. His unmade bed and his pajamas on the floor bothered him. But he decided that the room didn't look too bad. He picked up his pajamas and placed them on the bed and sat beside them. He waited.

Finally Grandpa came in and said, "Are you riding fence with me today?"

"Oh yes!"

"Fine. But why don't you make your bed? You'll probably feel pretty tired tonight. A well-made bed can be a warm welcome."

Justin moved slowly, reluctant to let Grandpa see him struggle with the bed. He started. What a surprise! Everything was tightly in place. He only had to smooth the covers. The

bed was made. No lumps and bumps. Justin looked at Grandpa and grinned broadly. "That was easy!" he shouted.

"Don't you think you should unpack your clothes? They won't need ironing if you hang them up. You gotta look razor sharp for the festival." He gave Justin some clothes hangers.

"Are we *really* going to the festival every day?" Justin asked.

"You bet, starting with the judging early tomorrow and the dance tomorrow night." Grandpa winked at him.

Justin's excitement faded when he started unpacking his rumpled shirts. "They sure are wrinkled, Grandpa," he said.

"Maybe that's because they weren't folded."

"I can't ever get them folded right," Justin cried.

"Well, let's see. Turn it so the buttons face down." Grandpa showed Justin how to bring the sleeves to the back, turning in the sides so that the sleeves were on top. Then he folded the tail of the shirt over the cuffs, and made a second fold up to the collar.

"Now you try it."

Justin tried it. "Oh, I see. That was easy, Grandpa." Justin smiled, pleased with himself.

"Everything's easy when you know how."

Justin, happy with his new-found skill, hurriedly placed his clothes on the hangers. He hoped the wrinkles would disappear in time for the festival.

"Now you'll look sharp," Grandpa said.

Justin felt a surge of love for his grandpa. He would always remember how to make a bed snug as a bug and fold clothes neatly. He grabbed Grandpa's hand. They walked downstairs, still holding hands, to get ready to ride fence.

Riding fence meant inspecting the fence all around the ranch to see where it needed mending. Riding fence took a great deal of a rancher's time. Justin and Grandpa planned to spend most of the day out on the plains. Grandpa said he'd pack a lunch for them to eat on the far side of the ranch.

Justin was surprised when Grandpa packed only flour, raisins, shortening, and chunks of smoked pork. Grandpa also packed jugs of water and makings for coffee.

The horses stood in the meadow as if they knew a busy day awaited them. While Grandpa saddled Pal, he let Justin finish the saddling of Black

Lightning. Justin tightened the cinches on Black, feeling the strong pull on his arm muscles. With their supplies in their saddlebags, they mounted Pal and Black, leaving Cropper behind to graze in the meadow.

The early sun shone fiery red on the hilltops while the foothills were cast in shades of purple. The dew still lingered heavily on the morning. They let their horses canter away past the house through the tall green grass. But on the outer edge of the ranch where the fence started, they walked the horses at a steady pace.

The fence had three rows of taut wire. "That's a pretty high fence," Justin said.

"We have to keep the cattle in. But deer sometimes leap that fence and eat hay with the cattle." When it got bitter cold and frosty, Grandpa rode around the ranch dropping bales of hay for the cattle. It took a lot of hay to feed the cattle during the winter months.

"I didn't think a cow could jump very high," Justin said.

"Aw, come on. Surely you know that a cow jumped over the moon." Grandpa had a serious look on his face.

"I guess that's a joke, eh?" Justin laughed.

Justin noticed that Grandpa had a map. When they came to a place in the fence that looked weak, Grandpa marked it on his map. Later, helpers who came to do the work would know exactly where to mend. That saved time.

Now the sun heated up the morning. The foothills were now varying shades of green. Shadows dotted the plains. Among the blackish green trees on the rolling hills, fog still lingered like lazy clouds. Insects buzzed. A small cloud of mosquitoes swarmed just behind their heads, and beautiful cardinals splashed their redness on the morning air. Justin felt a surge of happiness and hugged Black with his knees and heels.

Suddenly he saw a doe standing close to the fence. "Look, Grandpa!" he said. She seemed alarmed but did not run away. Doe eyes usually look peaceful and sad, Justin remembered. Hers widened with fear. Then Justin saw a fawn caught in the wire of the fence.

Quickly they got off their horses. They hitched them to a post and moved cautiously toward the fawn.

The mother rushed to the fence but stopped just short of the sharp wire. "Stay back and still," Grandpa said to Justin. "She doesn't know we will help her baby. She thinks we might hurt it. She wants to protect it."

The mother pranced restlessly. She pawed the ground, moving as close to the fence as she could. Near the post the fence had been broken. The wire curled there dangerously. The fawn's head, caught in the wire, bled close to an ear. Whenever it pulled its head the wire cut deeper.

Grandpa quickly untangled the fawn's head.

Blood flowed from the cut.

"Oh, Grandpa, it will die," Justin said sadly.

"No, no," Grandpa assured Justin. "Lucky we got here when we did. It hasn't been caught long."

The fawn moved toward the doe. The mother, as if giving her baby a signal, bounded off. The baby trotted behind.

As they mounted their horses, Justin suddenly felt weak in the stomach. Remembering the blood, he trembled. Black, too, seemed uneasy. He moved his nostrils nervously and strained against the bit. He arched his neck and sidestepped quickly. Justin pulled the reins. "Whoa, boy!"

"Let him run," Grandpa said.

Justin kicked Black's sides and off they raced across the plain. They ran and ran, Justin pretending he was rounding up cattle. Then Black turned and raced back toward Grandpa and Pal.

"Whoa, boy," Justin commanded. Justin felt better and Black seemed calm, ready now to go on riding fence.

The sun beamed down and sweat rolled off Justin as he rode on with Grandpa, looking for broken wires in the fence. They were well away from the house, on the far side of the ranch. Flies buzzed around the horses and now gnats swarmed in clouds just above their heads. The prairie resounded with songs of the bluebirds, the bobwhite quails, and the mockingbirds mimicking them all. The cardinal's song, as lovely as any, included a whistle.

Justin thought of Anthony and how Anthony whistled for Pepper, his dog.

It was well past noon and Justin was hungry. Soon they came upon a small, well-built shed, securely locked. Nearby was a small stream. Grandpa reined in his horse. When he and Justin dismounted, they hitched the horses, and unsaddled them.

"We'll have our lunch here," Grandpa said. Justin was surprised when Grandpa took black iron pots, other cooking utensils, and a table from the shed. Justin helped him remove some iron rods that Grandpa carefully placed over a shallow pit. These would hold the pots. Now Justin understood why Grandpa had brought uncooked food. They were going to cook outside.

First they collected twigs and cow dung. Grandpa called it cowchips. "These," Grandpa said, holding up a dried brown pad, "make the best fuel. Gather them up."

There were plenty of chips left from the cattle that had fed there in winter. Soon they had a hot fire.

Justin watched as Grandpa carefully washed his hands and then began to cook their lunch.

"When I was a boy about your age, I used to go with my father on short runs with cattle. We'd bring them down from the high country onto the plains."

"Did you stay out all night?"

"Sometimes. And that was the time I liked most. The cook often made for supper what I am going to make for lunch."

Grandpa put raisins into a pot with a little water and placed them over the fire. Justin was surprised when Grandpa put flour in a separate pan. He used his fist to make a hole right in the middle of the flour. In that hole he placed some shortening. Then he added water. With his long delicate fingers he mixed the flour, water, and shortening until he had a nice round mound of dough.

Soon smooth circles of biscuits sat in an iron skillet with a lid on top. Grandpa put the skillet on the fire with some of the red-hot chips scattered over the lid.

Justin was amazed. How could only those ingredients make good bread? But he said nothing as Grandpa put the chunks of smoked pork in a skillet and started them cooking. Soon the smell was so delicious, Justin could hardly wait.

Finally Grandpa suggested that Justin take the horses to drink at the stream. "Keep your eyes open and don't step on any snakes."

Justin knew that diamondback rattlers sometimes lurked around. They were dangerous. He must be careful. He watered Black first.

While watering Pal, he heard rustling in the grass. His heart pounded. He heard the noise again. He wanted to run, but was too afraid. He looked around carefully. There were two black eyes staring at him. He tried to pull Pal away from the water, but Pal refused to stop drinking. Then Justin saw the animal. It had a long tail like a rat's. But it was as big as a cat. Then he saw something crawling on its back. They were little babies, hanging on as the animal ran.

A mama opossum and her babies, he thought, and was no longer afraid.

By the time the horses were watered, lunch was ready. "*M-mm-m,*" Justin said as he reached for a plate. The biscuits were golden brown, yet fluffy inside. And the sizzling pork was now crisp. Never had he eaten stewed raisins before.

"Grandpa, I didn't know you could cook like this," Justin said when he had tasted the food. "I didn't know men could cook so good."

"Why, Justin, some of the best cooks in the world are men."

Justin remembered the egg on the floor and his rice burning. The look he gave Grandpa revealed his doubts.

"It's true," Grandpa said. "All the cooks on the cattle trail were men. In hotels and restaurants they call them chefs."

"How did you make these biscuits?"

"That's a secret. One day I'll let you make some."

"Were you a cowboy, Grandpa?"

"I'm still a cowboy."

"No, you're not."

"Yes, I am. I work with cattle, so I'm a cowboy."

"You know what I mean. The kind who rides bulls, broncobusters. That kind of cowboy."

"No, I'm not that kind. But I know some."

"Are they famous?"

"No, but I did meet a real famous Black cowboy once. When I was eight years old, my grandpa took me to meet his friend Bill Pickett. Bill Pickett was an old man then. He had a ranch in Oklahoma."

"Were there lots of Black cowboys?"

"Yes. Lots of them. They were hard workers, too. They busted broncos, branded calves, and drove cattle. My grandpa tamed wild mustangs."

"Bet they were famous."

"Oh, no. Some were. Bill Pickett

created the sport of bulldogging. You'll see that at the rodeo. One cowboy named Williams taught Rough Rider Teddy Roosevelt how to break horses; and another one named Clay taught Will Rogers, the comedian, the art of roping." Grandpa offered Justin the last biscuit.

When they had finished their lunch they led the horses away from the shed to graze. As they watched the horses, Grandpa went on, "Now, there were some more very famous Black cowboys. Jessie Stahl. They say he was the best rider of wild horses in the West."

"How could he be? Nobody ever heard about him. I didn't."

"Oh, there're lots of famous Blacks you never hear or read about. You ever hear about Deadwood Dick?"

Justin laughed. "No."

"There's another one. His real name was Nat Love. He could outride, outshoot anyone. In Deadwood City in the Dakota Territory, he roped, tied, saddled, mounted, and rode a wild horse faster than anyone. Then in the shooting match, he hit the bull's-eye every time. The people named him Deadwood Dick right on the spot. Enough about cowboys, now. While the horses graze, let's clean up here and get back to our men's work."

Justin felt that Grandpa was still teasing him, the way he had in Justin's

65

room when he had placed his hand on Justin's shoulder. There was still the sense of shame whenever the outburst about women's work and the tears were remembered.

As they cleaned the utensils and dishes, Justin asked, "Grandpa, you think housework is women's work?"

"Do you?" Grandpa asked quickly.

"I asked you first, Grandpa."

"I guess asking you that before I answer is unfair. No, I don't. Do you?"

"Well, it seems easier for them," Justin said as he splashed water all over, glad he was outside.

"Easier than for me?"

"Well, not for you, I guess, but for me, yeah."

"Could it be because you don't know how?"

"You mean like making the bed and folding the clothes."

"Yes." Grandpa stopped and looked at Justin. "Making the bed is easy now, isn't it? All work is that way. It doesn't matter who does the work, man or woman, when it needs to be done. What matters is that we try to learn how to do it the best we can in the most enjoyable way."

"I don't think I'll ever like housework," Justin said, drying a big iron pot.

"It's like any other kind of work. The better you do it, the easier it becomes, and we seem not to mind doing things that are easy."

With the cooking rods and all the utensils put away, they locked the shed and went for their horses.

"Now, I'm going to let you do the cinches again. You'll like that."

There's that teasing again, Justin thought. "Yeah. That's a man's work," he said, and mounted Black.

"There are some good horsewomen. You'll see them at the rodeo." Grandpa mounted Pal. They went on their way, riding along silently, scanning the fence.

Finally Justin said, "I was just kidding, Grandpa." Then without planning to, he said, "I bet you don't like boys who cry like babies."

"Do I know any boys who cry like babies?"

"Aw, Grandpa, you saw me crying."

"Oh, I didn't think you were crying like a baby. In your room, you mean? We all cry sometime."

"You? Cry, Grandpa?"

"Sure."

They rode on, with Grandpa marking his map. Justin remained quiet, wondering what could make a man like Grandpa cry.

As if knowing Justin's thoughts, Grandpa said, "I remember crying when you were born."

"Why? Didn't you want me?"

"Oh, yes. You were the most beautiful baby. But, you see, your grandma, Beth, had just died. When I held you I was flooded with joy. Then I thought, *Grandma will never see this beautiful boy.* I cried."

The horses wading through the grass made the only sound in the silence. Then Grandpa said, "There's an old saying, son. 'The brave hide their fears, but share their tears.' Tears bathe the soul."

Justin looked at his grandpa. Their eyes caught. A warmth spread over Justin and he lowered his eyes. He wished he could tell his grandpa all he felt, how much he loved him.

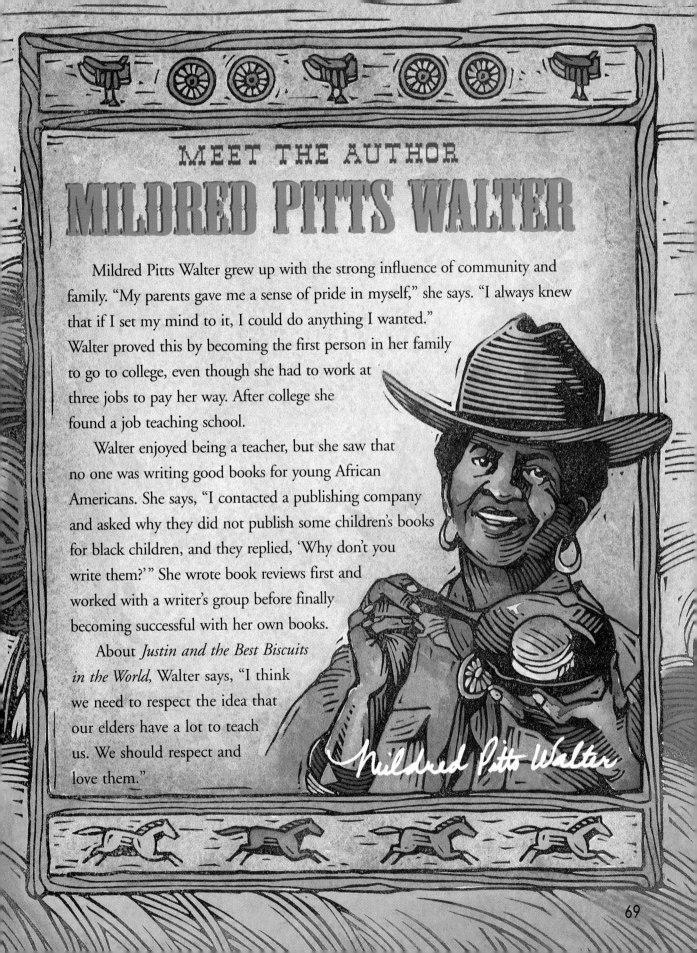

MEET THE AUTHOR
MILDRED PITTS WALTER

Mildred Pitts Walter grew up with the strong influence of community and family. "My parents gave me a sense of pride in myself," she says. "I always knew that if I set my mind to it, I could do anything I wanted." Walter proved this by becoming the first person in her family to go to college, even though she had to work at three jobs to pay her way. After college she found a job teaching school.

Walter enjoyed being a teacher, but she saw that no one was writing good books for young African Americans. She says, "I contacted a publishing company and asked why they did not publish some children's books for black children, and they replied, 'Why don't you write them?'" She wrote book reviews first and worked with a writer's group before finally becoming successful with her own books.

About *Justin and the Best Biscuits in the World*, Walter says, "I think we need to respect the idea that our elders have a lot to teach us. We should respect and love them."

Mildred Pitts Walter

from
The People, Yes

"I love you,"
said a great mother.
"I love you for what you are
knowing so well what you are.
And I love you more yet, child,
deeper yet than ever, child,
for what you are going to be,
knowing so well you are going far,
knowing your great works are ahead,
ahead and beyond,
yonder and far over yet."

by Carl Sandburg

Award-Winning
Poet

All Kinds of Grands

She
rocks in a chair and
She
walks with a sign
and they're both of them
Grands
and they're both of them
Mine!

She
taught me to knit and
She taught me to dance
and I wouldn't trade either
of them, not a chance!

She
rocks me to sleep and
She shouts me awake
and they both of them love me
and both, for my sake,

do all kinds of grand things
they wouldn't have guessed.
Oh, all kinds of Grands
are the Grands that are best!

by Lucille Clifton

Award-Winning
Poet

71

RESPONSE CORNER

BRAINSTORM A LIST

STICKS AND STONES...

A little praise can go a long way to make people feel good about themselves. Justin's feelings about himself were shaped and later changed by the way he was spoken to by family members. Work in a small group to list ways classmates can praise and encourage each other every day. Display your list.

MAKE A NOTEBOOK

AFRICAN AMERICAN COWBOYS

Round up information from the history section of a library about the African American cowboys Bill Pickett, Jessie Stahl, Deadwood Dick, and others. Take notes on the most important facts about each one's life. Then make a notebook of this information and add sketches of the cowboys.

"GRANDPA'S LITTLE INSTRUCTION BOOK"

One way Grandpa teaches Justin is by talking to him about life. Collect Grandpa's wisdom in a book. First, choose a title for the book. Then find some of the good advice that Grandpa offered Justin. Write his ideas plus a few of your own. The advice can be serious or funny, but it should be useful. Write or type the suggestions one to a page. Then decorate and bind the pages. Share your finished book with family and friends.

WHAT DO YOU THINK?

- What are some of the things Justin learned to do on his grandfather's ranch?

- Would you like to spend a week on a ranch like the one Justin's grandfather owned? Why or why not?

- Why do you think this story and the poems that follow it belong in a theme called "Guiding Your Way"?

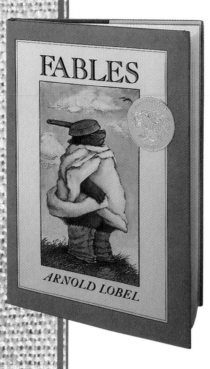

FABLES

ARNOLD LOBEL

Caldecott Medal

THE
YOUNG
ROOSTER

from
FABLES
Written and Illustrated by
ARNOLD LOBEL

A young Rooster was summoned to his Father's bedside.

"Son, my time has come to an end," said the aged bird. "Now it is your turn to crow up the morning sun each day."

The young Rooster watched sadly as his Father's life slipped away.

Early the next morning, the young Rooster flew up to the roof of the barn. He stood there, facing the east.

"I have never done this before," said the Rooster. "I must try my best." He lifted his head and crowed. A weak and scratchy croak was the only sound he was able to make.

The sun did not come up. Clouds covered the sky, and a damp drizzle fell all day. All of the animals of the farm came to the Rooster.

"This is a disaster!" cried a Pig.

"We need our sunshine!" shouted a Sheep.

"Rooster, you must crow much louder," said a Bull. "The sun is ninety-three million miles away. How do you expect it to hear you?"

Very early the next morning, the young Rooster flew up to the roof of the barn again. He took a deep breath, he threw back his head and CROWED. It was the loudest crow that was ever crowed since the beginning of roosters.

The animals on the farm were awakened from their sleep with a start.

"What a noise!" cried the Pig.

"My ears hurt!" shouted the Sheep.

"My head is splitting!" said the Bull.

"I am sorry," said the Rooster, "but I was only doing my job."

He said this with a great deal of pride, for he saw, far to the east, the tip of the morning sun coming up over the trees.

A first failure may prepare the way for later success.

Art and Literature

L ook at the paint-ing *The Country School* by Winslow Homer. What type of classroom do you think this is? How does this painting fit into a theme titled "Guiding Your Way"?

The Country School (1871) by Winslow Homer,
Oil on canvas (21 3/8" x 38 3/8").
The Saint Louis Art Museum, Purchase.

The Country School
by Winslow Homer

Homer liked to paint country settings and scenes of the sea.
His paintings often show natural light, or light from the sun.
Note how the sunlight in this painting brushes the children's hair,
the furniture, and the floor as it streams through the windows.

THE STORY OF
ANNIE SULLIVAN,
HELEN KELLER'S TEACHER

Helen Keller (1880–1968) dedicated her life to helping others with disabilities. Here, Helen (left) is pictured with Annie Sullivan, her beloved teacher.

BY BERNICE SELDEN

Although Helen Keller was both deaf and blind, she learned to read and write and became famous working to improve conditions for the deaf and blind all over the world. The teacher who helped make all this possible was Annie Sullivan, herself a graduate of the Perkins Institute for the Blind. When Annie first arrived at the Kellers' home, Ivy Green, in Tuscumbia, Alabama, she found a very frustrated and temperamental seven-year-old child.

This was a difficult time for Annie. Often she wondered if she could find the jewel of a child buried under the resistant wild creature.

Helen's movements were so angry that once her hand flew up and knocked out one of Annie's front teeth.

"To get her to do the simplest thing, such as combing her hair or washing her hands," Annie reported to Mrs. Hopkins, "it is necessary to use force." But then the family would get upset, particularly Captain Keller, who could not bear to see his daughter cry.

Annie Sullivan

Something had to be done—Annie thought—and quickly.

Was there a place she and Helen could be by themselves? she asked the Kellers. Surprised by this request, they promised to think it over.

Finally Captain Keller made available to them a garden house some distance away from Ivy Green. "But only for two weeks," he said firmly. "Then we want her back home."

Day by day Helen became easier to work with. But it was an up and down struggle. One morning, during the first week in the garden house, Captain Keller passed by and looked in the window. He saw Helen still in her nightgown long after the breakfast hours. He was outraged. "I've got a good mind to send that Yankee[1] girl back to Boston," he told a relative.

He had no idea what progress this "Yankee girl" was making. Helen was learning to sew, knit, and string beads. On her daily visits to the barnyard, she was beginning to identify living creatures.

"I spell into her hand everything we do all day long, although she has no idea yet what the spelling means," Annie wrote.

The two weeks in the garden house passed quickly, and soon teacher and student were back in the Keller home.

---

[1] Yankee: a person who is from or lives in the northern United States.

Helen was beginning to associate some of the words with some objects out there in the world. It was a kind of game that she played, partly to please Annie. But she was mixed up about a lot of things.

For instance, she knew that the words *mug* and *milk* had something to do with drinking. But she kept using one in place of the other. Now, when she was washing her hands, she asked to know the word for *water*. She did this by pointing to the water and patting her teacher's hand.

Annie took her out to the pumphouse in the garden. Helen felt the cold water pouring into her mug and all over her fingers. Annie spelled W–A–T–E–R into her free hand. Helen froze. She looked as if she was remembering something from very long ago. As Annie reported it: "The word coming so close upon the sensation of cold water rushing over her hand seemed to startle her. She dropped the mug . . . A new light came into her face."

Helen had suddenly realized that she was not just playing games, but that *words* stood for *things*. And if she could identify those things with words, she had the power to know anything she wanted to—out there in the world of light and sound.

She touched the ground and immediately wanted to know the word for it. Then the pump. When her baby sister was brought out for her to hold, she wanted to know what she was called. And finally she wanted to know Annie's name.

Helen Keller

"T–E–A–C–H–E–R," Annie spelled out. From that day on, Annie was called "Teacher" and nothing else.

A key had been turned in Helen's mind. Within an hour she had memorized thirty words.

"When I got into bed," Annie wrote, "she stole into my arms of her own accord and kissed me for the first time, and I thought my heart would burst, so full was it of joy!"

"Helen is a truly wonderful child," Annie wrote to the director of Perkins a few weeks later. "She knows almost three hundred words and is learning five or six a day."

Anagnos wrote back: "I am

deeply interested in your pupil. She certainly is a remarkable child. Keep an exact account of what she learns and does every day." And he began to keep records also, putting Annie's accounts of Helen's progress into his annual reports, reports that were widely read.

Whatever interested Helen in the wide world, her teacher would explain in detail. "Everything that could hum, or buzz, or sing, or bloom" was part of her education.

Helen became conscious of her appearance. She liked to wear pretty dresses and to have her hair put up in curls. She learned to count and to read simple books written in the raised letters of the alphabet. She seemed to want to know everything.

Then came the day she asked to be able to write letters to people. Teacher got her a specially designed board for blind people, grooved so that a pencil could form letters on the paper placed over it.

This is Helen's first letter, written to her mother, when Helen and her father were away on a trip.

Helen will write mother letter papa did give helen medicine . . . conductor did punch ticket papa did give helen drink of water . . . helen will hug and kiss mother. good-by.

The following letter was written to her mother just one year later, and shows how rapidly Helen got command of the written language:

My dear Mother, I think you will be very glad to know all about my visit to West Newton. Teacher and I had a very lovely time with many kind friends . . . I was delighted to see my dear little friends and I hugged and kissed them . . . Clifton did not kiss me because he does not like to kiss girls. He is shy . . . Will you please ask my father to come to the train to meet Teacher and me? . . . With much love and a thousand kisses from your dear little daughter.

In the year between the two letters, the "wild animal" had become a brilliant and joyful child.

Mirette on

Caldecott
Medal

ALA Notable
Book

SLJ Best Books
of the Year

MIRETTE
ON THE
HIGH
WIRE

Emily Arnold M©Cully

the High Wire

by Emily Arnold McCully

One hundred years ago in Paris, when theaters and music halls drew traveling players from all over the world, the best place to stay was at the widow Gâteau's, a boardinghouse on English Street.

Acrobats, jugglers, actors, and mimes from as far away as Moscow and New York reclined on the widow's feather mattresses and devoured her kidney stews.

Madame Gâteau worked hard to make her guests comfortable, and so did her daughter, Mirette. The girl was an expert at washing linens, chopping leeks, paring potatoes, and mopping floors. She was a good listener too. Nothing pleased her more than to overhear the vagabond players tell of their adventures in this town and that along the road.

One evening a tall, sad-faced stranger arrived. He told Madame Gâteau he was Bellini, a retired high-wire walker.

"I am here for a rest," he said.

"I have just the room for you, Monsieur Bellini: in the back, where it's quiet," she said. "But it's on the ground floor, with no view."

"Perfect," said the stranger. "I will take my meals alone."

The next afternoon, when Mirette came for the sheets, there was the stranger, crossing the courtyard on air! Mirette was enchanted. Of all the things a person could do, this must be the most magical. Her feet tingled, as if they wanted to jump up on the wire beside Bellini.

Mirette worked up the courage to speak. "Excuse me, Monsieur Bellini, *I* want to learn to do that!" she cried.

Bellini sighed. "That would not be a good idea," he said. "Once you start, your feet are never happy again on the ground."

"Oh, please teach me!" Mirette begged. "My feet are already unhappy on the ground." But he shook his head.

Mirette watched him every day. He would slide his feet onto the wire, cast his eyes ahead, and cross without ever looking down, as if in a trance.

Finally she couldn't resist any longer. When Bellini was gone, she jumped up on the wire to try it herself. Her arms flailed like windmills. In a moment she was back on the ground. Bellini made it look so easy. Surely she could do it too if she kept trying.

In ten tries she balanced on one foot for a few seconds. In a day, she managed three steps without wavering. Finally, after a week of many, many falls, she walked the length of the wire. She couldn't wait to show Bellini.

He was silent for a long time. Then he said, "In the beginning everyone falls. Most give up. But you kept trying. Perhaps you have talent as well."

"Oh, thank you," said Mirette.

She got up two hours earlier every day to finish her chores before the sun shone in the courtyard. The rest of the day was for lessons and practice.

Bellini was a strict master. "Never let your eyes stray," he told her day after day. "Think only of the wire, and of crossing to the end."

When she could cross dozens of times without falling, he taught her the wire-walker's salute. Then she learned to run, to lie down, and to turn a somersault.

"I will never ever fall again!" Mirette shouted.

"Do not boast," Bellini said, so sharply that Mirette lost her balance and had to jump down.

One night an agent from Astley's Hippodrome in London rented a room. He noticed Bellini on his way to dinner.

"What a shock to see him here!" he exclaimed.

"See who?" asked a mime.

"Why, the great Bellini! Didn't you know he was in the room at the back?"

"Bellini . . . the one who crossed Niagara Falls on a thousand-foot wire in ten minutes?" asked the mime.

"And on the way back stopped in the middle to cook an omelette on a stove full of live coals. Then he opened a bottle of champagne and toasted the crowd," the agent recalled.

"My uncle used to talk about that," said a juggler.

"Bellini crossed the Alps with baskets tied to his feet, fired a cannon over the bullring in Barcelona, walked a flaming wire wearing a blindfold in Naples—the man had the nerves of an iceberg," the agent said.

Mirette raced to Bellini's room.

"Is it true?" she cried. "You did all those things? Why didn't you tell me? I want to do them too! I want to go with you!"

"I can't take you," said Bellini.

"But why not?" asked Mirette.

Bellini hesitated a long time. "Because I am afraid," he said at last.

Mirette was astonished. "*Afraid*?" she said. "But *why*?"

"Once you have fear on the wire, it never leaves," Bellini said.

"But you must *make* it leave!" Mirette insisted.

"I cannot," said Bellini.

Mirette turned and ran to the kitchen as tears sprang to her eyes. She had felt such joy on the wire. Now Bellini's fear was like a cloud casting its black shadow on all she had learned from him.

Bellini paced his room for hours. It was terrible to disappoint Mirette! By dawn he knew that if he didn't face his fear at last, he could not face Mirette. He knew what he must do. The question was, could he succeed?

That night, when the agent returned, Bellini was waiting for him. The agent listened to Bellini's plan with mounting excitement. "I'll take care of it," he promised. To himself he added, "A big crowd will make me a tidy profit. What luck I just happened to be in Paris now."

Bellini went out to find a length of hemp with a steel core. He borrowed a winch and worked until daylight securing the wire.

The next evening, Mirette heard the commotion in the street.

"Go and see what it is," her mother said. "Maybe it will cheer you up."

In the square was a hubbub. The crowd was so thick she couldn't see, at first, that the agent was aiming a spotlight at the sky.

". . . return of the great Bellini!" he was yelling. Could it be? Mirette's heart hammered in her chest.

Bellini stepped out onto the wire and saluted the crowd. He took a step and then froze. The crowd cheered wildly. But something was wrong. Mirette knew at once what it was. For a moment she was as frozen as Bellini was.

Then she threw herself at the door behind her, ran inside, up flight after flight of stairs, and out through a skylight to the roof.

She stretched her hands to Bellini. He smiled and began to walk toward her. She stepped onto the wire, and with the most intense

pleasure, as she had always imagined it might be, she started to cross the sky.

"Brava! Bravo!" roared the crowd.

"Protégée of the Great Bellini!" shouted the agent. He was beside himself, already planning the world tour of Bellini and Mirette.

As for the master and his pupil, they were thinking only of the wire, and of crossing to the end.

Emily Arnold McCully

AUTHOR AND ILLUSTRATOR

A love of Paris, France, and a desire to try something new in writing and illustrating a book led Emily Arnold McCully to write *Mirette on the High Wire*. McCully won the Caldecott Medal for this book, which is perhaps the highest honor a children's book illustrator can earn.

McCully illustrated her first children's book in 1966. The book did well, and she went on to do more. She believes that an illustrator's job is not just to decorate the book, but to add to the story. When she starts working on a book, she decides "what the characters should look like and where they are. Sometimes I look at photographs, sometimes I think of friends, sometimes I make it all up."

Of her life as an artist, McCully says, "I was probably the only one who couldn't predict my future when I was young. Anyone observing me at seven or eight, sprawled on the floor or bent over my desk, might have known that my life's work would be exactly what it is."

Much to Learn

by Carmen Tafolla

TEACHERS

My child, there is much
for you to learn.
Wondrous things,
like how candles burn.

How *tortillas* puff up,
How the earth cools down,
How the sunset in the skies
changes colors all around.

How the *chile* turns red
When it's still on the bush.
How the hawk swoops down
to grab a field mouse with a swoosh!

How coyotes howl
In a voice that sounds like words.
How there's always food around
For even the smallest birds.

My child, there is much
For you to learn
And also much for you
To teach us in return.

Like how to make friends
With someone who is kind.
Like how to see the joy
In something old you find.

Like how to use a stick and string
As if it were a toy,
Or how to bring a smile
To another girl or boy.

Like how to dream the biggest dreams,
Or keep a tiny hope alive,
Or—when grownups say "Impossible!"—
To say, "We've never tried."

My child, there is much
for you to learn
And also much for you
To teach us in return.

Better than a thousand days
of diligent study is one day
with a great teacher.
—Japanese proverb

To become a teacher one must
first respect one's teacher.
—Vietnamese proverb

Your teacher can lead you to
learning; the actual learning
you have to do yourself.
—Chinese proverb

The Funny Papers

Have you ever heard someone's actions described as "walking a tightrope"? This saying doesn't mean that the person is an acrobat. It means that he or she is watching each step carefully. Create a cartoon showing what this phrase says, and then write what it really means. You might also draw and write about other sayings, such as "sitting on the fence," "skating on thin ice," and "having your head in the clouds."

response

"Most Give Up"

"In the beginning, everyone falls," Bellini tells Mirette. "Most give up." Mirette's teacher has known both kinds of people. Think of a time you either gave up doing something that was hard to do or kept on to the end. Write a paragraph or two in a letter to a friend, explaining what you were trying to do, why you did what you did, and what you would do if something like that happened again.

So Much to Learn, So Little Time!

Learn more about one of the topics from the poem "Much to Learn" or from the story "Mirette on the High Wire." After researching your topic, share with your classmates what you learned.

corner

What Do You Think?

- What do the two main story characters learn from one another?
- Could this story take place in real life today? Tell why you think as you do.
- How do "Much to Learn" and "Teachers" add to your understanding of the story's theme?

The characters in the selections in this theme faced many challenges. Which characters found inner strength to guide themselves? Which characters learned with the guidance of others?

Activity Corner

Has there been a time when someone else has helped to guide you in doing something? Think about the characters in the selections in this theme. Then write a thank-you letter to a person who has helped guide you in some way. Tell how you were able to accomplish a task because of the help or advice you received.

Think about how Mandy Sue and Justin each dealt with their problems. What advice do you think Mandy Sue would have given to Justin? Explain why you think that.

THEME

WORKING IT OUT

Have you ever had a problem that seemed almost impossible to solve? The characters in each selection in this theme discover ways to communicate with each other to help solve their problems.

IT OUT

CONTENTS

BOOKSHELF

Class President
by Johanna Hurwitz
illustrated by Sheila Hamanaka

Which leader will the class vote for—Julio Sanchez or Cricket Kaufman?

Award-Winning Author

Signatures Library

Mop, Moondance, and the Nagasaki Knights
by Walter Dean Myers

Members of a championship baseball team discover the value of communication as they try to win a trip to Japan by playing against international teams.

Award-Winning Author

Signatures Library

Charlotte's Web
by E. B. White
illustrated by
Garth Williams

Charlotte the spider communicates in her own special way to help Wilbur the pig.

Newbery Honor,
ALA Notable Book,
SLJ Best Books of the Year

A Guide Dog Puppy Grows Up
by Caroline Arnold
photographs by
Richard Hewett

Honey, a golden-retriever puppy, trains to be a guide dog for the blind.

Award-Winning Author

A Llama in the Family
by Johanna Hurwitz
illustrated by Mark Graham

The Fine family has a new addition, and it's the beginning of some funny business.

Award-Winning Author

Bonesy and Isabel

By Michael J. Rosen
Illustrated by James Ransome

Award-Winning
Author

Award-Winning
Illustrator

Bonesy
and
Isabel

Michael J. Rosen
Illustrated by
James Ransome

118

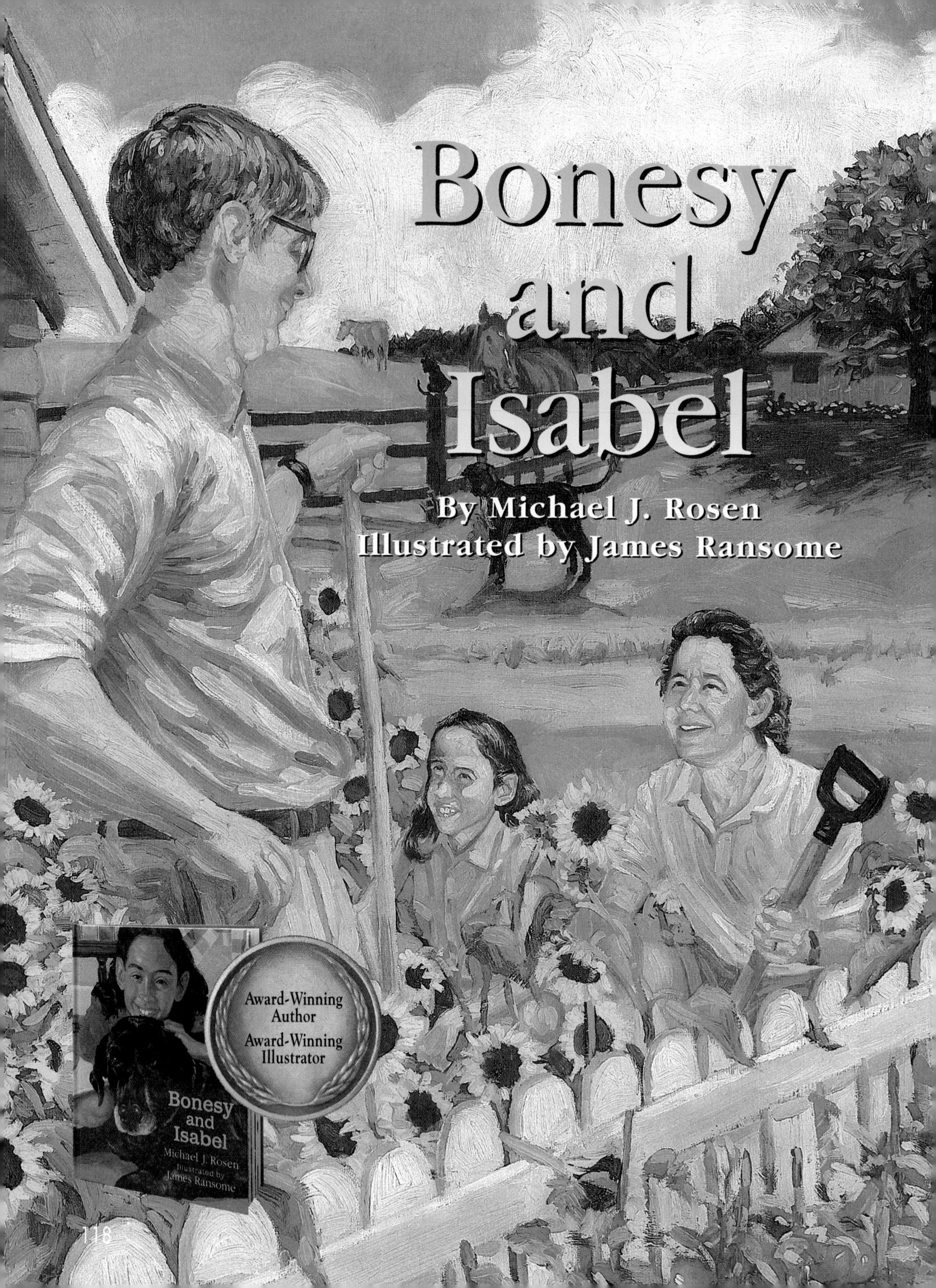

Before Isabel came to the house on Sunbury Road, thirty-five other creatures were living there. At least thirty-five—and that's not counting all the creatures that couldn't be counted. Three horses grazed the grassy fields. Eleven ducks paddled a pond that had been dug and filled only a few years earlier. Eight or nine cats prowled the place—some inside and some outside. And nine dogs called that house their home: all outside dogs that used to be strays (mixed-up breeds and many sizes), except for one inside dog, a twelve-year-old Labrador retriever named Bonesy.

And then there were two people who cared for all these countable creatures. They were the ones who had brought Isabel from El Salvador.

The main house on Sunbury Road had once been a cabin, but over the years, the many owners had made one addition after another. Now there are fifteen rooms, as well as a pair of barns, gardens in all the sunny and partly sunny spots, a tool shed, an empty corncrib, timber and picket fences, part of a pine forest, a deck, and a pasture, too. The whole place rambles like a long story. And each creature who lives in or around or above the house on Sunbury Road knows a different part of that story.

The barn swallows and nighthawks could tell you about the chimney smoke and the antenna's perches, where the roof slates have cracked and the gutters have clogged with leaves.

The horses know the barnyard's circles, the mole and rabbit holes in the fields, the scrambling gravel along the roads, and how far it is from here to most anywhere.

The cats spy on everyone, nosing into nooks and niches where crickets *chirr* and mice skedaddle. Still, whatever stories the cats discover they don't tell a living soul.

But the nine dogs in Isabel's new house share a single story. It's the story of the people who took them from the dangerous roads where each had been abandoned. Of course, they all know the faint wind's gossip of scents and the story of the fences where they bark to passersby: *Don't bother our house.* Yet the real story they like to tell is about the people of the house who speak to them in a strange language—words that, most of the time, just mean, *We care for you.*

When Isabel came to the house, she knew only a few words of that strange language, English—about as much as the dogs knew, which was a lot more than the horses would ever know, and a little more than the cats admitted knowing. As for the uncountable birds, Isabel quickly learned the nighthawks' *peent, peent*, and the swallows' rapid *tat-tat-tat-tat*.

And so Isabel spent her summer listening to the animals who showed her all they knew about the place. Though she didn't understand their busy language, it sounded good to her. The animals of Sunbury Road spoke like the wandering mules and chickens and goats from the roads of El Salvador Isabel remembered.

Isabel called the people who lived in the house "Vera" and "Ivan." They were the ones who groomed the horses, flea-dipped the cats, untangled burrs from the dogs' coats, and stuffed the bird feeders with suet. They were the ones who had brought Isabel from a country farther away than any of the resident birds could report from their high-up views.

123

People were always visiting Isabel's new house—especially at dinner-time when there would be clinking glasses and clouds of laughter. Although Isabel couldn't often understand what was funny, she at least understood that Vera and Ivan and their friends were happy. Laughing in English sounded just like laughing in Spanish.

It was Bonesy, the one inside dog, who became Isabel's closest companion. Isabel even recognized the word "companion" the first time Vera pronounced it slowly; it sounded so much like *compañero*.[1] Bonesy was allowed inside because he was old. And because he had lost most of his teeth, he was allowed to eat table scraps. And because he had arthritis, Bonesy was even allowed to stay under the dining room table, where scraps could be slipped to him under the tablecloth. He never begged. He just waited—or slept. While Vera and Ivan and their guests would laugh, Isabel would feed Bonesy the soft leftovers from her plate. She would slip off her shoes and stroke Bonesy's coat with her bare toes.

And so it was the always-awaiting Bonesy who helped Isabel study English. A little of it, anyway. Under the dining room table with the sleepy dog, Isabel would sound out the English words in her new books. Though Bonesy didn't know if it was right when Isabel said *hor-SES* or when she said *HOR-ses*, he rewarded her with licks just for practicing beside him.

---

[1] compañero (kōm•pän•yā´rō)

The warm breeze from Bonesy's nose would riffle the pages of her book. And whenever Isabel said *Bonesy* or *Good dog!* or *¡Perro bueno!*,[2] the old retriever would thump his tail against the rug. Whatever language Isabel spoke, Bonesy seemed to know she was saying what his other humans often said: *I care for you.*

One evening, Vera and Ivan invited another family of three to dinner. Isabel helped set the table with freshly ironed linens, with plates that someone in a nearby town had made from clay, and with flowers she had helped Ivan gather from the horses' field. Earlier in the day she had picked peaches from their own trees and rolled out a pie crust with Vera. She learned a word or two with each of these little jobs.

The guests, Mr. and Mrs. Jeffrey and their daughter Emmie, sat directly across the table from Ivan and Vera and Isabel. Of course, Bonesy, to whom everyone was introduced, slept among the six pairs of feet.

---

[2] Perro bueno (pā´rō bwā´nō)

Dinner began with Vera's minty soup and lots of words that Isabel hadn't studied. She slipped off her shoes and began to stroke Bonesy with her toes. Emmie passed Isabel the basket of chewy bread that her family had brought, and Isabel nudged Bonesy with her foot to offer him a piece from which she had torn the crust. Once the dinner plates arrived, Isabel peeked under the table and saw the bread still lying beside her shoe. Then someone pronounced the words for her old country, *El Salvador*, and this made her smile. Emmie repeated the words and smiled back at Isabel, and then, because Emmie didn't know any other Spanish, she turned back to her plate and began to arrange her green beans into rows.

Throughout dinner, Bonesy ignored Isabel's offer of a green bean, a chunk of potato, and even a piece of chicken skin. Isabel wiggled her toes on Bonesy's back, nudged him, lifted his sleepy tail from the floor with her foot. While everyone at the table continued to laugh and tell stories, Isabel slid slowly off her chair and ducked beneath the tablecloth.

On her hands and knees—on all fours like Bonesy—Isabel whispered the dog's name and then said, "*¡Despiértate!*[3]—Wake up!" But Bonesy didn't rouse, didn't lick Isabel's face, didn't wag his tail, didn't smell the chicken on her fingertips. She held her hand in front of his nose but couldn't feel the little drafts of warm air.

---

[3] Despiértate (dās•pē•är´tä•tā)

Isabel reached over to the dress covering Vera's knees and tugged its hem until Vera poked her head beneath the table and whispered, "What's wrong?" When Isabel pointed to Bonesy, Vera slid under the tablecloth, crawled over to the dog on her hands and knees, on all fours, and placed her hands softly on Bonesy's chest. After a quiet moment, Isabel could see Vera's eyes brimming, too, as if their tears were words that Isabel and Vera shared. Vera put one arm around Isabel and her other arm around the retriever.

Before Vera could say a word, Ivan peered under the table and saw his wife and Isabel hugging old Bonesy. He said "Excuse me" to the Jeffreys and slid under the tablecloth, creeping on all fours to join the family circle. He looked at his dog of twelve years, his wife of twenty-two years, and this beautiful girl—his new daughter—who had been living with them these last three weeks. Isabel waited for him to say something, but Ivan just shook his head as if to show her that this sadness had no translation other than their tears.

At the table, the Jeffreys looked at one another and picked at the cold remains of their dinners. Finally, Mr. Jeffrey lifted the edge of the tablecloth and peered beneath. "Can we join the fun?" he asked.

Isabel and Vera and Ivan turned to look at Mr. Jeffrey's sideways face; his smile quickly vanished.

"I'm afraid we've had a death in the family," Vera said.

Isabel could now hear gentler words outside the tablecloth and then the sound of three chairs scooting away from the table. She smelled the peach pie in the kitchen and heard the jingling of one of the outside dogs' collar tags. Isabel knew there must be English words for what she felt, but the two new people on either side of her were just as quiet as she was, as if they, too, had just arrived without English in this suddenly sad place from a faraway country.

Then the front door closed, and Isabel heard the gravel skitter along the road. But under the tablecloth, where the four of them huddled together, it was as silent as when Bonesy slept there all by himself.

A little later, the world outside the tablecloth would begin again— all the words for "clearing the table" or "feeding the animals" or "washing the dishes"—but that hadn't begun just yet. For now, three people shared a story about a house on Sunbury Road where a retriever named Bonesy had lived. It was a story that didn't need words—a long story and a happy story and a story with a quiet ending.

And then "a little later" arrived. It was, of course, waiting for them right there in the dining room. It was as shy and unexpected as another stray dog, and it needed them—as Bonesy had. It needed Vera and Ivan and Isabel. And so Isabel helped to welcome this next part of the story into her family's house.

Later still, in the light of the summer stars, Isabel helped Vera and Ivan bury Bonesy beside a tree near the old barn. And in the days that followed, Isabel shared the story of Bonesy's death with each of the animals who lived on Sunbury Road. She told her story to the outside dogs, to the in- and outside cats, to the horses, and even to the swallows and nighthawks who didn't sit still and listen. In their different languages, each of the animals understood this new friend Isabel, and they helped her practice the strange language that mostly means, *We care for you.*

Michael J. Rosen

MICHAEL J. ROSEN is the author of several other books in addition to *Bonesy and Isabel*. Writer Ilene Cooper interviewed him to find out how he came up with the idea for this special story.

Cooper: **Bonesy and Isabel** *seems like a very personal story. Where did the idea come from?*

Rosen: I was thinking about a number of different things when I wrote this book. At the time, El Salvador was in the news. Also, a friend's dog had recently died. Then there was my ongoing decision to make about whether to move to the country. All these images were in my head, but I didn't have a story yet. I don't know how a story is going to evolve until I begin to write it.

Cooper: *If you don't know where the story is going, how do you begin?*

Rosen: Well, in this case, I began with the house. It is based on a real house I drive past every once in a while, the kind of place that I would like to own. Then came the animals and then the people.

Cooper: *Do you own dogs?*

Rosen: I have two—Paris, a golden retriever, and Madison, a Labrador retriever. I also have a kennel of carved dogs and portraits that people do of their pets—another extended family.

139

Response Corner

To a Best Friend

Bonesy, Isabel's animal friend, has died. Write a short poem or speech telling how Bonesy helped Isabel in his own quiet way and how you think Isabel feels about his death.

Walk the Talk

We learn a lot about Ivan and Vera by their actions. With a partner, make a list of their character traits. Then, using your list, work with a partner to make up a conversation between Ivan and Vera. The topic? They have just learned that a Salvadoran girl named Isabel is coming to live with them. Act out their conversation for your classmates.

From the Heart

Have you ever had an experience like Isabel's in which you were in a new place and needed a good friend? Perhaps you have lost a pet that was dear to you. Write a few paragraphs that compare your own experience to Isabel's.

What Do You Think?

• How would you describe Isabel to someone? What story details support your description?

• Describe the mood of the story. How did the mood affect you?

• Do you think Isabel and her new parents will become closer as a result of what they have experienced? Why or why not?

HUGGER TO THE RESCUE

BY DOROTHY HINSHAW PATENT
PHOTOGRAPHS BY WILLIAM MUÑOZ

Someone is lost in the woods. He might be hurt, or the weather could turn bad. It is important to find him as fast as possible. But he didn't follow a trail, and footprints don't show on the forest floor. What to do?

Panda and Susie are set to search.

Children's Choice

Panda sniffs clothing belonging to the person playing "lost" during a training session.

Now Panda is ready to go.

Call in the search and rescue dogs. Dogs have a very fine sense of smell. They can find people lost by following their scents, because each person has his or her own, unique scent.

Panda is a Newfoundland dog trained to locate lost people. She and her owner, Susie Foley, know how to search through the woods, under the snow, or in the water. Sometimes a piece of the lost person's clothing is available for the dog to smell. But even without knowing the special scent, a trained dog knows to sniff the air, searching for the smell of a human.

Panda catches the scent and off she goes. She checks the ground if she loses the odor trail in the air. Once she finds the lost person, she licks him happily. Finding him is her best reward.

She searches . . .

finds the "victim," and shows him to Susie.

Search and rescue dogs work around the world to find lost hunters, hikers, and children. They are called in after avalanches to find people buried in the snow. After earthquakes, they look for people hidden in the rubble. Thousands of people owe their lives to these wonderful animals.

Many breeds of dogs are used for search and rescue. But most require a great deal of training to learn the work. Newfoundlands, however, are special. They have natural lifesaving instincts, so they learn their work quickly.

The Newfoundland—called a "Newfie" or "Newf" for short—originated on Newfoundland Island in Canada. It was developed as a working dog that performed a variety of tasks like pulling carts and carrying heavy loads. The breed was most useful as a fisherman's companion, for Newfoundlands are as much at home in the water as on dry land. Their webbed feet help them swim, and their thick coats protect them from the icy cold of northern seas.

Dogs like Indigo can find avalanche victims in the snow quickly.

Newfoundland puppies are born with the instinct to find lost people.

But saving people is the Newfie's greatest natural talent. Even without training, they will rescue people. During storms, Newfies may patrol the shore. When there have been shipwrecks, Newfies have rescued people without being trained to do so. Newfoundlands are famous for their rescuing skills, especially in water. They have carried lifelines to sinking ships and pulled countless drowning people to shore. A single untrained Newfoundland dog saved a hundred people in one rescue. The water was too rough for rescue boats, but just one dog was able to do the job.

Newfoundlands are natural swimmers and love the water.

Susie Foley with Panda and Hugger.

A dog has to be big to perform such work. Newfoundlands weigh from 100 to 160 pounds. They have heavy, muscular bodies and large heads. Most Newfoundlands are black. But they can also be brown, gray, or white and black. They are gentle, good-natured dogs that have a natural love for people.

Newfies make fine family pets. But such a huge dog is a big responsibility. It needs lots of food. A Newfoundland will eat twenty pounds of dry dog food each week, along with five pounds of meat. In addition, it can consume a pound of rawhide treats and two pounds of dog biscuits. Even with all that food, it will still enjoy table scraps and soup bones for chewing.

Susie and Murphy Foley of Bigfork, Montana, raise and train Newfoundland dogs. Their animals are family pets that have a special job. Their volunteer organization, called "Black Paws Search, Rescue & Avalanche Dogs," has chapter groups sprinkled throughout the United States and in other countries. There are two good reasons for the name. Most Newfies do have black fur on their paws. But because of their love of wet places, all Newfoundlands are likely to have "black paws" any time they have a chance to get their feet muddy.

LEFT *Hugger is big, even for a Newfie.*

Panda is always enthusiastic about her work.

Hydra will soon be out searching with the other dogs.

Susie and Murphy use several dogs in their work. Chelsie is a black female. She is loving and obedient, but she is also very determined to do things her way. When she finds a conscious victim, the searchers know right away because they can usually hear the person protesting her enthusiastic dog kisses.

Panda is white and black. Newfoundlands with this special color pattern are called "Landseers." Panda is huge, happy, and especially loyal to Susie. Only when she is at work looking for lost people does she willingly leave Susie's side.

Hydra is just a puppy, but she is learning quickly how to become a fine search and rescue dog. She is curious and lively. Hydra acts as if she really wishes she could talk, she seems so eager to communicate with people.

150

Hugger, as his name suggests, is calm and lovable. He is especially eager to please, and his large size gives him extra strength that can come in handy in a challenging search. All these dogs, however, are really "huggers"—they love people and enjoy human companionship.

Panda.

Even though they may rescue people without being taught, Newfoundland dogs need training. So do their human handlers. The dog must learn some important commands. The command "Wait" tells the dog to stop and wait for its handler to catch up—four legs work much better than two on rough or steep ground. If the dog gets distracted by wildlife or the tempting cool water of a creek, it must know to obey and get back to work when its handler calls out, "Leave it."

Susie and Bill Weppler, a Black Paws member, get ready to work with the dogs.

Hugger and Susie know how to communicate with one another.

Meanwhile, the handler must get into top physical condition—searching is very hard work! He or she also needs to learn how to "read" the dog—how to know what the dog is trying to tell its handler. Each dog may have its own ways of "alerting" when it makes a find. The type of alert may vary, too, depending on whether the victim responds to the dog or not. For example, when Hugger finds a conscious victim, he wags his tail and waits to be invited over. But if the person is unresponsive, Hugger gives a "woof" while looking at Susie if she is nearby, then another woof. When he sees that she is coming to join him, he woofs one more time.

Training is best started when the dog is still young. Around eight weeks of age, a puppy is eager to learn and quite unafraid of the unfamiliar. This is a good time to accustom it to situations that might be frightening later on. The puppy and its handler need to get acquainted by playing together, and cuddling creates a special bond. It is also important to become comfortable around other dogs.

From the time they are very young, Newfies become used to humans and their gadgets.

Susie plays "hide and seek" with Hydra, a good game for search and rescue training.

Love and kisses bond a puppy to its handler.

Even a Newfie puppy knows how to follow a human scent and locate a person. It is important to give the puppy practice in searching and to reward success with plenty of praise and petting.

Black Paws' dogs must get used to wearing a uniform. The uniform is a very important part of their work. It carries first aid materials for both the dog and the victim, headlamps for work in the dark, dog cookies, and a canine energy drink.

The uniform has a harness used when the animal needs to be hoisted by helicopter or rope. The harness straps are tucked into pockets on the uniform when not in use to keep them out of the way. When Susie puts a uniform on one of her dogs, it gets excited. It recognizes the call of duty.

The harness straps are taken from their pockets when they are needed.

Murphy reassures Hugger before taking a helicopter ride.

The Newfies also need training for water rescue. They need to get used to riding in a boat and to signaling where a person is underwater when they catch the scent in the air. One way a dog can show the right spot is by leaning over and biting at the water. Then divers know to search in that spot.

The dogs must learn how to search from boats.

Black Paws   Search & Rescue Dogs

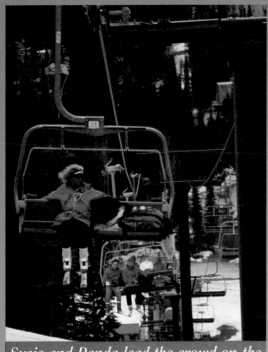

Susie and Panda lead the crowd on the chair lift during a training session.

For avalanche work, the dog needs to become used to riding on a chair lift which might be swaying in the wind. The dog must climb onto the lift willingly and ride calmly to the top. Once there, the dog has to search quickly. A person buried in the snow can suffocate or get dangerously cold very quickly.

Most search and rescue dogs need rewards like the chance to play ball or to eat a special treat, but not Newfies. Their reward is finding a person, saving a life. Their joy is obvious as they wag their tails and lick the faces of the people they rescue. No one wants to get lost in the woods or buried in the snow. But if it happens, there is no better way to be rescued than by a big, loving Newfoundland dog.

Being "found" by a Newfoundland means getting kissed.

DOROTHY HINSHAW PATENT

nlike many authors, Dorothy Hinshaw Patent never dreamed of being a writer when she was young. She did read a lot, but only books about animals. She even read encyclopedia entries about animals. At last, she got her own dog, a cocker spaniel she named Buffy. Then Patent became interested in show dogs, breeding, and training.

Later, she decided she wanted to be a zoologist like her father, so she studied animal behavior in college. When she had two young sons, she began writing, because it was work that she could do at home. When she was writing a book about horses, her publisher teamed her with a photographer named Bill Muñoz. They became good friends and have worked on many books together since then.

Speaking about her work, Patent says, "I hope that my writing can help children get in touch with the world of living things and realize how dependent we are on them."

RESPONSE CORNER

A HUMAN'S BEST FRIEND

Almost everyone wants to love and be loved by a pet, but owning a pet is a big responsibility. What must a pet owner know and do? Do some research in the library or visit a pet store. Then write and present a short talk that will tell your classmates how to be the best pet owners they can be.

SPEAK!

Imagine that you work as a writer for Black Paws Search and Rescue Company. Create a pamphlet that Black Paws might use for advertising. Explain the kind of special training the dogs are given as well as the things they can do. Remember to use vivid words to get your readers' attention.

RESCUE COMMITTEE

Wouldn't Hugger, Panda, and Chelsie like to tell their own tales! With a few of your classmates, write a short movie script with a Newfie as the hero. Remember that you can use a narrator, have the animals talk, or do both. You will need to write descriptions of the action. (Scriptwriters sometimes put these in a separate column, beside the actors' lines.) Use details, description, and what you have learned about Newfies to make your story come to life.

WHAT DO YOU THINK?

- How do the search and rescue dogs and their human handlers work together?
- Do you think you would be good at working with search and rescue dogs? Why or why not?
- Do you think it is right to make Newfoundland dogs work for people? Explain your answer.

ART AND LITERATURE

The sisters in the painting *A Game of Chess* must solve problems to play their game. Look at their faces. What do you think each of them is about to say, and why? How is working together important in playing a game?

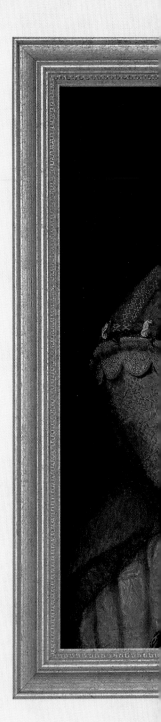

A Game of Chess
by Sofonisba Anguissola

Sofonisba Anguissola was born in Italy in 1532. She was one of the few women in the 1500s who trained and worked as an artist. Look at the designs on the girls' dresses. Anguissola knew how to sew such delicate patterns. This skill helped her paint the image of the dresses exactly as they appeared.

A Game of Chess (1555) by Sofonisba Anguissola.
Oil on canvas (27 9/16″ × 37″).
Muzeum Narodowe, Poznan, Poland.
Courtesy Erich Lessing/Art Resource.

161

When the new school year begins, Felita is happy to find that she and her three friends are in the same class. She becomes even more excited when their new teacher tells them that they will be working together to present a Thanksgiving play. However, Felita finds that her best friend, Gigi, doesn't seem interested in what is going on.

Notable
Trade Book
in Social Studies

Felita

WRITTEN BY

NICHOLASA MOHR

ILLUSTRATED BY

MIKE REED

A wonderful thing happened this new school year. Gigi, Consuela, Paquito, and I were all going into the fourth grade, and we were put in the same class. It had never happened before. Once I was in the same class with Consuela, and last year Gigi and Paquito were together. But this—it was too good to be true! Of course knowing Gigi and I were in the same class made me the happiest.

Our teacher, Miss Lovett, was friendly and laughed easily. In early October, after we had all settled into our class and gotten used to the routine of school once more, Miss Lovett told us that this year our class was going to put on a play for Thanksgiving. The play we were going to perform was based on a poem by Henry Wadsworth Longfellow, called "The Courtship of Miles Standish." It was about the Pilgrims and how they lived when they first landed in America.

We were all so excited about the play. Miss Lovett called for volunteers to help with the sets and costumes. Paquito and I agreed to help with the sets. Consuela was going to work on makeup. Gigi had not volunteered for anything. When we asked her what she was going to do, she shrugged and didn't answer.

Miss Lovett said we could all audition for the different parts in the play. I was really interested in being Priscilla. She is the heroine. Both Captain Miles Standish and the handsome, young John Alden are in love with her. She is the most beautiful maiden in Plymouth, Massachusetts. That's where the Pilgrims used to live. I told my friends how much I would like to play that part. Everyone said I would be perfect . . . except Gigi. She said that it was a hard part to do, and maybe I wouldn't be able to play it. I really got annoyed and asked her what she meant.

"I just don't think you are right to play Priscilla. That's all," she said.

"What do you mean by right?" I asked. But Gigi only shrugged and didn't say another word. She was beginning to get on my nerves.

Auditions for the parts were going to start Tuesday. Lots of kids had volunteered to audition. Paquito said he would try out for the brave Captain Miles Standish. Consuela said she was too afraid to get up in front of everybody and make a fool of herself. Gigi didn't show any interest in the play and refused to even talk to us about it. Finally the day came for the girls to read for the part of Priscilla. I was so excited I could hardly wait. Miss Lovett had given us some lines to study. I had practiced real hard. She called out all the names of those who were going to read. I was surprised when I heard her call out "Georgina Mercado." I didn't even know Gigi wanted to try out for Priscilla. I looked at Gigi, but she ignored me. We began reading. It was my turn. I was very nervous and kept forgetting my lines.

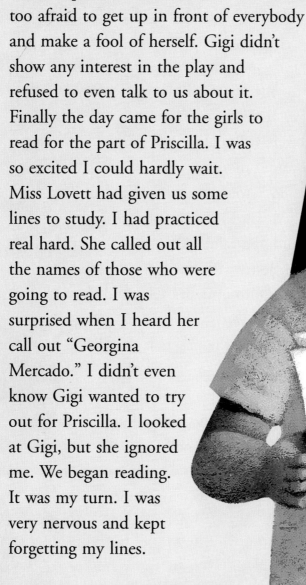

I had to look down at the script a whole lot. Several other girls were almost as nervous as I was. Then it was Gigi's turn. She recited the part almost by heart. She hardly looked at the script. I noticed that she was wearing one of her best dresses. She had never looked that good in school before. When she finished, everybody clapped. It was obvious that she was the best one. Miss Lovett made a fuss.

"You were just wonderful, Georgina," she said, "made for the part!" Boy, would I have liked another chance. I bet I could have done better than Gigi.

Why hadn't she told me she wanted the part? It's a free country, after all. She could read for the same part as me. I wasn't going to stop her! I was really angry at Gigi.

After school everyone was still making a fuss over her. Even Paquito had to open his stupid mouth.

"Oh, man, Gigi!" he said. "You were really good. I liked the part when John Alden asked you to marry Captain Miles Standish and you said, 'Why don't you speak for yourself, John?' You turned your head like this." Paquito imitated Gigi and closed his eyes. "That was really neat!" Consuela and the others laughed and agreed.

I decided I wasn't walking home with them.

"I have to meet my brothers down by the next street," I said. "I'm splitting.

See you." They hardly noticed. Only Consuela said goodbye. The rest just kept on hanging all over Gigi. Big deal, I thought.

Of course walking by myself and watching out for the tough kids was not something I looked forward to. Just last Friday Hilda Gonzales had gotten beat up and had her entire allowance stolen. And at the beginning of the term Paquito had been walking home by himself and gotten mugged. A bunch of big bullies had taken his new schoolbag complete with pencil and pen case, then left him with a swollen lip. No, sir, none of us ever walked home from school alone if we could help it. We knew it wasn't a safe thing to do. Those mean kids never bothered us as long as we stuck together. Carefully I looked around to make sure none of the bullies were in sight. Then I put some speed under my feet, took my chances, and headed for home.

Just before all the casting was completed, Miss Lovett offered me a part as one of the Pilgrim women. All I had to do was stand in the background like a zombie. It wasn't even a speaking part.

"I don't get to say one word," I protested.

"Felicidad Maldonado, you are designing the stage sets and you're assistant stage manager. I think that's quite a bit. Besides, all the speaking parts are taken."

"I'm not interested, thank you," I answered.

"You know"—Miss Lovett shook her head—"you can't be the best in everything."

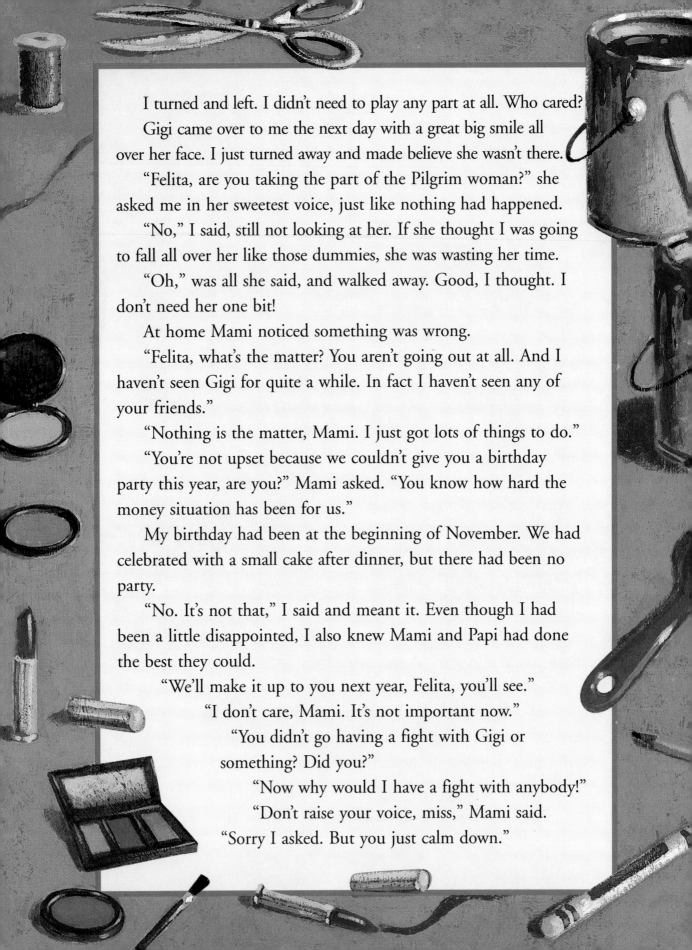

I turned and left. I didn't need to play any part at all. Who cared?

Gigi came over to me the next day with a great big smile all over her face. I just turned away and made believe she wasn't there.

"Felita, are you taking the part of the Pilgrim woman?" she asked me in her sweetest voice, just like nothing had happened.

"No," I said, still not looking at her. If she thought I was going to fall all over her like those dummies, she was wasting her time.

"Oh," was all she said, and walked away. Good, I thought. I don't need her one bit!

At home Mami noticed something was wrong.

"Felita, what's the matter? You aren't going out at all. And I haven't seen Gigi for quite a while. In fact I haven't seen any of your friends."

"Nothing is the matter, Mami. I just got lots of things to do."

"You're not upset because we couldn't give you a birthday party this year, are you?" Mami asked. "You know how hard the money situation has been for us."

My birthday had been at the beginning of November. We had celebrated with a small cake after dinner, but there had been no party.

"No. It's not that," I said and meant it. Even though I had been a little disappointed, I also knew Mami and Papi had done the best they could.

"We'll make it up to you next year, Felita, you'll see."

"I don't care, Mami. It's not important now."

"You didn't go having a fight with Gigi or something? Did you?"

"Now why would I have a fight with anybody!"

"Don't raise your voice, miss," Mami said.

"Sorry I asked. But you just calm down."

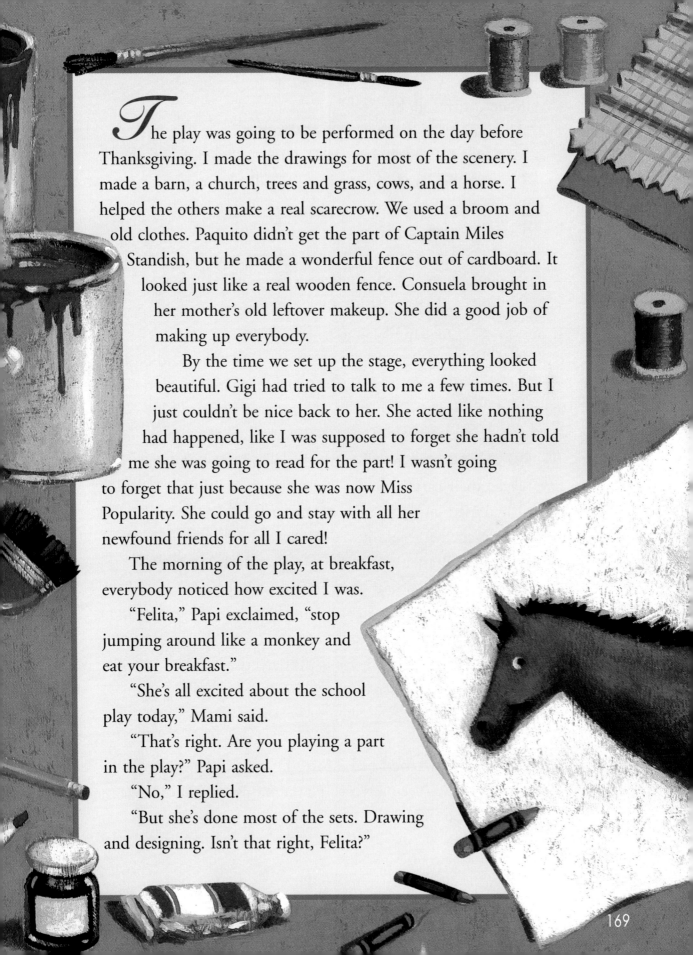

The play was going to be performed on the day before Thanksgiving. I made the drawings for most of the scenery. I made a barn, a church, trees and grass, cows, and a horse. I helped the others make a real scarecrow. We used a broom and old clothes. Paquito didn't get the part of Captain Miles Standish, but he made a wonderful fence out of cardboard. It looked just like a real wooden fence. Consuela brought in her mother's old leftover makeup. She did a good job of making up everybody.

By the time we set up the stage, everything looked beautiful. Gigi had tried to talk to me a few times. But I just couldn't be nice back to her. She acted like nothing had happened, like I was supposed to forget she hadn't told me she was going to read for the part! I wasn't going to forget that just because she was now Miss Popularity. She could go and stay with all her newfound friends for all I cared!

The morning of the play, at breakfast, everybody noticed how excited I was.

"Felita," Papi exclaimed, "stop jumping around like a monkey and eat your breakfast."

"She's all excited about the school play today," Mami said.

"That's right. Are you playing a part in the play?" Papi asked.

"No," I replied.

"But she's done most of the sets. Drawing and designing. Isn't that right, Felita?"

"Mami, it was no big deal."

"That's nice," said Papi. "Tell us about it."

"What kind of sets did you do?" Johnny asked.

"I don't know. Look, I don't want to talk about it."

"Boy, are you touchy today," Tito said with a laugh.

"Leave me alone!" I snapped.

"Okay." Mami stood up. "Enough. Felita, are you finished?" I nodded. "Good. Go to school. When you come back, bring home a better mood. Whatever is bothering you, no need to take it out on us." Quickly I left the table.

"Rosa," I heard Papi say, "sometimes you are too hard on her."

"And sometimes you spoil her, Alberto!" Mami snapped. "I'm not raising fresh kids."

I was glad to get out of there. Who needs them, I thought.

The play was a tremendous hit. Everybody looked wonderful and played their parts really well. The stage was brilliant with the color I had used on my drawings. The background of the countryside, the barn, and just about everything stood out clearly. Ernesto Bratter, the stage manager, said I was a good assistant. I was glad to hear that, because a couple of times I'd had to control my temper on account of his ordering me around. But it had all worked out great.

No doubt about it. Gigi was perfect as Priscilla. Even though the kids clapped and cheered for the entire cast, Gigi got more applause than anybody else. She just kept on taking a whole lot of bows.

Afterward Miss Lovett had a party for our class. We had lots of treats. There was even a record player and we all danced. We had a really good time.

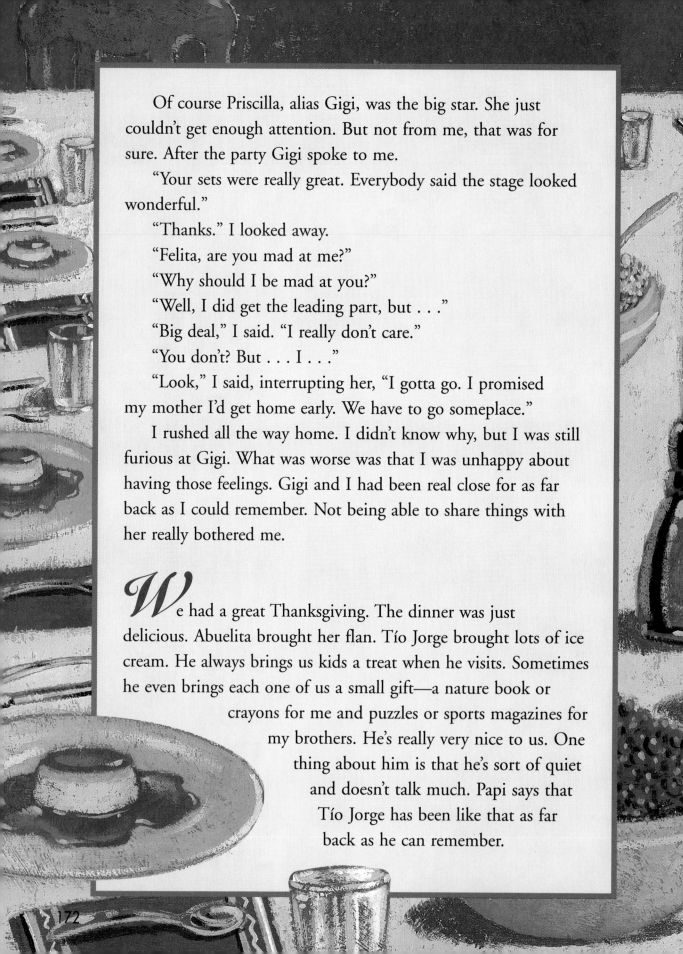

Of course Priscilla, alias Gigi, was the big star. She just couldn't get enough attention. But not from me, that was for sure. After the party Gigi spoke to me.

"Your sets were really great. Everybody said the stage looked wonderful."

"Thanks." I looked away.

"Felita, are you mad at me?"

"Why should I be mad at you?"

"Well, I did get the leading part, but . . ."

"Big deal," I said. "I really don't care."

"You don't? But . . . I . . ."

"Look," I said, interrupting her, "I gotta go. I promised my mother I'd get home early. We have to go someplace."

I rushed all the way home. I didn't know why, but I was still furious at Gigi. What was worse was that I was unhappy about having those feelings. Gigi and I had been real close for as far back as I could remember. Not being able to share things with her really bothered me.

*W*e had a great Thanksgiving. The dinner was just delicious. Abuelita brought her flan. Tío Jorge brought lots of ice cream. He always brings us kids a treat when he visits. Sometimes he even brings each one of us a small gift—a nature book or crayons for me and puzzles or sports magazines for my brothers. He's really very nice to us. One thing about him is that he's sort of quiet and doesn't talk much. Papi says that Tío Jorge has been like that as far back as he can remember.

Abuelita asked me if I wanted to go home with her that evening. Boy, was I happy to get away from Mami. I just couldn't face another day of her asking me questions about Gigi, my friends, and my whole life. It was getting to be too much!

It felt good to be with Abuelita in her apartment. Abuelita never questioned me about anything really personal unless I wanted to talk about it. She just waited, and when she sensed that I was worried or something, then she would ask me. Not like Mami. I love Mami, but she's always trying to find out every little thing that happens to me. With my abuelita sometimes we just sit and stay quiet, not talk at all. That was nice too. We fixed the daybed for me. And then Tío Jorge, Abuelita, and I had more flan as usual.

"Would you like to go to the park with me this Sunday?" Tío Jorge asked me.

"Yes."

"We can go to the zoo and later we can visit the ducks and swans by the lake."

"Great!" I said.

Whenever Tío Jorge took me to the zoo, he would tell me stories about how he, Abuelita, and their brothers and sisters had lived and worked as youngsters taking care of farm animals. These were the only times I ever heard him talk a whole lot.

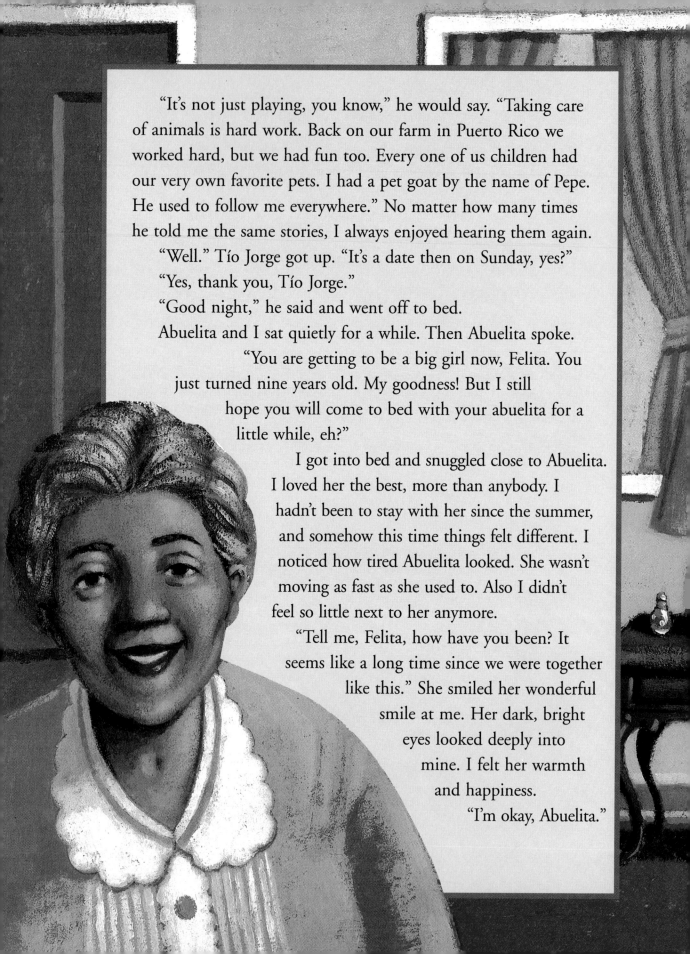

"It's not just playing, you know," he would say. "Taking care of animals is hard work. Back on our farm in Puerto Rico we worked hard, but we had fun too. Every one of us children had our very own favorite pets. I had a pet goat by the name of Pepe. He used to follow me everywhere." No matter how many times he told me the same stories, I always enjoyed hearing them again.

"Well." Tío Jorge got up. "It's a date then on Sunday, yes?"

"Yes, thank you, Tío Jorge."

"Good night," he said and went off to bed.

Abuelita and I sat quietly for a while. Then Abuelita spoke.

"You are getting to be a big girl now, Felita. You just turned nine years old. My goodness! But I still hope you will come to bed with your abuelita for a little while, eh?"

I got into bed and snuggled close to Abuelita. I loved her the best, more than anybody. I hadn't been to stay with her since the summer, and somehow this time things felt different. I noticed how tired Abuelita looked. She wasn't moving as fast as she used to. Also I didn't feel so little next to her anymore.

"Tell me, Felita, how have you been? It seems like a long time since we were together like this." She smiled her wonderful smile at me. Her dark, bright eyes looked deeply into mine. I felt her warmth and happiness.

"I'm okay, Abuelita."

"Tell me about your play at school. Rosa tells me you worked on the stage sets. Was the play a success?"

"It was. It was great. The stage looked beautiful. My drawings stood out really well. I never made such big drawings in my life. There was a farm in the country, a barn, and animals. I made it the way it used to be in the olden days of the Pilgrims. You know, how it was when they first came to America."

"I'm so proud of you. Tell me about the play. Did you act in it?"

"No." I paused. "I didn't want to."

"I see. Tell me a little about the story."

I told Abuelita all about it.

"Who played the parts? Any of your friends?"

"Some."

"Who?"

"Well, this boy Charlie Martinez played John Alden. Louie Collins played Captain Miles Standish. You don't know them. Mary Jackson played the part of the narrator. That's the person who tells the story. You really don't know any of them."

I was hoping she wouldn't ask, but she did.

"Who played the part of the girl both men love?"

"Oh, her? Gigi."

"Gigi Mercado, your best friend?" I nodded. "Was she good?"

"Yes, she was. Very good."

"You don't sound too happy about that."

"I don't care." I shrugged.

"But if she is your best friend, I should think you would care."

"I . . . I don't know if she is my friend anymore, Abuelita."

"Why do you say that?"

I couldn't answer. I just felt awful.

"Did she do something? Did you two argue?" I nodded. "Can I ask what happened?"

"Well, it's hard to explain. But what she did wasn't fair."

"Fair about what, Felita?"

I hadn't spoken about it before. Now with Abuelita it was easy to talk about it.

"Well, we all tried out for the different parts. Everybody knew what everybody was trying out for. But Gigi never told anybody she was going to try out for Priscilla. She kept it a great big secret. Even after I told her that I wanted to try for the part, she kept quiet about it. Do you know what she did say? She said I wasn't right for it . . . it was a hard part and all that bunch of baloney. She just wanted the part for herself, so she was mysterious about the whole thing. Like . . . it was . . . I don't know." I stopped for a moment, trying to figure this whole thing out. "After all, I am supposed to be her best friend . . . her very best friend. Why shouldn't she let me know that she wanted to be Priscilla? I wouldn't care. I let her know my plans. I didn't go sneaking around."

"Are you angry because Gigi got the part?"

It was hard for me to answer. I thought about it for a little while. "Abuelita, I don't think so. She was really good in the part."

"Were you as good when you tried out for Priscilla?"

"No." I looked at Abuelita. "I stunk." We both laughed.

"Then maybe you are not angry at Gigi at all."

"What do you mean?"

"Well, maybe you are a little bit . . . hurt?"

"Hurt?" I felt confused.

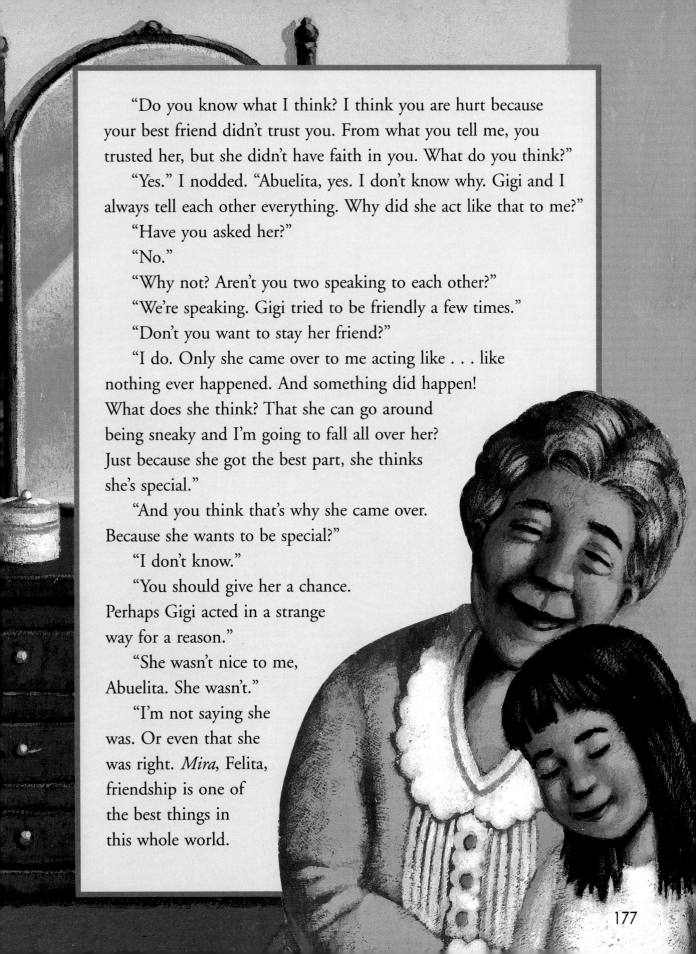

"Do you know what I think? I think you are hurt because your best friend didn't trust you. From what you tell me, you trusted her, but she didn't have faith in you. What do you think?"

"Yes." I nodded. "Abuelita, yes. I don't know why. Gigi and I always tell each other everything. Why did she act like that to me?"

"Have you asked her?"

"No."

"Why not? Aren't you two speaking to each other?"

"We're speaking. Gigi tried to be friendly a few times."

"Don't you want to stay her friend?"

"I do. Only she came over to me acting like . . . like nothing ever happened. And something did happen! What does she think? That she can go around being sneaky and I'm going to fall all over her? Just because she got the best part, she thinks she's special."

"And you think that's why she came over. Because she wants to be special?"

"I don't know."

"You should give her a chance. Perhaps Gigi acted in a strange way for a reason."

"She wasn't nice to me, Abuelita. She wasn't."

"I'm not saying she was. Or even that she was right. *Mira*, Felita, friendship is one of the best things in this whole world.

177

It's one of the few things you can't go out and buy. It's like love. You can buy clothes, food, even luxuries, but there's no place I know of where you can buy a real friend. Do you?"

I shook my head. Abuelita smiled at me and waited. We were both silent for a long moment. I wondered if maybe I shouldn't have a talk with Gigi. After all, she had tried to talk to me first.

"Abuelita, do you think it's a good idea for me to . . . maybe talk to Gigi?"

"You know, that's a very good idea." Abuelita nodded.

"Well, she did try to talk to me a few times. Only there's just one thing. I won't know what to say to her. I mean, after what's happened and all."

"After so many years of being close, I am sure you could say 'Hello, Gigi. How are you?' That should be easy enough."

"I feel better already, Abuelita."

"Good," Abuelita said. "Now let's you and I get to sleep. Abuelita is tired."

"You don't have to tuck me in. I'll tuck you in instead." I got out of bed and folded the covers carefully over my side. Then I leaned over her and gave her a kiss. Abuelita hugged me real tight.

"My Felita has become a young lady," she whispered.

I kept thinking of what Abuelita had said, and on Monday I waited for Gigi after school. It was as if she knew I wanted to talk. She came over to me.

"Hello, Gigi," I said. "How are you?"

"Fine." Gigi smiled. "Wanna walk home together?"

"Let's take the long way so we can be by ourselves," I said.

We walked without saying anything for a couple of blocks. Finally I spoke.

"I wanted to tell you, Gigi, you were really great as Priscilla."

"Did you really like me? Oh, Felita, I'm so glad. I wanted you to like me, more than anybody else. Of course it was nothing compared to the sets you did. They were something special. Everybody liked them so much."

"You were right too," I said. "I wasn't very good for the part of Priscilla."

"Look." Gigi stopped walking and looked at me. "I'm sorry about . . . about the way I acted. Like, I didn't say anything to

you or the others. But, well, I was scared you all would think I was silly or something. I mean, you wanted the part too. So, I figured, better not say nothing."

"I wouldn't have cared, Gigi. Honest."

"Felita . . . it's just that you are so good at a lot of things. Like, you draw just fantastic. You beat everybody at hopscotch and kick-the-can. You know about nature and animals, much more than the rest of us. Everything you do is always better than . . . what I do! I just wanted this part for me. I wanted to be better than you this time. For once I didn't wanna worry about you. Felita, I'm sorry."

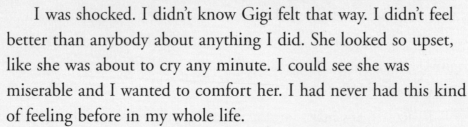

I was shocked. I didn't know Gigi felt that way. I didn't feel better than anybody about anything I did. She looked so upset, like she was about to cry any minute. I could see she was miserable and I wanted to comfort her. I had never had this kind of feeling before in my whole life.

"Well, you didn't have to worry. 'Cause I stunk!" We both laughed with relief. "I think I was the worst one!"

"Oh, no, you weren't." Gigi laughed. "Jenny Fuentes was the most awful."

"Worse than me?"

"Much worse. Do you know what she sounded like? She sounded like this. 'Wha . . . wha . . . why don't you . . . speeek for your . . . yourself *Johnnnn?*'" Gigi and I burst into laughter.

"And how about that dummy, Louie Collins? I didn't think he read better than Paquito."

"Right," Gigi agreed. "I don't know how he got through the play. He was shaking so much that I was scared the sets would fall right on his head."

It was so much fun, Gigi and I talking about the play and how we felt about everybody and everything. It was just like before, only better.

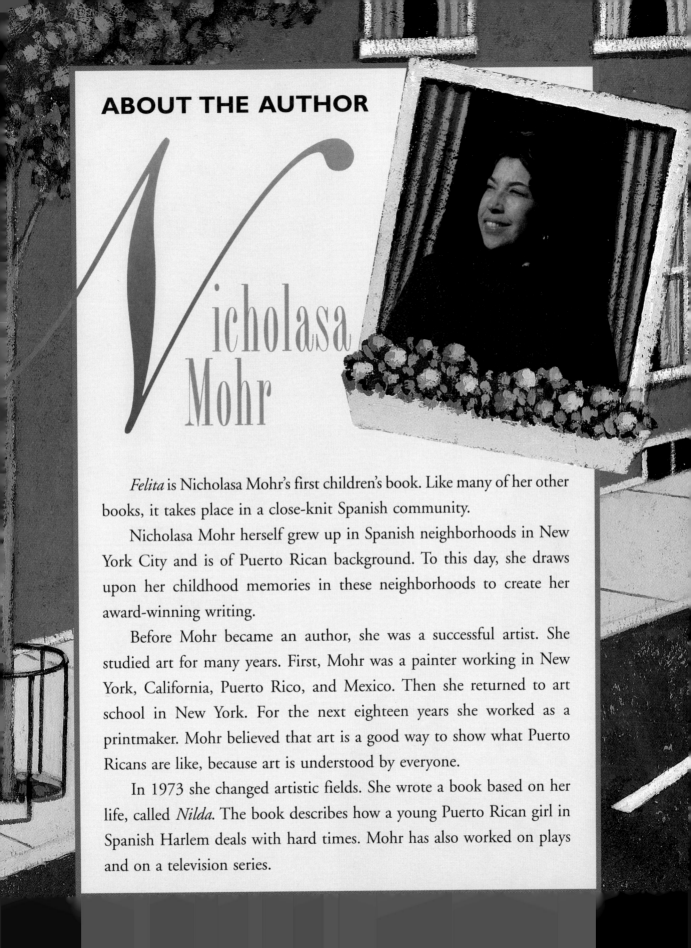

ABOUT THE AUTHOR

Nicholasa Mohr

Felita is Nicholasa Mohr's first children's book. Like many of her other books, it takes place in a close-knit Spanish community.

Nicholasa Mohr herself grew up in Spanish neighborhoods in New York City and is of Puerto Rican background. To this day, she draws upon her childhood memories in these neighborhoods to create her award-winning writing.

Before Mohr became an author, she was a successful artist. She studied art for many years. First, Mohr was a painter working in New York, California, Puerto Rico, and Mexico. Then she returned to art school in New York. For the next eighteen years she worked as a printmaker. Mohr believed that art is a good way to show what Puerto Ricans are like, because art is understood by everyone.

In 1973 she changed artistic fields. She wrote a book based on her life, called *Nilda*. The book describes how a young Puerto Rican girl in Spanish Harlem deals with hard times. Mohr has also worked on plays and on a television series.

RESPONSE CORNER

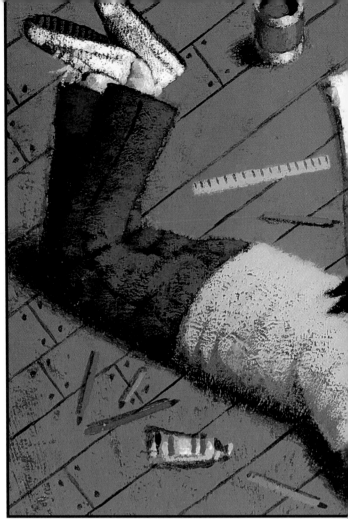

Be Upbeat!

Songs about friendship are as old as friendship itself. With a small group, write a song about Felita and Gigi. Choose a tune you like. Then write words for the song that explain their problem and how they solved it. Practice your song before presenting it to classmates.

Making Up Is Hard to Do

Felita thinks she and Gigi got along better after their argument than before it. Design and create a greeting card that one girl could give to the other. Inside the card, write a message or greeting that tells about friendship. Your greeting may rhyme, if you'd like.

First Aid for Friendship

It's important to know what to do when friendships break down. Write a letter for an advice column. Then write an answer in which you list ways friends can work out problems. Tell why this is important. You may want to discuss your ideas with classmates before you write. Make copies of your column for classmates.

What Do You Think?

- What causes Felita to stop talking to her best friend? What causes her to start talking again?

- Think about what you know about Felita. If you were Gigi, would you have kept quiet about your plans to audition for the play? Why or why not?

- What do you think Felita means at the end of the story when she says that her friendship with Gigi is "just like before, only better"?

185

WRITTEN BY PETER GOLENBOCK

TEAM

Notable Trade Book in Social Studies

Jackie Robinson

MATES

ILLUSTRATED BY PAUL BACON

"Pee Wee" Reese

Once upon a time in America, when automobiles were black and looked like tanks and laundry was white and hung on clotheslines to dry, there were two wonderful baseball leagues that no longer exist. They were called the Negro Leagues.

The Negro Leagues had extraordinary players, and adoring fans came to see them wherever they played. They were heroes, but players in the Negro Leagues didn't make much money and their lives on the road were hard.

SATCHEL PAIGE

Laws against segregation didn't exist in the 1940s. In many places in this country, black people were not allowed to go to the same schools and churches as white people. They couldn't sit in the front of a bus or trolley car. They couldn't drink from the same drinking fountains that white people drank from.

Back then, many hotels didn't rent rooms tc black people, so the Negro League players slept in their cars. Many towns had no restaurants that would serve them, so they often had to eat meals that they could buy and carry with them.

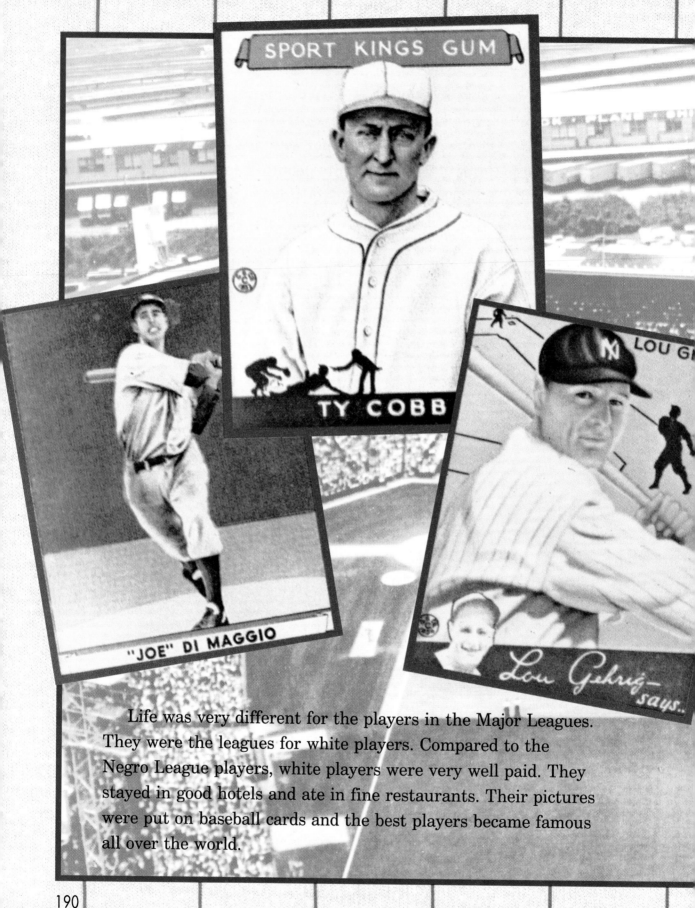

SPORT KINGS GUM

TY COBB

"JOE" DI MAGGIO

LOU G[...]

Lou Gehrig says...

Life was very different for the players in the Major Leagues. They were the leagues for white players. Compared to the Negro League players, white players were very well paid. They stayed in good hotels and ate in fine restaurants. Their pictures were put on baseball cards and the best players became famous all over the world.

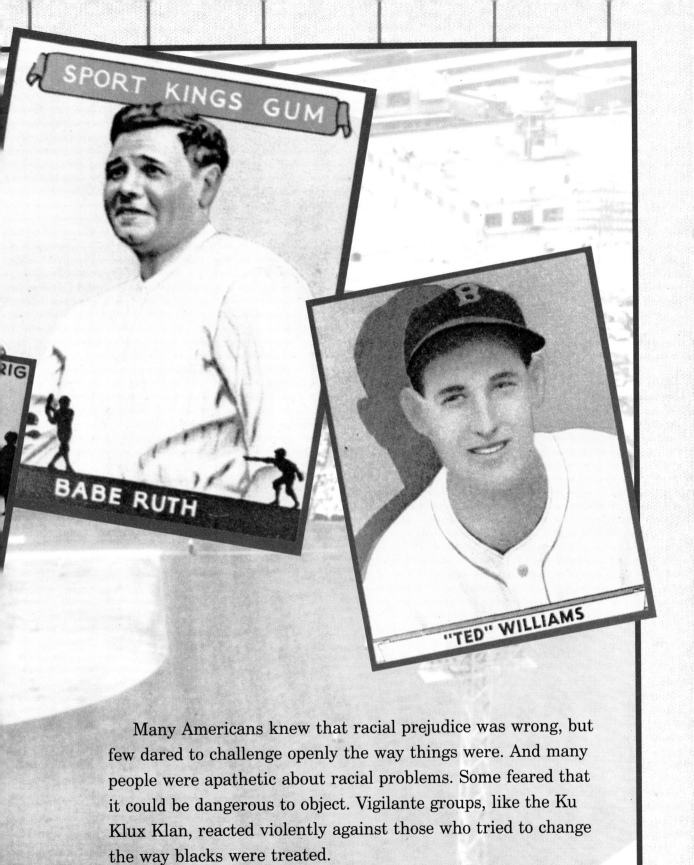

Many Americans knew that racial prejudice was wrong, but few dared to challenge openly the way things were. And many people were apathetic about racial problems. Some feared that it could be dangerous to object. Vigilante groups, like the Ku Klux Klan, reacted violently against those who tried to change the way blacks were treated.

The general manager of the Brooklyn Dodgers baseball team was a man by the name of Branch Rickey. He was not afraid of change. He wanted to treat the Dodger fans to the best players he could find, regardless of the color of their skin. He thought segregation was unfair and wanted to give everyone, regardless of race or creed, an opportunity to compete equally on ballfields across America.

To do this, the Dodgers needed one special man.

Branch Rickey launched a search for him. He was looking for a star player in the Negro Leagues who would be able to compete successfully despite threats on his life or attempts to injure him. He would have to possess the self-control not to fight back when opposing players tried to intimidate or hurt him. If this man disgraced himself on the field, Rickey knew, his opponents would use it as an excuse to keep blacks out of Major League baseball for many more years.

JACKIE ROBINSON AND BRANCH RICKEY

Rickey thought Jackie Robinson might be just the man.

Jackie rode the train to Brooklyn to meet Mr. Rickey. When Mr. Rickey told him, "I want a man with the courage not to fight back," Jackie Robinson replied, "If you take this gamble, I will do my best to perform." They shook hands. Branch Rickey and Jackie Robinson were starting on what would be known in history as "the great experiment."

At spring training with the Dodgers, Jackie was mobbed by blacks, young and old, as if he were a savior. He was the first black player to try out for a Major League team. If he succeeded, they knew, others would follow.

Initially, life with the Dodgers was for Jackie a series of humiliations. The players on his team who came from the South, men who had been taught to avoid black people since childhood, moved to another table whenever he sat down next to them. Many opposing players were cruel to him, calling him nasty names from their dugouts. A few tried to hurt him with their spiked shoes. Pitchers aimed at his head. And he received threats on his life, both from individuals and from organizations like the Ku Klux Klan.

Despite all the difficulties, Jackie Robinson didn't give up. He made the Brooklyn Dodgers team.

But making the Dodgers was only the beginning. Jackie had to face abuse and hostility throughout the season, from April through September. His worst pain was inside. Often he felt very alone. On the road he had to live by himself, because only the white players were allowed in the hotels in towns where the team played.

The whole time Pee Wee Reese, the Dodger shortstop, was growing up in Louisville, Kentucky, he had rarely even seen a black person, unless it was in the back of a bus. Most of his friends and relatives hated the idea of his playing on the same field as a black man. In addition, Pee Wee Reese had more to lose than the other players when Jackie joined the team.

Jackie had been a shortstop, and everyone thought that Jackie would take Pee Wee's job. Lesser men might have felt anger toward Jackie, but Pee Wee was different. He told himself, "If he's good enough to take my job, he deserves it."

When his Southern teammates circulated a petition to throw Jackie off the team and asked him to sign it, Pee Wee responded, "I don't care if this man is black, blue, or striped"— and refused to sign. "He can play and he can help us win," he told the others. "That's what counts."

Very early in the season, the Dodgers traveled west to Ohio to play the Cincinnati Reds. Cincinnati is near Pee Wee's hometown of Louisville.

The Reds played in a small ballpark where the fans sat close to the field. The players could almost feel the breath of the fans on the backs of their necks. Many who came that day screamed terrible, hateful things at Jackie when the Dodgers were on the field.

More than anything else, Pee Wee Reese believed in doing what was right. When he heard the fans yelling at Jackie, Pee Wee decided to take a stand.

With his head high, Pee Wee walked directly from his shortstop position to where Jackie was playing first base. The taunts and shouting of the fans were ringing in Pee Wee's ears. It saddened him, because he knew it could have been his friends and neighbors. Pee Wee's legs felt heavy, but he knew what he had to do.

As he walked toward Jackie wearing the gray Dodger uniform, he looked into his teammate's bold, pained eyes. The first baseman had done nothing to provoke the hostility except that he sought to be treated as an equal. Jackie was grim with anger. Pee Wee smiled broadly as he reached Jackie. Jackie smiled back.

Stopping beside Jackie, Pee Wee put his arm around Jackie's shoulders. An audible gasp rose up from the crowd when they saw what Pee Wee had done. Then there was silence.

Outlined on a sea of green grass stood these two great athletes, one black, one white, both wearing the same team uniform.

"I am standing by him," Pee Wee Reese said to the world. "This man is my teammate."

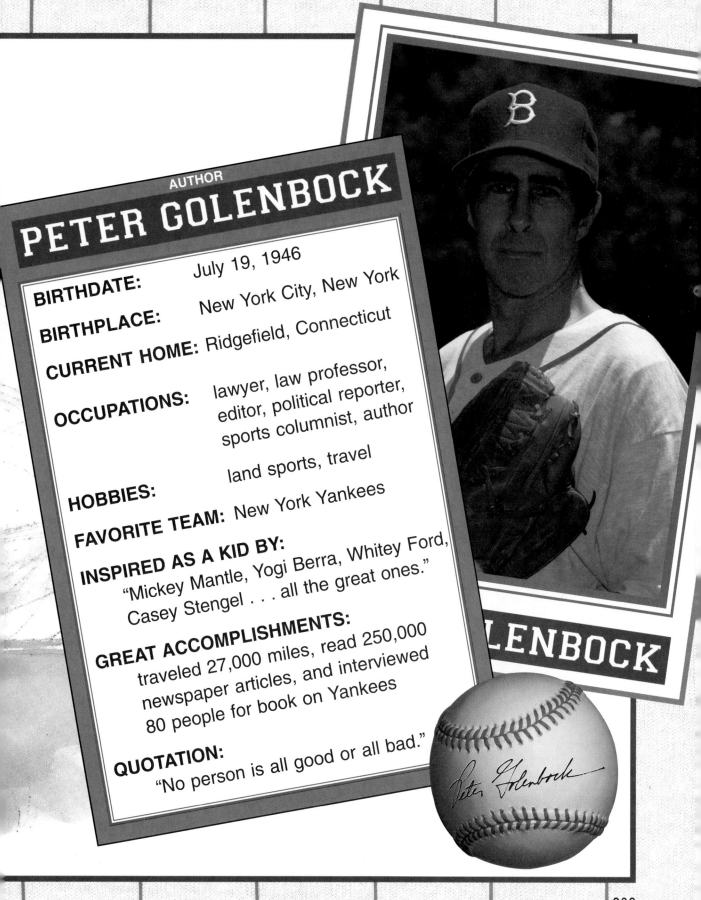

AUTHOR

PETER GOLENBOCK

BIRTHDATE: July 19, 1946

BIRTHPLACE: New York City, New York

CURRENT HOME: Ridgefield, Connecticut

OCCUPATIONS: lawyer, law professor, editor, political reporter, sports columnist, author

HOBBIES: land sports, travel

FAVORITE TEAM: New York Yankees

INSPIRED AS A KID BY: "Mickey Mantle, Yogi Berra, Whitey Ford, Casey Stengel . . . all the great ones."

GREAT ACCOMPLISHMENTS: traveled 27,000 miles, read 250,000 newspaper articles, and interviewed 80 people for book on Yankees

QUOTATION: "No person is all good or all bad."

We Have Our

from Sports Pages *by Arnold Adoff*
illustrated by Ron Mahoney

Moments.

Sometimes we leap and land.
Sometimes we trip and fall.
Sometimes we catch the other team   before they score.
Sometimes we jump too soon and get faked out of our
                                                          socks.

                        We can be sharp on the pick-off play at third.
            Or

                        we can have rocks in our heads and miss that
                                                softly batted ball,
                                                and miss that
                                                      one
                                        sweet chance to
                                                    save
                                                    the
                                                    day.

I lose. I win. We lose. We win.
The team   finishes in last place.
The team is
            in the play-offs at last
            and past defeats f a d e
                    fast.

We have our moments.

RESPONSE CORNER

RAH, RAH, RAH!

Did the Dodgers act like a team the year Jackie Robinson came aboard? Discuss your ideas in a small group. Then work as a "team" to create a poster that shows why teamwork is important in sports.

SPRING INTO ACTION

Practice "making a statement" without words, as Pee Wee did. Read aloud the poem "We Have Our Moments" while a partner silently acts out what the words describe. You may want to research baseball terms before reading or acting.

GOOD SHOW!

Branch Rickey was one person who was active in ending racial segregation. Research other people from this time period who helped change the way things were for African Americans. Choose one person who interests you, such as Martin Luther King, Jr., or Mary McLeod Bethune, and prepare a short report on his or her life for your classmates.

WHAT DO YOU THINK?

◆ How did Pee Wee Reese show his support for Jackie Robinson?

◆ If you had been Branch Rickey, would you have hired Jackie Robinson? Why or why not?

◆ How does the poem "We Have Our Moments" help you understand the message in "Teammates"?

207

WRAP-UP

CLUBHOUSE

The selections in this theme show the importance of communicating with one another in solving problems. What do you think would have been different if Felita had not tried to work things out by talking with Abuelita about her problem? Explain why you think that.

Both Isabel and Felita missed their best friend. How could Felita use what she learned about friendship from Abuelita to help Isabel adjust to life with her new family?

ACTIVITY CORNER

Think about a time when you had to depend on someone else to help you solve a problem. Maybe you had an experience similar to one you read about in this theme, such as losing a pet or having a problem with a friend. Maybe you have even been rescued from a difficult situation. Briefly describe your situation, and write the steps you took to work out the problem.

THEME

NATURAL CHANGES

Over time, the Earth's features
have changed along with the
creatures that inhabit the land, sky,
and sea. Many of the changes have
occurred naturally, but some have
been caused by humans. In this
theme, you will meet some of
the creatures who face having
to adapt to changes
in their environment.

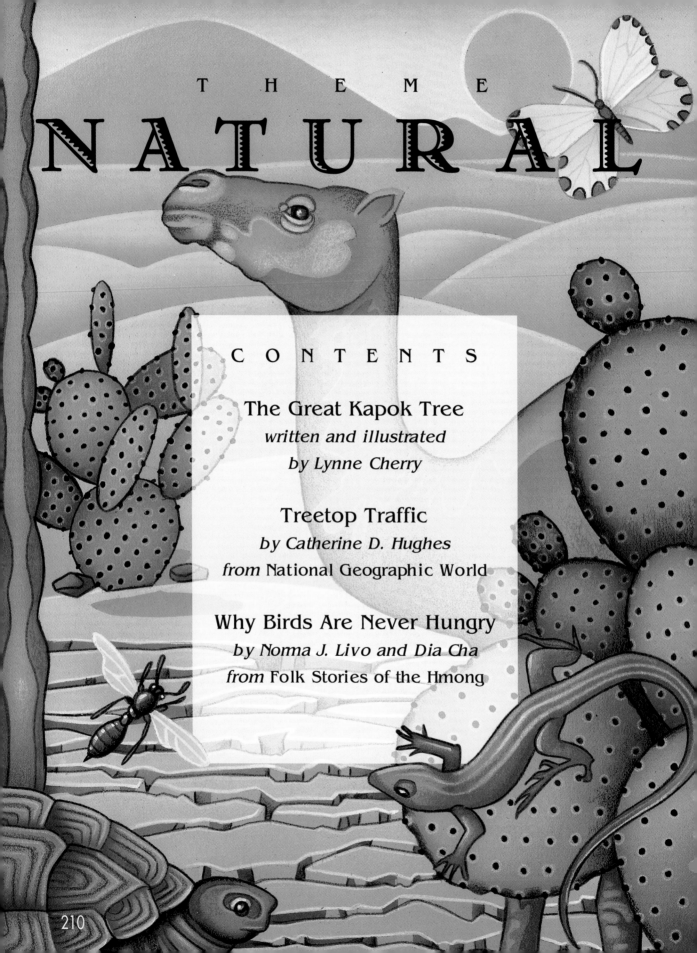

CONTENTS

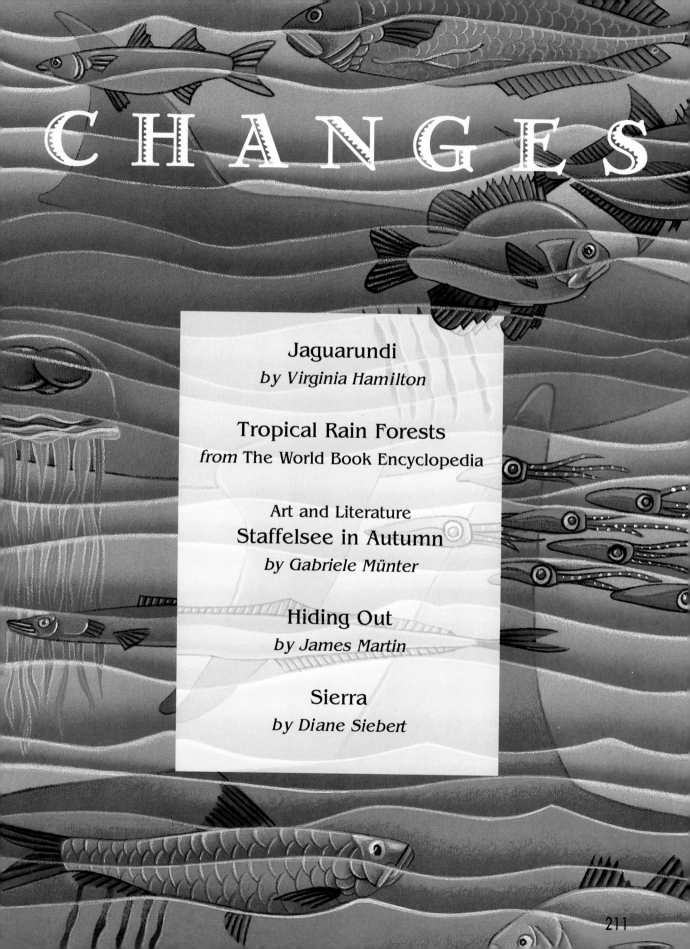

CHANGES

BOOKSHELF

Come Back, Salmon

COME BACK, SALMON

HOW A GROUP OF DEDICATED KIDS ADOPTED
PIGEON CREEK AND BROUGHT IT BACK TO LIFE

by Molly Cone • Photog

Come Back, Salmon

*by Molly Cone
photographs by
Sidnee Wheelwright*

Some students set an
example in caring for
the world around us.

Teachers' Choice, Outstanding
Science Trade Book, Notable Trade
Book in the Field of Social Studies
Signatures Library

This Place Is Wet

This Place Is Wet
*by Vicki Cobb
illustrated by
Barbara Lavallee*

Try to imagine what it
would be like to live
in one of the wettest
places on Earth!

Award-Winning Author
Signatures Library

IMAGINE LIVING HERE

THIS PLACE IS WET

BY
VICKI COBB
ILLUSTRATED BY
BARBARA LAVALLEE

The Dragon and the Unicorn
written and illustrated by Lynne Cherry

The relationship between two creatures and a princess heals misunderstandings and ensures the future of the forest.

Award-Winning Author and Illustrator

Marjory Stoneman Douglas: Friend of the Everglades
by Tricia Andryszewski

Douglas—champion of Florida's endangered wetlands—spent her long life working for a worthy cause.

Chameleons: Dragons in the Trees

by James Martin photographs by Art Wolfe

The facts about these colorful creatures may change how you view them.

ALA Notable Book, Outstanding Science Trade Book

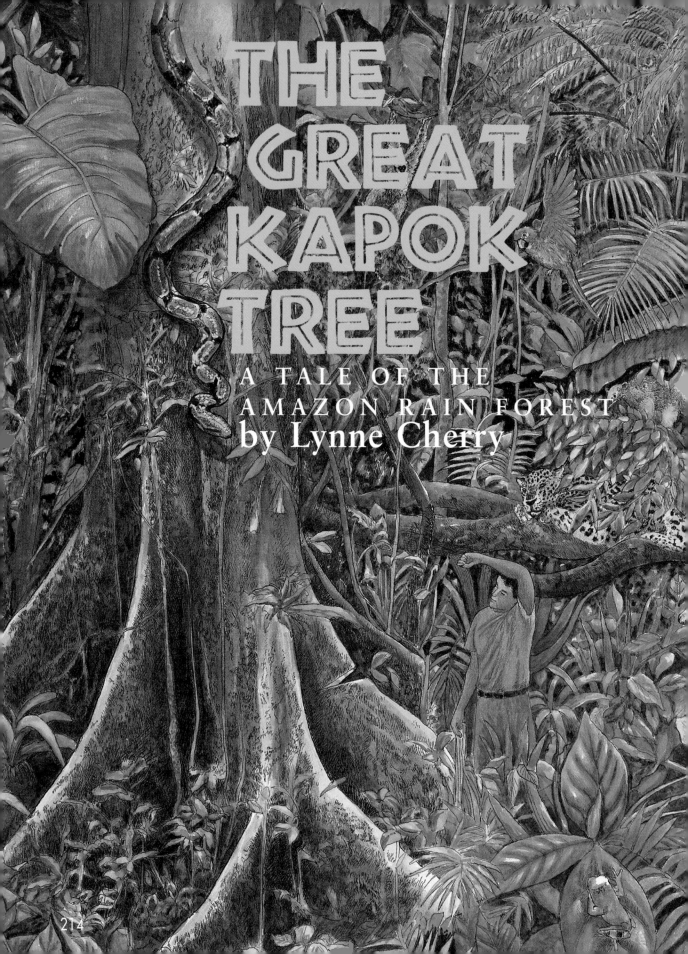

THE GREAT KAPOK TREE

A TALE OF THE AMAZON RAIN FOREST
by Lynne Cherry

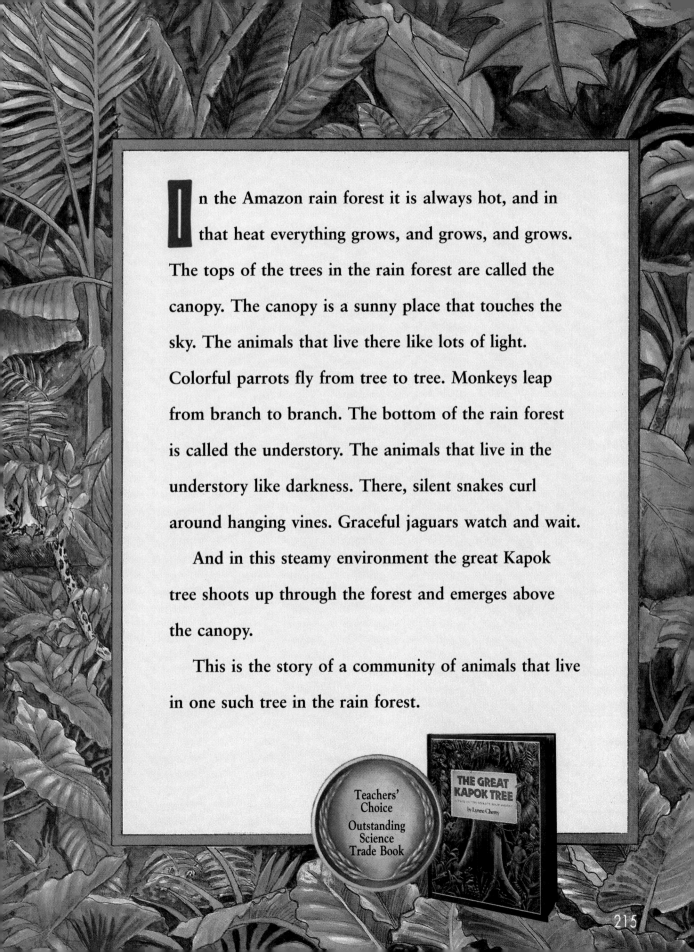

In the Amazon rain forest it is always hot, and in that heat everything grows, and grows, and grows. The tops of the trees in the rain forest are called the canopy. The canopy is a sunny place that touches the sky. The animals that live there like lots of light. Colorful parrots fly from tree to tree. Monkeys leap from branch to branch. The bottom of the rain forest is called the understory. The animals that live in the understory like darkness. There, silent snakes curl around hanging vines. Graceful jaguars watch and wait.

And in this steamy environment the great Kapok tree shoots up through the forest and emerges above the canopy.

This is the story of a community of animals that live in one such tree in the rain forest.

Teachers'
Choice

Outstanding
Science
Trade Book

THE GREAT
KAPOK TREE
A TALE OF THE AMAZON RAIN FOREST
by Lynne Cherry

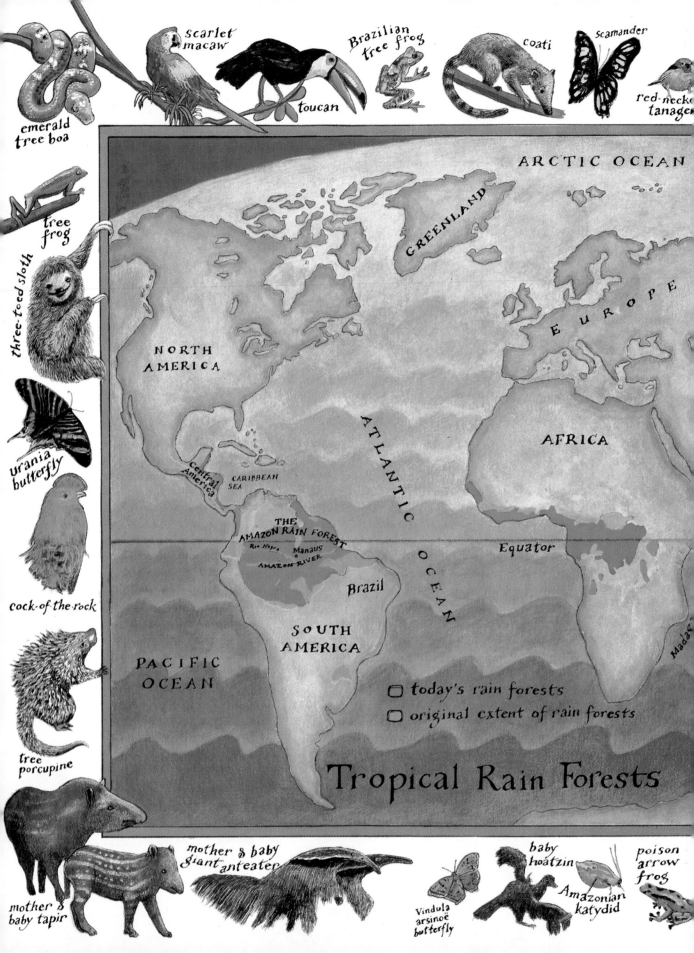

emerald
tree boa

scarlet
macaw

toucan

Brazilian
tree frog

coati

scamander

red-necke
tanage

tree
frog

three-toed sloth

urania
butterfly

cock-of-the-rock

tree
porcupine

ARCTIC OCEAN

GREENLAND

NORTH
AMERICA

EUROPE

ATLANTIC

AFRICA

Central
America

CARIBBEAN
SEA

THE
AMAZON RAIN FOREST
Rio Negro   Manaus
AMAZON RIVER

Equator

OCEAN

Brazil

SOUTH
AMERICA

Madag

PACIFIC
OCEAN

☐ today's rain forests
☐ original extent of rain forests

Tropical Rain Forests

mother & baby tapir

mother & baby
giant anteater

Vindula
arsinoë
butterfly

baby
hoatzin

Amazonian
katydid

poison
arrow
frog

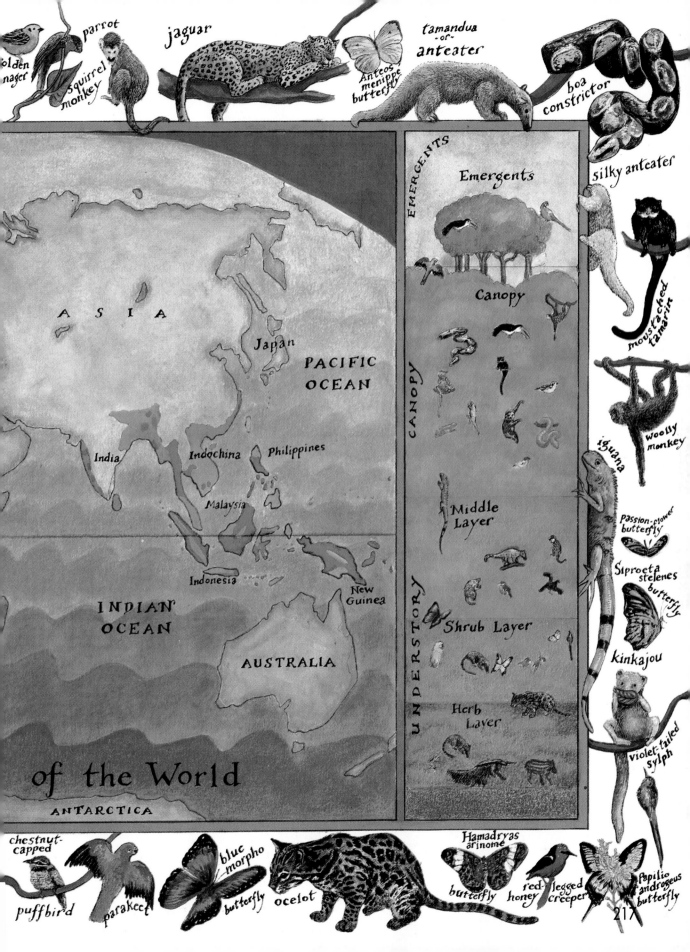

golden
tanger

parrot

squirrel
monkey

jaguar

Anteos
menippe
butterfly

tamandua
-or-
anteater

boa
constrictor

silky anteater

EMERGENTS

Emergents

moustached
tamarin

ASIA

Japan

PACIFIC
OCEAN

CANOPY

Canopy

woolly
monkey

India

Indochina

Philippines

iguana

Malaysia

Middle
Layer

passion-flower
butterfly

Indonesia

New
Guinea

UNDERSTORY

Siproeta
stelenes
butterfly

INDIAN
OCEAN

Shrub Layer

kinkajou

AUSTRALIA

Herb
Layer

of the World

violet-tailed
sylph

ANTARCTICA

chestnut-
capped

puffbird

parakeet

blue
morpho
butterfly

ocelot

Hamadryas
arinome

butterfly

red-
honey
legged
creeper

Papilio
androgeus
butterfly

217

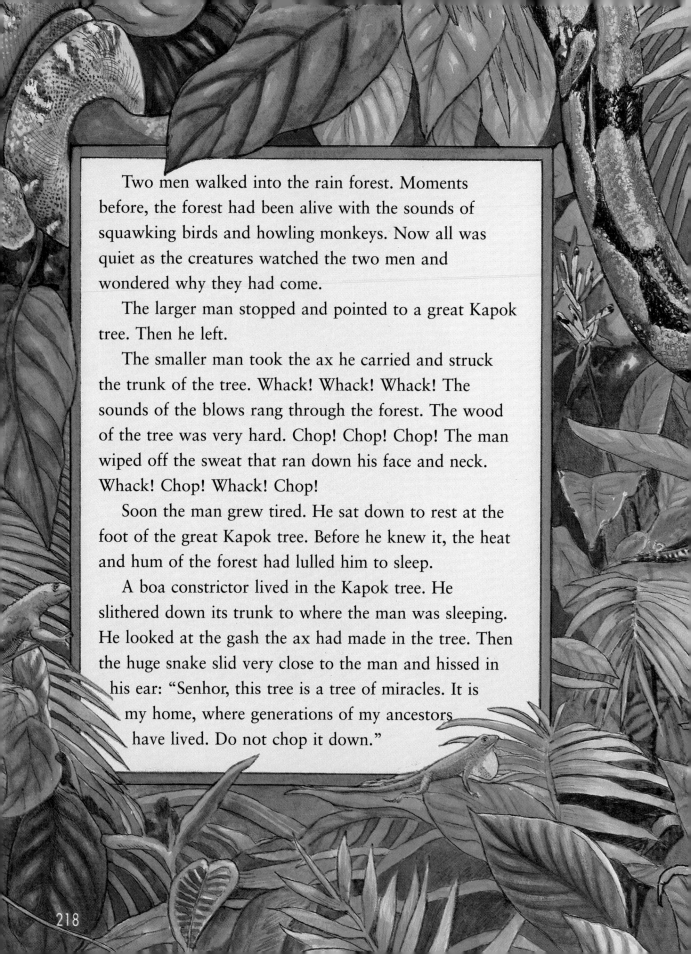

Two men walked into the rain forest. Moments before, the forest had been alive with the sounds of squawking birds and howling monkeys. Now all was quiet as the creatures watched the two men and wondered why they had come.

The larger man stopped and pointed to a great Kapok tree. Then he left.

The smaller man took the ax he carried and struck the trunk of the tree. Whack! Whack! Whack! The sounds of the blows rang through the forest. The wood of the tree was very hard. Chop! Chop! Chop! The man wiped off the sweat that ran down his face and neck. Whack! Chop! Whack! Chop!

Soon the man grew tired. He sat down to rest at the foot of the great Kapok tree. Before he knew it, the heat and hum of the forest had lulled him to sleep.

A boa constrictor lived in the Kapok tree. He slithered down its trunk to where the man was sleeping. He looked at the gash the ax had made in the tree. Then the huge snake slid very close to the man and hissed in his ear: "Senhor, this tree is a tree of miracles. It is my home, where generations of my ancestors have lived. Do not chop it down."

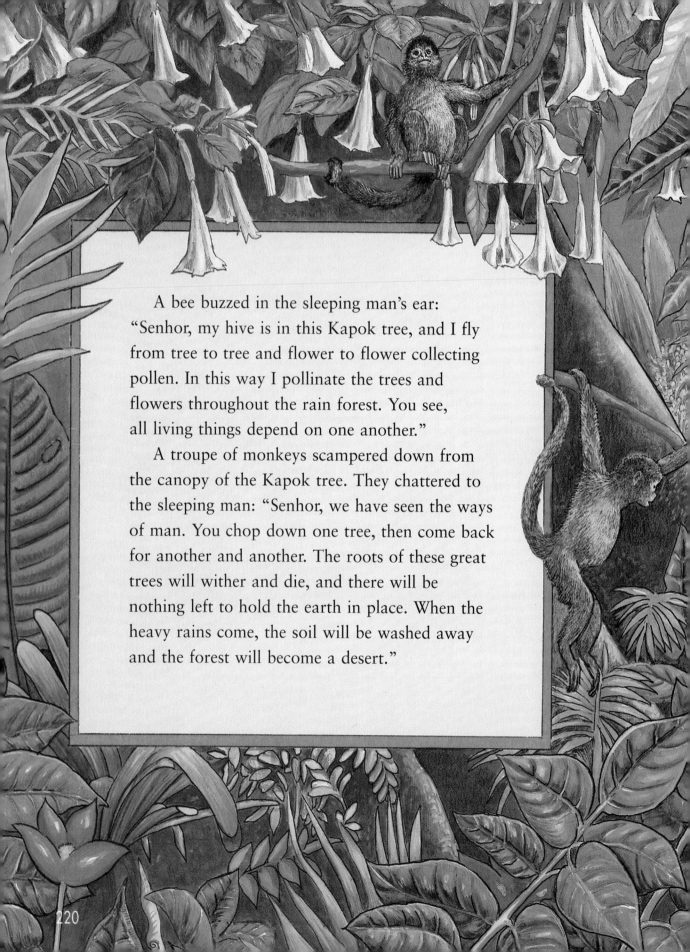

A bee buzzed in the sleeping man's ear: "Senhor, my hive is in this Kapok tree, and I fly from tree to tree and flower to flower collecting pollen. In this way I pollinate the trees and flowers throughout the rain forest. You see, all living things depend on one another."

A troupe of monkeys scampered down from the canopy of the Kapok tree. They chattered to the sleeping man: "Senhor, we have seen the ways of man. You chop down one tree, then come back for another and another. The roots of these great trees will wither and die, and there will be nothing left to hold the earth in place. When the heavy rains come, the soil will be washed away and the forest will become a desert."

A toucan, a macaw, and a cock-of-the-rock flew down from the canopy. "Senhor!" squawked the toucan, "you must not cut down this tree. We have flown over the rain forest and seen what happens once you begin to chop down the trees. Many people settle on the land. They set fires to clear the underbrush, and soon the forest disappears. Where once there was life and beauty only black and smoldering ruins remain."

A bright and small tree frog crawled along the edge of a leaf. In a squeaky voice he piped in the man's ear: "Senhor, a ruined rain forest means ruined lives . . . many ruined lives. You will leave many of us homeless if you chop down this great Kapok tree."

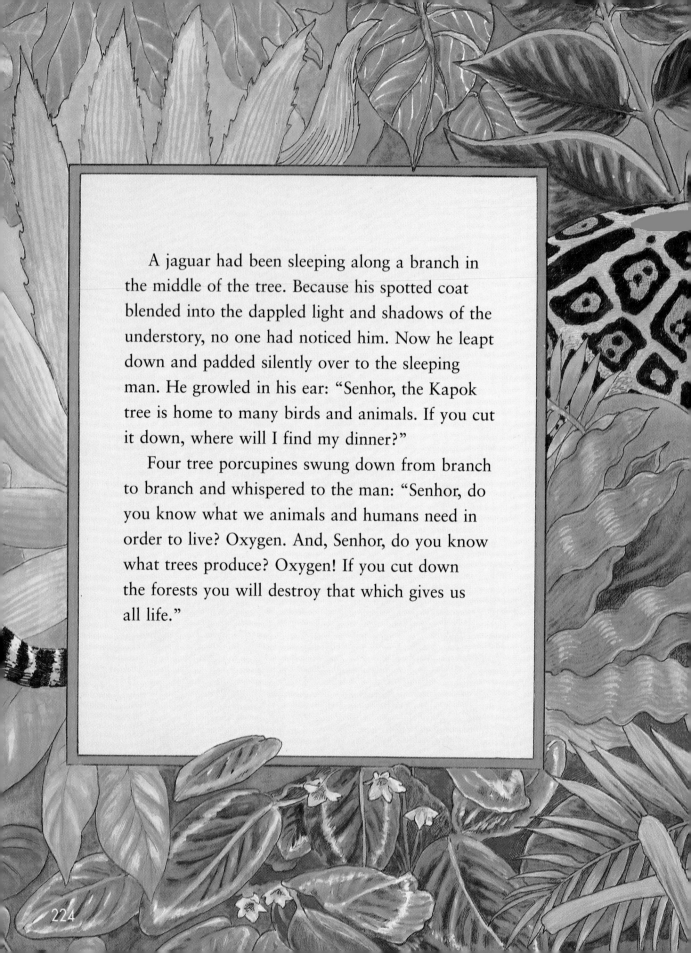

A jaguar had been sleeping along a branch in the middle of the tree. Because his spotted coat blended into the dappled light and shadows of the understory, no one had noticed him. Now he leapt down and padded silently over to the sleeping man. He growled in his ear: "Senhor, the Kapok tree is home to many birds and animals. If you cut it down, where will I find my dinner?"

Four tree porcupines swung down from branch to branch and whispered to the man: "Senhor, do you know what we animals and humans need in order to live? Oxygen. And, Senhor, do you know what trees produce? Oxygen! If you cut down the forests you will destroy that which gives us all life."

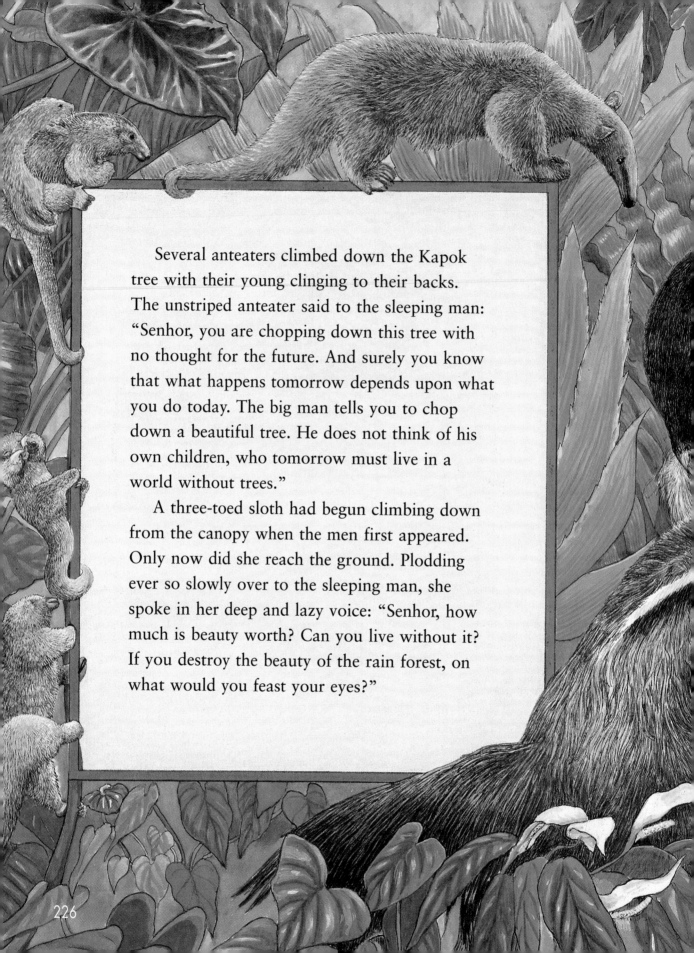

Several anteaters climbed down the Kapok tree with their young clinging to their backs. The unstriped anteater said to the sleeping man: "Senhor, you are chopping down this tree with no thought for the future. And surely you know that what happens tomorrow depends upon what you do today. The big man tells you to chop down a beautiful tree. He does not think of his own children, who tomorrow must live in a world without trees."

A three-toed sloth had begun climbing down from the canopy when the men first appeared. Only now did she reach the ground. Plodding ever so slowly over to the sleeping man, she spoke in her deep and lazy voice: "Senhor, how much is beauty worth? Can you live without it? If you destroy the beauty of the rain forest, on what would you feast your eyes?"

A child from the Yanomamo tribe who lived in the rain forest knelt over the sleeping man. He murmured in his ear: "Senhor, when you awake, please look upon us all with new eyes."

The man awoke with a start. Before him stood the rain forest child, and all around him, staring, were the creatures who depended upon the great Kapok tree. What wondrous and rare animals they were!

The man looked about and saw the sun streaming through the canopy. Spots of bright light glowed like jewels amidst the dark green forest. Strange and beautiful plants seemed to dangle in the air, suspended from the great Kapok tree.

The man smelled the fragrant perfume of their flowers. He felt the steamy mist rising from the forest floor. But he heard no sound, for the creatures were strangely silent.

The man stood and picked up his ax. He swung back his arm as though to strike the tree. Suddenly he stopped. He turned and looked at the animals and the child.

He hesitated. Then he dropped the ax and walked out of the rain forest.

An Interview with the Author and Illustrator
LYNNE CHERRY

Have you ever wondered how the famous writer and illustrator Lynne Cherry became interested in writing stories such as *The Great Kapok Tree*? Read what she told interviewer Ilene Cooper as she discussed how her interest in nature conservation developed.

Cooper: Did your interest in conservation start as an adult or as a child?

Cherry: I grew up interested in conservation before I even knew the word. As a child, I loved to play in the woods near my home in Pennsylvania. I practically lived in those woods. One day when I was in the fourth grade, I came home and there were bulldozers all over the land. I knew those woods. I knew the hollowed-out trees where the raccoons lived and which holes the possums lived in. Watching the land being bulldozed was like watching a bomb hitting my house.

Cooper: How did you deal with your feelings about what was happening?

Cherry: I wrote little books about it. Today, children have much more power to change things. Today, they might also testify in front of the city council or work with a nature conservancy group to protect the land before the bulldozers come.

Treetop Traffic

By Catherine D. Hughes • Illustrated By Patricia Wynne

If you could take an elevator to the top of the rain forest, you might find hundreds of animals gathered around a single plant. Find out why.

Take a peek at this bustling mini-world. You're seeing a day in the life of a bromeliad (broh-MEE-lee-ad), an odd—but common—rain forest plant. Its leaves form pools that collect rainwater high in the rain forest canopy where the plant grows. The bromeliad's nourishment comes from the rainwater and from the decaying plant and animal matter that collects in the pools. Up to 300 kinds of animals—from insects to mammals—depend on bromeliads for food and shelter.

Bromeliads come in many sizes. The kind shown here is about two feet in diameter. If you were to watch it for several hours, you'd see a lot of visitors!

At dawn a *mosquito* lays her eggs in one of the pools. The eggs will hatch, and the *mosquito larvae* will develop in the water. Later a *frog* deposits her eggs in the pool. When the eggs hatch, the tadpoles may make a meal of a few of the mosquito eggs or larvae. Warmed by the midday sun, a *snake* peers into the bromeliad in search of small creatures to eat. A *harvestman*, a relative of spiders, hunts for small prey, such as *sowbugs* or *ants*. They're crawling about the branch and around the bromeliad.

In late afternoon a *hummingbird* pauses in midair to sip nectar from the reddish bromeliad flower. A *bee*, also attracted by nectar, buzzes in. At dusk a *warbler* pokes its beak between leaves, searching for insects to eat.

A *monkey* perched on a nearby tree rips apart an entire bromeliad, feasting on little creatures it finds hiding in the leaves. A *jay* uses a bromeliad pool for a refreshing birdbath and a drink. High up in the trees, where water evaporates quickly in the sunlight, the bromeliad is like a desert oasis for many rain forest residents. It is often the only source of water in the canopy.

CANOPY

UNDERSTORY

FOREST FLOOR

VINE SNAKE

BEE

HIGH LIVING. Plants called bromeliads grow on branches, not in soil. The tree branches are in the rain forest canopy—the uppermost layer. Several bromeliads may grow on a single branch.

WHITE-FACED MONKEY

POISON DART FROG

BLACKBURNIAN WARBLER

PURPLE-THROATED MOUNTAIN GEM HUMMINGBIRD

SOWBUG

MOSS

MOSQUITOES

MOSQUITO LARVA

ANTS

BROWN JAY

Reprinted by permission of National Geographic World, the official magazine for Junior Members of the National Geographic Society.

HARVESTMAN

RESPONSE CORNER

WRITE AN EDITORIAL

Recycled Ideas

"Think globally, act locally" is a well-known environmental saying. Think about what the saying means. Then write an editorial for a school or class newspaper in which you explain ways students can help preserve the world's rain forests.

CREATE A GAME

"Tree"vial Pursuits

With a group, make a rain forest board game. First, make a card for every animal character in "The Great Kapok Tree." Write on the card four questions about that character based on the story or on information from a science textbook or encyclopedia. Next, create a game board on which the starting point shows the man walking into the rain forest, and the finish shows him walking out. Then make a four-color spinner. Color-code the questions and gameboard spaces to match it.

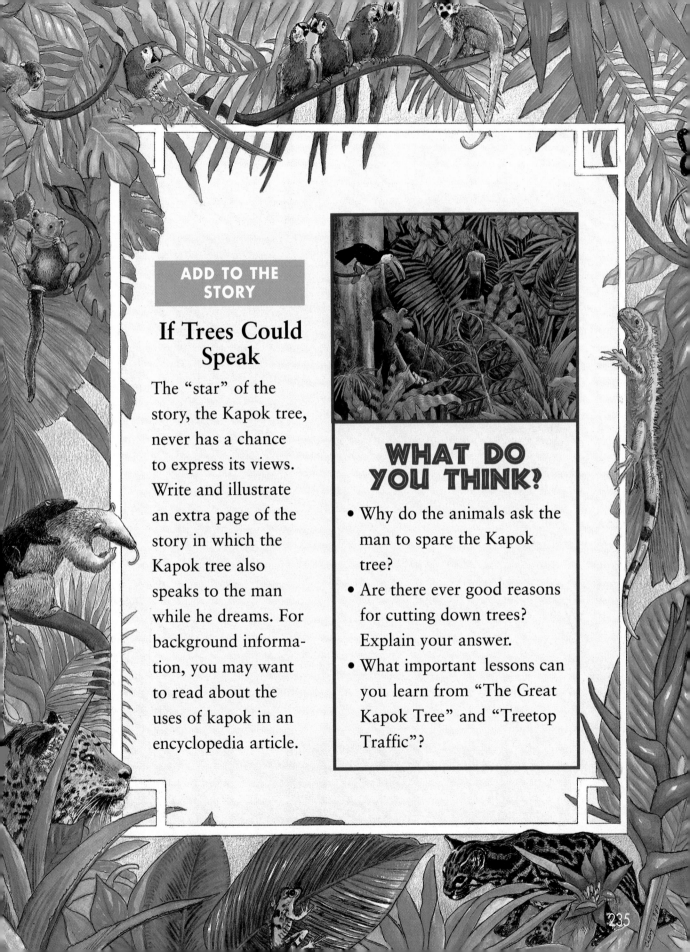

If Trees Could Speak

The "star" of the story, the Kapok tree, never has a chance to express its views. Write and illustrate an extra page of the story in which the Kapok tree also speaks to the man while he dreams. For background information, you may want to read about the uses of kapok in an encyclopedia article.

WHAT DO YOU THINK?

- Why do the animals ask the man to spare the Kapok tree?
- Are there ever good reasons for cutting down trees? Explain your answer.
- What important lessons can you learn from "The Great Kapok Tree" and "Treetop Traffic"?

235

Why Birds Are Never Hungry

**from *Folk Stories of the Hmong*
by Norma J. Livo and Dia Cha**

A long time ago, when the world was new, there were two brothers who went hunting. After the long day of walking through the jungle, they got lost. They were worried and could not remember which way to go to get back home to their parents. For many days, they wandered in the jungle. They did not have anything to eat and became very hungry.

One day the older brother decided that he had to go to find food and wood for the fire. The younger brother also wanted to go to gather water. After they discussed their plans, they each went their own way. They agreed to meet back at the clearing in the forest where they were camping when they had gathered the necessary things.

The younger brother went up and down everywhere through the jungle, but he could not find any water. Finally, he was so tired he sat down on a stone to think. He tried to face in a different direction, thinking he might find water that way. While he was thinking, a bluebird was jumping from one tree to another, singing, "I know where your parents are, I know where your parents are!"

The younger brother was surprised, because he wasn't sure what he was really hearing. He stared at the bluebird and tried to listen more carefully. He hoped the bluebird would sing to him and say those words again. He watched the bluebird wherever it went. After a time the bluebird started to sing again, saying the same words. The younger brother asked the bluebird, "Did you say you know where our parents are?"

"Yes, I did. But this is a bargain. If you can give me three insects then I will lead you to your parents," the bluebird chirped.

The boy paused a while and then he said, "Are you sure? If you are sure, will you also follow me now while I go to get my older brother?"

The bird agreed.

As the bargain had been set, the bluebird followed the younger boy to the clearing in the forest, where the older brother was sitting and waiting. He had been there for a long time and had returned without either the food or the wood. The younger brother told the older brother about his bargain with the bluebird. Then the brothers left the bird in the clearing and went to find the insects. It took them quite some time, but they finally returned to the clearing and gave the insects to the bluebird.

After the bluebird had eaten the insects he said, "You boys must follow me wherever I fly and I will lead you to your parents."

The bluebird flew away, leading the two boys. They followed the bird closely, and after many days they finally got home. They were very happy, and they thanked the bluebird many times for leading them safely home.

Before the bluebird left the two brothers to go back to the forest, the boys told him, "We will never forget how you helped us. We hope that we can help you one day—to save your life, too. We will always give you food when you are hungry."

And that is why birds are always around people's houses now—because of the promise given to the bluebird by the two grateful brothers.

JAGUA

Award-Winning
Author
and Illustrator

JAGUARUNDI

Virginia Hamilton   WITH PAINTINGS BY Floyd Cooper

RUNDI

BY VIRGINIA HAMILTON
WITH PAINTINGS BY FLOYD COOPER

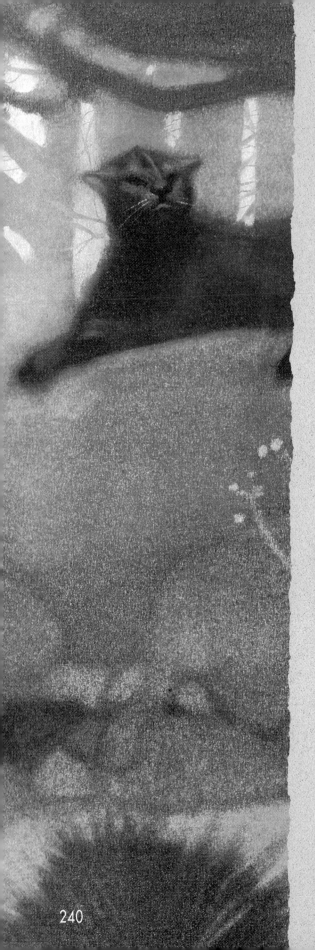

RUNDI JAGUARUNDI stalks in the sunset shadows. His coat is the blue-gray shade of scrubland at twilight. Once, this was the rain forest wild, but years ago, settlers began clearing the timber. They built houses and barns, and fences. Pineapple ranchers and longhorn cattle herders came to stay.

Rundi stays out of sight. Always on the move, he prowls, keeps watch. He murmurs, "The forest canopy is going. I'm afraid we wild animals will go with it."

In the morning, he creeps along the lowland edge. He comes upon Coati Coatimundi, who is nosing and sniffing in the plowed field hedges. "You old Coati," he growls, softly, "what in the hot breezes are you up to today?"

Coati crawls out from beneath a scrub. His bushy tail stands straight up, like a walking stick with a curved tip. "Old friend!" Coati says. His great nose wiggles. He tiptoes and sways, almost dancing over to Rundi.

They go off to a shady spot among the spiny bromeliads. "I'm going to be moving on," Rundi says. "But to leave friends always makes me sad. Coati, would you like to come along?"

"Come along—where to? To do what?" asks Coati.

"To find a better place to live," answers Rundi. "Where high, leafy branches still make a crown canopy."

"Don't mind if I do!" says Coati. "Which way do we go?"

"I've heard that to the north lies a great river called Rio Bravo," Rundi says. "They say there is timberland and a few small farms. There are animals like you and me, Coati. We could settle down for good."

Off they go, Rundi and Coati. They greet Kit Fox, wandering. Fox yips a swift hello.

"You're a long way from home," says Rundi.

"I was captured for my coat and carried south. But I got away," says Fox.

"There's danger here, too," says Rundi. "So we're going north to the Rio Bravo waters. Come north with us, Fox. We hope to find a canopy."

"I'll think about it," Fox says.

"Tell everyone where to find us," says Rundi. "Before we leave, we'll meet at midnight at the Great Pineapple Field of the Fallen Timber. Everyone knows where that is."

"I know the field," says Fox. "Whoever I see I will tell."

Running on, Fox spies Owl Monkey, who sleeps by day. "Wake up!" he yips. "Rundi and Coati plan to go north to the Rio Bravo waters. Tonight they'll be in the Great Pineapple Field of the Fallen Timber. Come say good-bye. Tell everybody."

"I will," hoots the monkey. He makes a funnel of his lips and barks, "ANIMALS, SAY GOOD-BYE TONIGHT TO OUR FRIENDS, JAGUARUNDI AND COATIMUNDI. THEY'RE LEAVING THIS PLACE. . . ." He passes along the whole message.

Bush Dog hears Owl Monkey's news. So does shy Spotted Cavy. Bush Dog shouts at Maned Wolf, streaking by, "Stop, brother Wolf, so far from your home. Stop!"

Wolf stops, and Bush Dog tells him the news.

Maned Wolf is a fine, wild beast, with tall, black legs like stilts. "I'll come," he tells Bush Dog. He races off at high speed. Far and wide, east and west, he tells the news.

So many animal friends hear about Rundi and Coati leaving. That night, they all make their way to the Great Pineapple Field of the Fallen Timber. Howler Monkey comes alone, whistling softly. He is followed by Kit Fox. Fox's plume-shaped tail trembles in the air. White-throated Capuchin Monkey is there. All three are rarely seen in the open.

Capuchin leaps upon a fallen timber log, as does Howler. The log is broken and split. They scramble back and forth, from log-piece to chunk, looking for places to hide. Soon, they vanish in the deep dark of the vast Great Pineapple Field.

Ringtail Cat finds its way, and so does White-tailed Deer. Tayra, Kinkajou, and Bobcat are among the last. All move around, talking low. They find their places.

Rundi leaps upon a split piece of log. His glowing eyes and glistening coat gleam in the full-moon night.

His friends crouch and stretch. Their coats ripple. They lie low. They are dark shapes, shielded by the swordlike pineapple leaves. The moon above is a cottony light, spread like a long, thin mesh over the vast field, and them.

"So glad you've come," begins Rundi. Shy Coati Coatimundi reveals himself behind pineapples. He jumps gingerly on a broken chunk of log. Coati's bushy tail sways, lifting him off his feet. He settles down next to Rundi.

"We wanted to see our friends before we leave here and head north," Rundi tells them. "I don't think we'll be back. If anyone would like to come along, we'd be glad to have you."

"I don't want you to go," says Big Brown Bat. "Why are you leaving us?"

Coati wiggles his nose and says, "I want to travel away from dangerous hunt-dogs."

"I want to find a place with more forest wild and fewer fences," answers Rundi.

"There will always be danger," says Big Brown Bat. "Do as I do—adapt to the changes. Bats can live in barns, in churches, and almost anywhere. If you try, so can you."

247

"I do try," says Coati, "but I must always watch my back. Even puppies practice chasing me. Settlers want to catch me and eat me!"

The animals shudder. They growl low, muttering.

Then Rundi says, "I feel unsafe to be out in the open, in the cleared land. And there are no more jaguarundis here."

Says the orange-yellow ocelot, "My friend, I, too, am alone. And everywhere I go, there are walls to stop me, traps and hunters to catch me. Some day, I'll have to leave, too. Then I'll go south over the mountains."

As the moon slides across the night, the animals talk on. Much later, Rundi sums up: "Some of us are many, and others of us are few. But we're all afraid of what might come."

Ringtail squeaks, "In the future, I think there'll be more farms, less canopy, and fewer of us."

"Change your ways, or else!" warns Big Brown Bat. "Adapt is what we must do."

249

The powerful jaguar with the golden, spotted coat speaks up: "Day in, year out, hunters keep up their war. They want to sell my hide. But they will never destroy *me*!"

Some animals cringe in fear. Others bare their teeth.

"Each time I catch their scent," says Jaguar, "I turn about and race away. Oh, no!" he gloats. "I'll never flee, nor change my ways. I'll stay in these parts, hiding when I have to."

"That's the way to do it!" Kit Fox says. "That's it! Rundi, I've made up my mind. I will stay here and take my chances."

"Unwise! Unwise!" chatters Coati. "Run. Run with us!"

"No, you stay, too, Coati and Rundi! Stay with us," cry others.

The night is nearly over. The animals have spoken together. Each thinks and wonders how much time it has to be safe here.

"We plan to keep moving until we reach the north," Rundi tells them.

"If you must go, then good luck, Rundi! Take care, Coati!" Animals call softly up and down the field, "Good-bye, good friends, good-bye!"

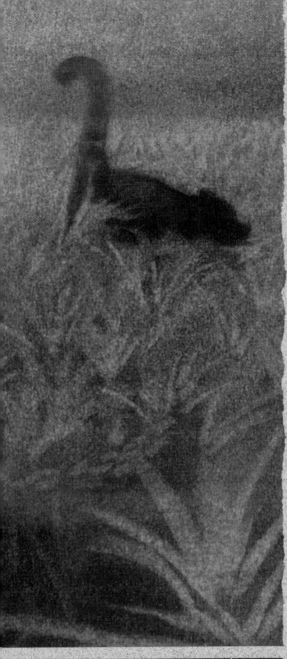

"Good-bye, friends, and good night!" Rundi and Coati answer.

The moon goes down. The animals leave. Finally the Great Pineapple Field is silent. The fallen timber log seems more lifeless than ever, slowly sinking into the ground. Before sunrise, Rundi and Coati begin their journey to the Rio Bravo.

Days later, they reach the river. "Oh, no!" cries Rundi. They find desert heat and more scrubland, houses and settlers, cats and dogs, cotton patches and cornfields. In the distance are cities, one on each side of the river. And everywhere, fences.

Rundi and Coati look on in silence. Finally, Rundi says, "Let's cross the waters, see if it's better over there."

"I'm too tired to travel anymore," old Coati answers. But he clings to Rundi's tail as the agile cat swims the way across. There, the Rio Bravo is called the Rio Grande. They squeeze beneath a high fence.

At once, a pack of dogs catches their scent. Rundi and Coati outrun them. Wet and shivering, they hide for hours in the shadowy corner of a lean-to. Finally, the dogs give up.

"Nothing much changes," whines Coati.

"Big Brown Bat said it. It is we who must change."

Coati follows Rundi. They find a prickly pear bush, and Coati stops to eat a piece. "Ummm, good!" he chatters.

"I'll go on ahead," calls Rundi.

With his mouth full of juicy pear, Coati calls softly back—"Be careful!"

The search for a home drives Rundi on. At evening, he is surprised to come upon a red jaguarundi on the move.

"So glad to meet you!" he greets the female cat.

"And you! Hello!" says she. Together, they prowl along the night. Each is happy to have the other's company.

A pretty pair, Rundi and Red Rundi Cat together go hunting for a habitat.

"Look! There are thickets!" Rundi exclaims. They thread their way within the tangled reach of brush and thorny mesquite.

"How cool the shade is all around," says Red Rundi Cat.

"Ah, yes," purrs Rundi, stretching out. "Oh, I'm tired! Let's stay here now and make our den." Red Rundi Cat agrees, and they settle in.

Not far away, Coati comes upon shrubs and stunted acacia trees. He finds lizards and scorpions and more prickly pear bushes. He roots for tubers and grubs. He naps. It is his old habit to stay by himself. He knows he will see Rundi on the trails.

One blistering day, he spies a band of coatimundis on the move. "I can't keep up

with you," he murmurs. "But I'm glad to see you are close by."

When Coati is ready to sleep for the night, he climbs a tree. He dreams he's running with his family band. Coati Coatimundi is content.

Long, dry days and pleasant, cool nights go by. In Rundi's den, a litter of three spotted kittens is born. The kittens eat and play. "See how they grow!" says Rundi. "One turns dark; one, gray; and one, red."

"They'll soon be on their own," Red Rundi says. "But will they be safe?"

"Let's hope so," Rundi answers. He gazes wistfully at the kittens playing. "The north must be farther on," Rundi adds. "I know we'll find it. We must!"

"Oh, I'm sure of it," says Red Rundi Cat. "There are land dwellers who take care to protect their forests. They plant saplings. I have seen them."

"Then someday, we'll go north, and there we'll find our crown canopy at last," Rundi tells her. "But for now . . ."

"For now. . . ?" Red Rundi asks.

"For now, we stay put," says Rundi. "As Big Brown Bat said, we adapt."

"We know how to take care of ourselves," Red Rundi says.

Rundi Jaguarundi and Red Rundi fit into their habitat. They teach the kittens how to stalk and prowl, how to find food.

They *live*.

THE END

257

ABOUT THE ANIMALS IN THIS BOOK

While some of the animals in this book are endangered, others are shy and so rarely seen that we do not know how many exist. We do know that our destruction of their habitat makes their struggle for survival more and more difficult.

The **jaguarundi** (pronounced ja´gwa run´dē) is a small, solitary wild cat from the Central and South American rain forests. It has a sleek coat, a long body, and short legs. Jaguarundis are dichromatic—having two or three color varieties. Red, gray, or black kittens are often born in the same litter. These color variations help jaguarundis blend into the brush and grass landscape. The cats often live near water on the edges of forests, and they are excellent runners. Their prey are mainly rodents and ground birds. Jaguarundis are shy, secretive cats, now found in Arizona and Texas. Rarely seen, they may well be endangered.

The **coati** (pronounced kwa´ ti) is a member of the raccoon family that lives in the forests of Central and South America. Coatis look like raccoons with bushy tails, but they also have long, flexible snouts, and their coats can be shades of red, brown, yellow, or black. A middle-aged male coati is called a coatimundi, and the term is often used for all coatis. Older males are usually solitary. But coatis are social animals that travel in troops. They eat anything, from small animals and insects to fruits and seeds. Immensely curious, they are very adaptable.

The **kit fox** is found in deserts from the southwestern United States down to northern Mexico. Kit foxes have such large ears that they are also known as big-eared foxes. They are trusting, nocturnal animals that live in burrows and eat rabbits, insects, mice, and rats. Kit foxes are threatened with extinction from predators and humans.

The **owl monkey** is also called the night monkey, and it lives in the South American forests. It is the only nocturnal monkey in the New World (the Americas). At sundown the monkeys start moving around, searching for fruit, leaves, insects, small birds, and mammals. Owl monkeys have huge eyes, which help them see at night, when they are most active. They live in small family groups, sleeping in trees high above the ground. Owl monkeys are now rare animals.

The **bush dog's** varied habitat stretches from Panama to much of northeastern South America. Bush dogs look like small bears, or badgers, with their stocky bodies and short legs. Shy and seldom seen, they are nocturnal animals found in forests and grasslands. They live and hunt in packs, are good swimmers, and they eat small animals. Bush dogs are rare.

The **maned wolf** is found in marshlands and grassy areas from Brazil to Argentina. Despite its name, the maned wolf is a member of the dog family (Canidae). It looks like a long-legged fox with pointed ears held straight up, and has a reddish-brown mane of thick fur along its back. It is an elusive animal, living in remote areas alone or in pairs. It hunts by lying in wait, then ambushing small creatures, which it immediately swallows. Farmers believe it eats livestock. The maned wolf has been virtually wiped out.

The **capuchin monkey** (pronounced kap´yo͞o chin) is also known as the ringtail monkey. Capuchin monkeys are usually black or dark brown with white faces, and they live in groups among the treetops of Central and South America. They descend to the ground only to drink. They eat mostly fruit, and swing and jump from tree to tree.

The **ringtail cat** has a striped tail longer than its body. Ringtail cats are yellowish-gray in color, with catlike bodies and foxlike faces. They live in forests and rocky terrain from Oregon to Mexico. Sharp claws allow them to climb walls or trees. The bobcat, great horned owl, and humans are its chief predators. Ringtail cats adapt well to gardens and city parks.

The **tayra** (pronounced tī´ ra), of the weasel family, has a long neck supporting a head that is quite large in relation to its slender body. Tayras range from southern Mexico to Argentina. They live in forests, woodlands, and other areas rich in vegetation. They are solitary, but hunt in groups for guinea pigs, squirrels, and, often, poultry. They particularly like sweet fruits.

The **kinkajou** (pronounced king´ ka jo͞o), a member of the raccoon family and related to the coatimundi, has soft, brownish fur and rounded ears. Kinkajous are agile as acrobats, hanging by their long, grasping tails from tree limbs. Rarely leaving the trees, they inhabit forests from Mexico to Brazil. They are commonly kept as pets and treated gently. But when frightened or angry, they are known to bite sharply.

The **big brown bat** is a widespread North American species found from southern Canada to Colombia and Venezuela, and the West Indies. They are medium-sized bats with dark, broad muzzles, simple noses, and long, brown fur. Originally forest dwellers, they now inhabit nearly all situations from caves to urban buildings and under bridges. Big brown bats are somewhat slow, heavy flyers that sleep all day and fly out at night to hunt insects. They live in large groups and are known to keep themselves very clean. They hibernate in winter.

The **ocelot** (pronounced os´ lot) is an American wildcat living in forests or brush-covered regions from Texas to much of South America. Ocelots hunt reptiles, birds, and medium-sized mammals, chiefly at night. Largely solitary animals, they rest in trees, often hunting in them. They live in pairs. Their beautifully patterned coats are greatly sought after commercially. The result has been that the species has disappeared over a great part of its range. The ocelot is considered endangered.

The **jaguar** (pronounced jag´ war) has a yellow-and-black-spotted coat and is the largest wildcat of the Americas. Jaguars are powerfully built, are approximately 6–9 feet in length, including tails of 2–3 feet, and can weigh as much as 350 pounds. Often, they live near water on the edge of canopied forests. They are good climbers and swimmers; they eat large and small animals, from rodents and fish to alligators and cattle. Jaguars are hunted relentlessly for their sleek, orange-tan fur with black spots arranged in rosettes. A solitary predator, the jaguar is seriously endangered.

The **spotted cavy**, or paca, lives in the forests of Central and South America. It is a rodent that has features resembling those of the guinea pig. Spotted cavies have huge eyes and feed at night on fruit, leaves, and bark. Their dark brownish coats with white markings and stripes on the back help them hide in the brush. Nocturnal, they sleep in burrows during the day. Spotted cavies are hunted for their fat and tasty flesh.

The **bobcat** lives in mountains, deserts, forests, and grasslands from southern Canada to Mexico. Its soft coat varies in color but is usually brown with black markings. A solitary animal, it lives in well-marked territories and burrows or dens in places where it rests. It is known to migrate. Bobcats prey upon small animals, especially rabbits, and are resourceful in their search for food. They are hunted and trapped by humans for their thick fur.

The **white-tailed deer** is a common woodland deer ranging from southern Canada to South America. Its summer coat is reddish-brown. In winter, it wears gray-brown. Only males have antlers. Its habitat is temperate to tropical deciduous forest. White-tailed deer gather in small herds and are not endangered.

The **howler monkey** is the largest South American monkey, and it lives in the rain forests from southern Mexico to Argentina. Howlers are noted for their deep hooting, and roaring calls, which carry two or three miles. They live in groups and have black, brown, or red fur; they eat leaves, bugs, flowers, fruit, and nuts. Some species of howler monkey are endangered.

VIRGINIA HAMILTON

Virginia Hamilton is perhaps one of the most important children's book authors living today. Her book *M.C. Higgins, the Great* was the first book in history to win two of the nation's highest writing awards, the National Book Award and the Newbery Medal. She used her gift for storytelling again to write the book *Jaguarundi*.

Hamilton was born in southern Ohio. Her family was descended from a runaway slave who settled in the town of Yellow Springs and became a successful farmer. Her father loved telling stories, so it became natural for her to be a storyteller, too. She began writing stories when she was ten. Although most of her stories contain some element of fantasy, family life is an important theme in all of her books.

"Books can, and do, help us to live," she says, "and some may even change our lives."

. . . and in the African-American tradition of animal folktales, as found in *The People Could Fly*, the animals in *Jaguarundi* can talk.

The story parallels humans who escape their homelands in search of better, safer lives. I was astounded to discover the added bonus, with the animals, of a classic symbolism of fleeing North—crossing the Great River into a Promised Land. I didn't plan it; nothing was further from my mind. But the symbolism was indeed organic and was to me a wonderful revelation about this book.

— *excerpt from a speech by Virginia Hamilton at the Tenth Annual Virginia Hamilton Conference in Kent, Ohio, on April 15, 1994*

TROPICAL RAIN FORESTS

From *The World Book Encyclopedia*

Tropical rain forest is a forest of tall trees in a region of year-round warmth and plentiful rainfall. Almost all such forests lie near the equator. They occupy large regions in Africa, Asia, and Central and South America, and on Pacific islands. The largest tropical rain forest is the Amazon rain forest, also called the *selva*. It covers about a third of South America (see **Amazon rain forest**). Tropical rain forests stay green throughout the year.

A tropical rain forest has more kinds of trees than any other area in the world. Scientists have counted 179 species in one 2 1/2 acre (1-hectare) area in South America. Most forests of this size in the United States have fewer than seven species. About half of the world's species of plants and animals also live in tropical rain forests. More species of amphibians, birds, insects, mammals, and reptiles live in tropical rain forests than anywhere else.

The tallest trees of a rain forest may grow as tall as 200 feet (61 meters). The *crowns* (tops) of other trees form a covering of leaves about 100 to 150 feet (30 to 45 meters) above the ground. This covering is called the *upper canopy*. The crowns of smaller trees form one or two *lower canopies*. All the canopies shade the forest floor so that it receives less than 1 percent as much sunlight as does the upper canopy.

Huge growths called buttresses extend from the trunk to the roots of many trees in tropical rain forests. The buttresses may help support the trees. Yagua Indians hunt small birds with blowguns in the upper Amazon Valley of South America.

Tropical rain forests lie chiefly near the equator. These areas receive some of the world's heaviest rainfall.

Most areas of the forest floor receive so little light that few bushes or herbs can grow there. As a result, a person can easily walk through most parts of a tropical rain forest. Areas of dense growth called *jungles* occur within a tropical rain forest in areas where much sunlight reaches the ground. Most jungles grow near broad rivers or in former clearings. See **Jungle**.

The temperature in a rain forest rarely rises above 93°F (34°C) or drops below 68°F (20°C). In many cases, the average temperature of the hottest month is only 2 to 5°F (1 to 3°C) higher than the average temperature of the coldest month. At least 80 inches (200 centimeters) of rain falls yearly in a tropical rain forest. Thunder showers may occur more than 200 days a year. The air beneath the lower canopy is almost always humid. The trees themselves give off water through the pores of their leaves. This process, called *transpiration,* may account for as much as half of the rain in the Amazon rain forest.

All tropical rain forests resemble one another. But each of the three largest ones—the American, the African, and the Asian—has a different group of animal and plant species. For instance, each rain forest has many species of monkeys, all of which differ from the species of the other two rain forests. In addition, different areas of the same rain forest may have different species. For example, many kinds of trees that grow in the mountains of the Amazon rain forest do not grow in the lowlands of that forest.

Squirrel monkeys live only in the tropical rain forests of Central and South America. These monkeys scamper along tree branches and climbing vines.

WRITE A LETTER

DEAR RUNDI

Have you ever felt like Big Brown Bat, who said "change your ways, or else"? Work with one or two classmates to describe a situation in school or in your neighborhood when you were forced to adapt to get along with others. How did it work out? Would you do the same thing the next time? As a group, write a letter of advice for other children your age to help them face similar situations.

DEBATE AN ISSUE

SHOULD I STAY, OR SHOULD I GO?

What would you do if you were one of the animals in "Jaguarundi"? Would you go with Rundi and Coati, or would you stay and adapt? On paper, list five reasons to support your decision. Then find a classmate who made the opposite choice and see if you can persuade that person to see it your way.

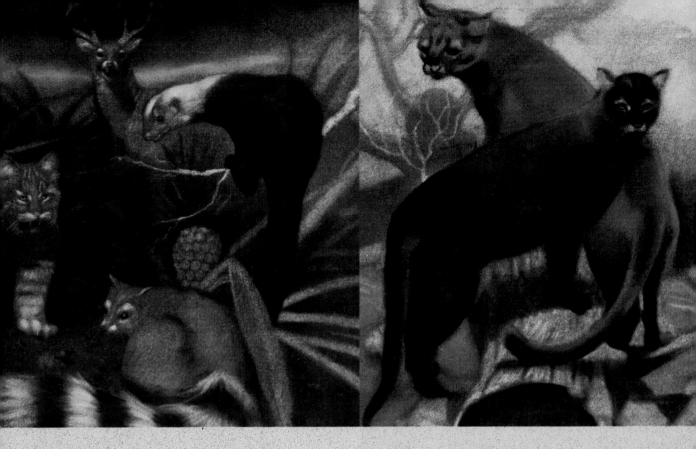

SPREAD THE WORD

Do you think that people should try harder to preserve animal habitats, or should animals learn to adapt because they will have no choice in the future? Create a billboard advertisement that states your viewpoint. Show one or more animals from "Jaguarundi" or other animals you know of that have their habitats threatened.

WHAT DO YOU THINK?

- How are Rundi and Coati alike? How are they different?
- Do you think "Jaguarundi" has a happy ending? Why or why not?
- How do you think the information in the encyclopedia article helps you better understand the story?

ART
AND
LITERATURE

The stories in this theme discuss the changes that can occur when people move into natural, unsettled areas. Gabriele Münter's painting *Staffelsee in Autumn* shows a scene in Germany in 1934. What changes may have occurred in this rural area since then? How might these changes have affected the forest, the lake, and the sheep?

Staffelsee in Autumn
by Gabriele Münter

Gabriele Münter was born in Berlin, Germany, in 1877. Later she lived in Murnau, a town near the lake Staffelsee. Münter often chose the lake, mountains, and houses as subjects. She painted bold colors and solid shapes. What colors and shapes do you see in *Staffelsee in Autumn*?

Staffelsee in Autumn (1923) by Gabriele Münter. Oil on board (13 3/4″ × 19 1/4″).
The National Museum of Women in the Arts, Washington D.C.,
Gift of Wallace and Wilhelmina Holladay.

CAMOUFLAGE
IN THE
WILD

HIDING OUT

BY
JAMES MARTIN

PHOTOGRAPHS BY
ART WOLFE

ALA
Notable Book

Children's Choice

Outstanding
Science
Trade Book

The Kenyan sand boa snuggles into the ground and depends on its coloration and pattern to hide as it pokes its head out from among a pile of stones.

▲ An orchid mantis hiding against a background of petals, holding a grasshopper with its powerful front legs.

IN the busy rain forest of Malaysia, a grasshopper leaps into a spray of orchids. Suddenly, one of the "flowers" turns on the grasshopper. An orchid mantis, with wings like petals, grips it tightly. For the grasshopper, there will be no escape.

The orchid mantis is a master of camouflage—the art of hiding while in plain sight. Camouflage enables predators like the orchid mantis to hide while they lie in wait for their prey. For other animals, camouflage is a method of protection from their enemies.

Animals blend into the background in several ways. Their colors and patterns may match their surroundings. The shape of their bodies may resemble some other object, such as a stick, a leaf, or a flower. Crests and frills may break up the outline of their bodies, disguising their real shape and fooling the eye. They may even behave like something else—a fluttering leaf or a dangerous animal, for example.

◀ The colors of the Solomon Island leaf frog match those of the forest floor. The shape of its head, with its horn-like protrusions, resembles that of a leaf.

▲ The color and pattern of this owl's feathers blend in with a background of tree bark.

▼ Frills and crests, together with a confusing pattern of stripes, help hide the "fish shape" of this anglerfish, making it hard to spot in its home in the Coral Sea near Australia.

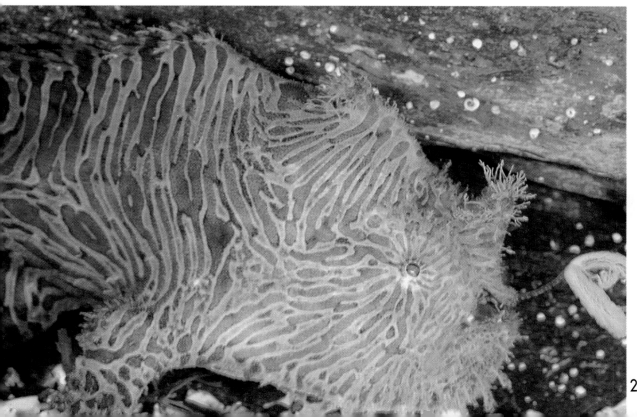

271

▲ Red-eyed tree frog (Panama).

▲ Comet moths (Madagascar).

▼ Sand dab.

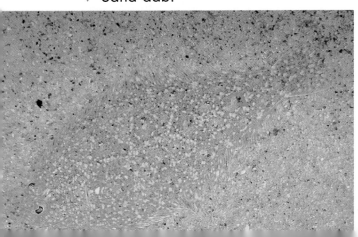

Some animals depend on color alone for concealment. The skin of the red-eyed tree frog is the universal green of the rain forest. Others use both color and pattern. The comet moth matches the colors and patterns of the drying leaves of the undergrowth.

The Kenyan sand boa snuggles into the ground and depends on its coloration and pattern to hide as it pokes its head out from among a pile of stones. *(See photograph on page 269.)*

Sand dabs use the same technique underwater. These fish settle on the sand and flutter their fins to partially bury themselves. Soon only a faint fish "shadow" remains.

Brightly colored animals can be masters of camouflage. Scorpionfish, warbonnets, and other tropical fish look shocking in open water, but when swimming in the reef, they match the vivid tints of the coral. As well as being camouflaged by their colors, these fish are also hidden by their complicated shapes: with their jagged outlines and frilled fins, they look "unfishlike" among the coral branches. When a predator looks for a fish shape, its eyes detect only bits and pieces.

▲ Japanese decorated warbonnets.

▼ Scorpionfish.

273

▲ Hawkfish (Coral Sea, Australia).

▼ Zebras (Kenya).

The striped hawkfish has bright bands of color that break up its outline and fool predators in a similar way. This technique is called "disruptive coloration."

Zebras also benefit from disruptive coloration. Although they are easy to see on the grasslands at noon, at dawn and dusk their stripes make them harder to see. Since lions and other predators prefer to hunt in low light, the pattern helps the zebra survive.

Chameleons are famous for their ability to change color. However, they don't change color in order to match their surroundings. Their usual color matches the place they live; they *change* color to communicate with other chameleons. When they change color, they become more noticeable, not less.

▼ Jewel chameleon (Madagascar).

Chameleons combine many camouflage techniques. Their flat, oval shape resembles a leaf, and many species grow crests along the edges of the oval to hide their chameleon shape. They spend most of the day motionless except for swiveling their eyes to look for food. But when they do walk or climb, they rock back and forth so their movements seem as random as those of a leaf in the breeze.

▲ Leaf-tail gecko (Madagascar).

The leaf-tail gecko shares the rain forest of Madagascar with several species of chameleon. A flat reptile with jagged frills and a broad tail, it clings with its disk-like toes to tree trunks that are mottled with lichen (tiny plants that grow on rocks and trees).

Gradually, the gecko's skin changes to the color and pattern of the lichen patches. Within twenty minutes, the lizard seems part of the tree. Its frills help to break up its outline. Then, when an insect flies near, the gecko leaps into the air and snatches it with its jaws.

276

Animals in cooler climates change with the seasons. Summer camouflage is often useless when winter snow changes the green and brown forests and fields to white, so many birds and animals turn white in the winter.

The snowshoe hare wears a drab brown in summer but changes to white for the winter. If it did not change, it would be an easy target for foxes and birds of prey. Ptarmigans—slow, squat birds that live in the same parts of the northern United States and Canada as the snowshoe hare— use identical tactics, switching from brown to white and back again as the seasons change.

▲ Caught against a background of brown trees in Montana, a snowshoe hare in its winter coat stands out plainly.

▲ Against the white of a snowfield, it almost disappears.

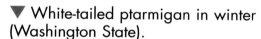

▼ White-tailed ptarmigan in winter (Washington State).

▼ Willow ptarmigan in summer (Alaska).

▲ Blacktail fawn (Washington State).

▼ Baby pardalis chameleon.

The most dangerous time of any animal's life is babyhood, and baby animals have some of the most effective camouflage. The mottled pattern of a fawn (a young deer) makes it hard for predators to see. Baby chameleons wear the color of tree bark—dull browns and grays—turning leaf green only when they are large enough to mimic a leaf.

Birds' eggs are often colored to match their surroundings, camouflaging the baby birds even before they are born. Once born, baby birds are usually a gray puff of feathers, difficult to see in the nest. When they reach adulthood, they will acquire the more colorful plumage of their parents.

▲ Western sandpiper's eggs (Alaska).

▼ Baby night herons (Falkland Islands).

▲ Walking stick (Malaysia).

▼ Leaf insect (Malaysia).

Some animals don't simply blend into the background: they pretend to be something they're not—part of a plant, or another animal. In the tropical rain forest, many insects survive disguised as parts of plants. Among them are many species of walking stick. Some look like bare sticks; others resemble dead twigs with dried leaves attached.

The jungles of the world are full of leaf insects. The most common are bright green and have broad, flat bodies. They wander slowly among the leafy underbrush searching for food.

▲ Some insects imitate dead leaves. It's easy to miss this arsenura moth of Panama as it rests on a carpet of fallen leaves.

▲ A caterpillar in the Panamanian rain forest, with its two snake-eye-like spots.

▼ King snake.

Animals in disguise must act the part. When walking sticks aren't walking, they are difficult to see. If they run, predators will suspect a trick. A chameleon wouldn't be mistaken for a leaf if it hopped like a kangaroo, so chameleons move slowly, rocking like a leaf in the breeze.

For animals that mimic other animals, every day is Halloween— they pretend to be fearsome beasts! By adopting the color and shape of dangerous animals, they fool predators into leaving them alone.

In the jungles of Central America, a brown caterpillar lives among the brown leaves of the forest floor. When noticed by an enemy, the caterpillar turns, revealing two black spots that look like snake eyes. Startled predators usually decide to leave the caterpillar alone.

At first glance, the bright, glossy red-and-black bands of the king snake resemble those of a coral snake. Because coral snakes have a very poisonous bite, most animals steer clear of them. By mimicking the coral snake, the harmless king snake benefits from their caution.

▲ Polar bear (Canada).

Unlike animals that depend on camouflage for defense, larger camouflaged hunters have little to fear from other animals. They employ camouflage only to avoid detection when they hunt.

Even though they are the largest carnivore on earth, growing to over a thousand pounds in weight, white polar bears on the snow will escape notice by all but the keenest eye. On an overcast day, or during a storm, the first sign of an approaching bear is the swinging of its black nose against the white background.

▶ Leopard (South Africa).

Anyone could spot a leopard walking down the street—but in the dry grasses of Africa the leopard almost disappears. The harsh African sun casts dark shadows in the grass, which are matched by the leopard's black spots and tan fur. By the time an antelope or other prey notices the leopard, it's often too late.

▲ Gaboon vipers (central Africa).

▲ The colors of many species of big cat effectively camouflage them in their hunting grounds. ▼

The velvety skin of the Gaboon viper resembles dead leaves. It lives on the soggy jungle floor of the Congo Basin in central Africa. Sunlight is blocked by a snarl of branches and leaves far above and seldom brightens the forest floor. Encountering this snake is a nasty surprise for any animal—including man. It has the longest fangs of any snake, over two inches long, and its venom kills swiftly.

When we notice an animal concealing itself through color, pattern, or mimicry, we are looking at part of the competition between hunters and the hunted. Of course, camouflage is difficult to see. But if our eyes are sharp enough, what we can see is a powerful weapon in the struggle for survival.

JAMES MARTIN
AUTHOR

Playing hide-and-seek can be fun, unless you're a hungry predator. In *Hiding Out: Camouflage in the Wild*, author James Martin reveals how many animals stay alive by using natural disguises. To learn more about these clever creatures, Martin and photographer Art Wolfe traveled from Montana to Malaysia, from Alaska to Africa, and studied reptiles, amphibians, insects, and other animals.

The results of their work were so interesting that both this book and their book *Chameleons: Dragons in the Trees* were each named Outstanding Science Trade Book for Children and Notable Book for Children. Another book filled with mysterious creatures is Martin's book *Tentacles: The Amazing World of Octopus, Squid, and Their Relatives*.

When Martin is not busy exploring the lives and habits of unique animals, he writes nature articles for magazines like *Smithsonian* and *Sports Illustrated*.

RESPONSE CORNER

MAKE A POSTER

Now You See It!

Which of the animals you met in this selection is your favorite? Use an encyclopedia to find out more about this animal, such as where it lives, what it eats, and other important facts about it. Make a poster about the animal, and share it with your classmates.

Eye Spy

Do you think camouflage works for people? How might someone "hide in plain sight" in a mall, in a supermarket, or in a school? Work with a partner to create and act out a humorous camouflage scene for your classmates.

A New Address

The animals in the story have perfect camouflage for their environment. But what would happen if they had to find a new home? Write a want ad by one of the animals. Have the animal describe something that has happened to its environment to cause it to leave. Then have it explain what it needs to have in its new home.

What Do You Think?

- What are three ways in which animals blend into their backgrounds?
- Which of the animals described in the selection would you most like to see in real life? Why?
- How do you think animals survive if they are unable to blend into their backgrounds?

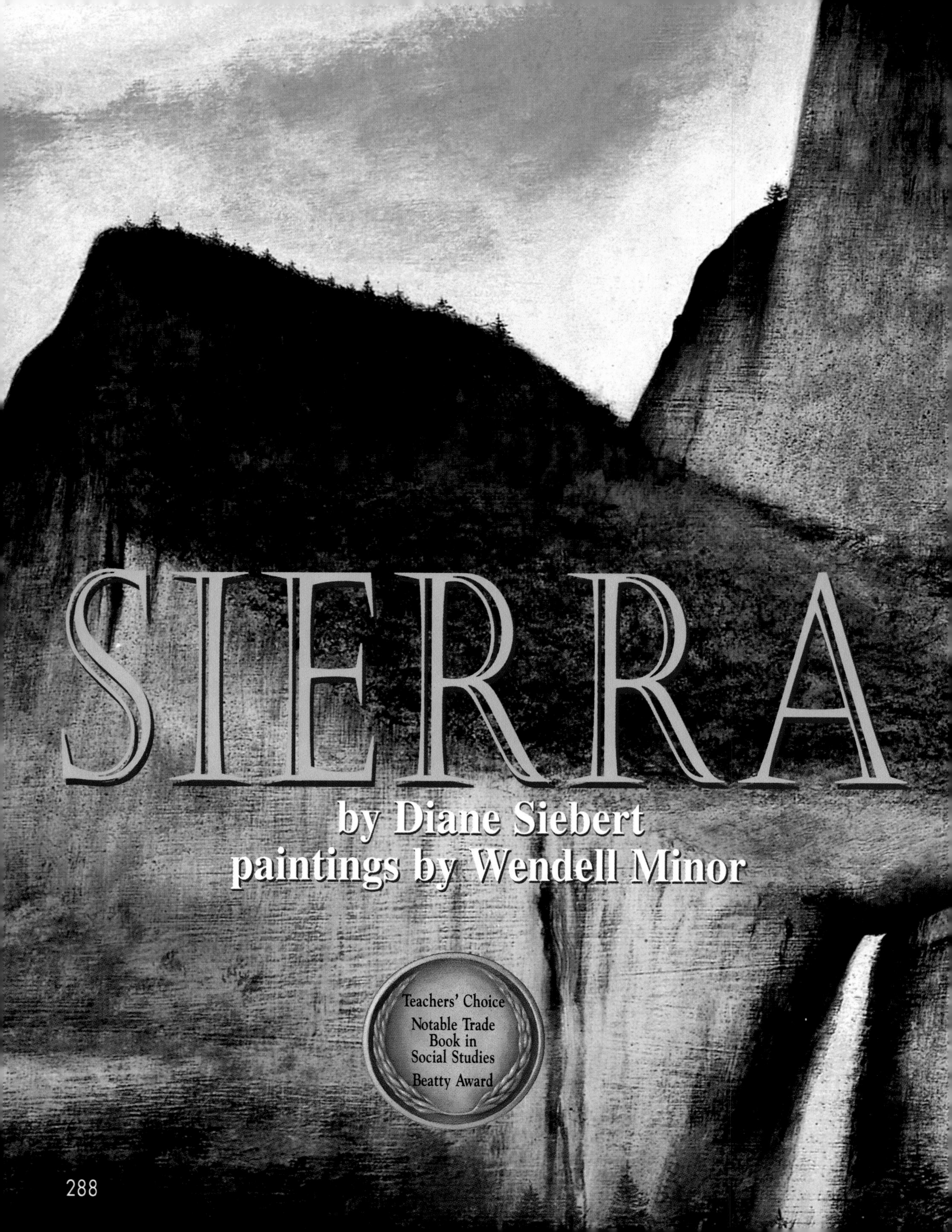

SIERRA

by Diane Siebert
paintings by Wendell Minor

Teachers' Choice
Notable Trade
Book in
Social Studies
Beatty Award

SIERRA

By Diane Siebert • Paintings by Wendell Minor

I am the mountain,
Tall and grand.
And like a sentinel I stand.

Surrounding me, my sisters rise
With watchful peaks that pierce
the skies;
From north to south we form a chain
Dividing desert, field, and plain.

I am the mountain.
Come and know
Of how, ten million years ago,
Great forces, moving plates of earth,
Brought, to an ancient land, rebirth;
Of how this planet's faulted crust
Was shifted, lifted, tilted, thrust
Toward the sky in waves of change
To form a newborn mountain range.

I am the mountain,
Young, yet old.
I've stood, and watching time unfold,
Have known the age of ice and snow
And felt the glaciers come and go.
They moved with every melt and freeze;
They shattered boulders, leveled trees,
And carved, upon my granite rocks,
The terraced walls of slabs and blocks
That trace each path,
    each downward course,
Where through the years,
    with crushing force,
The glaciers sculpted deep ravines
And polished rocks to glossy sheens.

At last this era, long and cold,
Began to lose its frigid hold
When, matched against a warming sun,
Its final glacier, ton by ton,
Retreated, melting, making way
For what I have become today:

A place of strength and lofty height;
Of shadows shot with shafts of light;
Where meadows nestle in between
The arms of forests, cool and green;
Where, out of clefted granite walls,
Spill silver, snow-fed waterfalls.

Here stand the pines, so straight and tall,
Whose needles, dry and dying, fall
Upon my sides to slowly form
A natural blanket, soft and warm;
Their graceful, swaying branches sing
In gentle breezes, whispering
To junipers, all gnarled and low,
That here, in stubborn splendor, grow.

And on my western slope I hold
My great sequoias, tall and old;
They've watched three thousand years go by,
And, in their endless quest for sky,
This grove of giants slowly grew
With songs of green on silent blue.

I am the mountain.
In each breath
I feel the pull of life and death
As untamed birds and beasts obey
The laws of predator and prey.

On me, the hunted ones reside,
Sustained by foods my plants provide:

I keep the pikas, small and shy,
That spread their gathered grass to dry.

I shelter rodents. In my trees
Live pinecone-loving chickarees,
While tunnels, crevices, and holes
Hold marmots, ground squirrels,
    chipmunks, voles.

I cradle herds of graceful deer
That drink from waters cold and clear;
I know each buck with antlers spread
Above his proud, uplifted head.
I know each doe, each spotted fawn,
In sunshine seen, in shadows, gone.

I know these creatures, every one.
They, to survive, must hide or run;
As food for those that stalk and chase,
Within life's chain, they have a place.

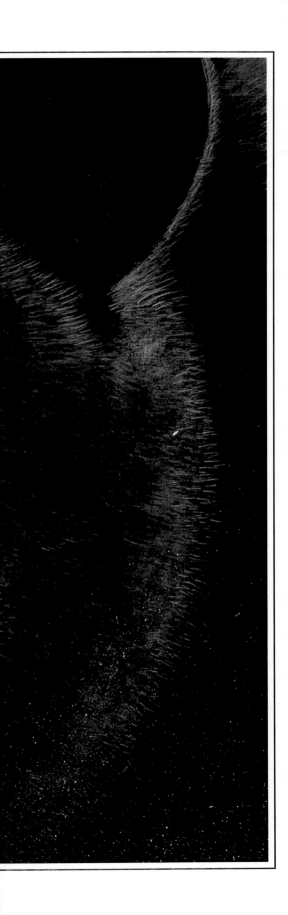

Then, too, the predators are mine,
Each woven into earth's design.
I feel them as they wake and rise;
I see the hunger in their eyes.

These are the coyotes, swift and lean;
The bobcats, shadowy, unseen;
The martens in their tree-branch trails;
The masked raccoons with long,
    ringed tails;
The mountain lions and big black bears
That live within my rocky lairs;
The owls that prowl the skies at night;
The hawks and eagles, free in flight.

I know them all. I understand.
They keep the balance on the land.
They take the old, the sick, the weak;
And as they move, their actions speak
In tones untouched by right or wrong:
            We hunt to live.
            We, too, belong.

I am the mountain.
From the sea
Come constant winds to conquer me—
Pacific winds that touch my face
And bring the storms whose clouds embrace
My rugged shoulders, strong and wide;
And in their path, I cannot hide.

And though I have the strength of youth,
I sense each change and know the truth:
By wind and weather, day by day,
I will, in time, be worn away;
For mountains live, and mountains die.
As ages pass, so, too, will I.

But while my cloak of life exists,
I'll cherish winds and storms and mists,
For in them, precious gifts are found
As currents carry scent and sound;
As every gust and playful breeze
Helps sow the seeds of parent trees;
As silver drops and soft white flakes
Fill laughing streams and alpine lakes;
As lightning fires, hot and bright,
Thin undergrowth, allowing light
To reach the fresh, cleared soil below
So roots can spread and trees can grow.

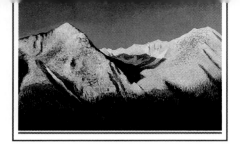

I am the mountain,
Tall and grand,
And like a sentinel I stand.
Yet I, in nature's wonders draped,
Now see this mantle being shaped
By something new—a force so real
That every part of me can feel
Its actions changing nature's plan.
Its numbers grow. Its name is MAN.
And what my course of life will be
Depends on how man cares for me.

I am the mountain,
Tall and grand.
And like a sentinel I stand.

DIANE SIEBERT

MEET THE AUTHOR

Diane Siebert loves to explore and has traveled all over the United States and Mexico. One of her favorite places, and the inspiration for this book, is the Sierra Nevada mountain range in California. She has spent a great deal of time there camping, hiking, and running with her husband.

Siebert has written several books about mountains, plains, valleys, and deserts— including *Mojave* and *Heartland.* She says that the beauty of nature continually provides her with her ideas for writing.

She and her husband have lived close to the Mojave Desert and in Oregon. Although these places are very different, they have both been rich sources of inspiration. In addition to keeping pet dogs and rats, the Sieberts have been able to observe deer, coyotes, and other wildlife up close.

RESPONSE CORNER

WRITE A POSTCARD

WISH YOU WERE HERE!

Have you ever imagined what it would be like to hike to a mountaintop? Write a postcard describing a view of nature you would enjoy, such as the way the world looks from the top of a mountain. Use ideas from the selection to help you, as well as ideas from books, movies, or television shows you have seen or from trips you have taken.

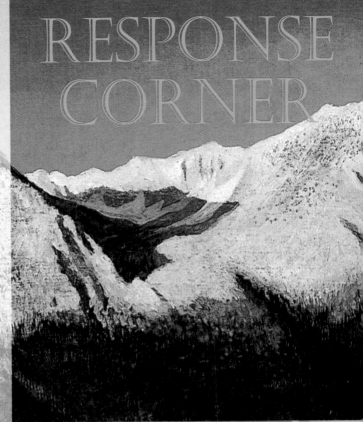

CREATE A PICTURE DICTIONARY

LOOK IT UP

Some of the science terms in "Sierra" may be new to you. With a group, create a picture dictionary. First, list in alphabetical order the terms you will include. Then write and illustrate each definition. Use a dictionary to help you. You may want to publish your dictionary by typing your entries on a word processor and binding the printed pages together. Place your dictionary in the science center or library.

302

RANGING FAR AND WIDE

Make a 3-D mountain map. You'll need tracing paper, an atlas, a big piece of cardboard, and clay. First, trace an outline map of North America. The atlas will show you where and how high the mountain ranges are. Build up the mountains with clay and label them. Finally, make a chart comparing the heights and lengths of the ranges.

WHAT DO YOU THINK?

- What natural changes have taken place in the Sierra Nevada? What natural changes continue to take place?
- What place do you think humans have in life's chain?
- In what ways might humans be threatening the Sierra Nevada?

WRAP-UP

Think about the animal and plant life you read about in the selections in this theme. How do you think Rundi or the chameleons and other creatures in "Hiding Out" would adapt to living in your city or community?

Suppose that Rundi and Coati had traveled through the same Amazon rain forest that was described in "The Great Kapok Tree." What might they have said if they had stopped to talk to the man who slept under the Kapok tree?

ACTIVITY CORNER

Sometimes the changes that occur in our lives create changes in our feelings. Think about the changes discussed in the selections in this theme. Think about the changes you face in your own life. Write a journal entry describing your concerns about a change you are experiencing or know about. Save your writing in your personal journal.

THEME
IN
SEARCH
OF A
DREAM

HAVE YOU EVER DREAMED of exploring a new place? What made you want to go to that place? The characters you'll meet in the selections in this theme are searching for a new home or seeking fortune. Read to find out whether their dreams come true.

IN SEARCH OF A DREAM

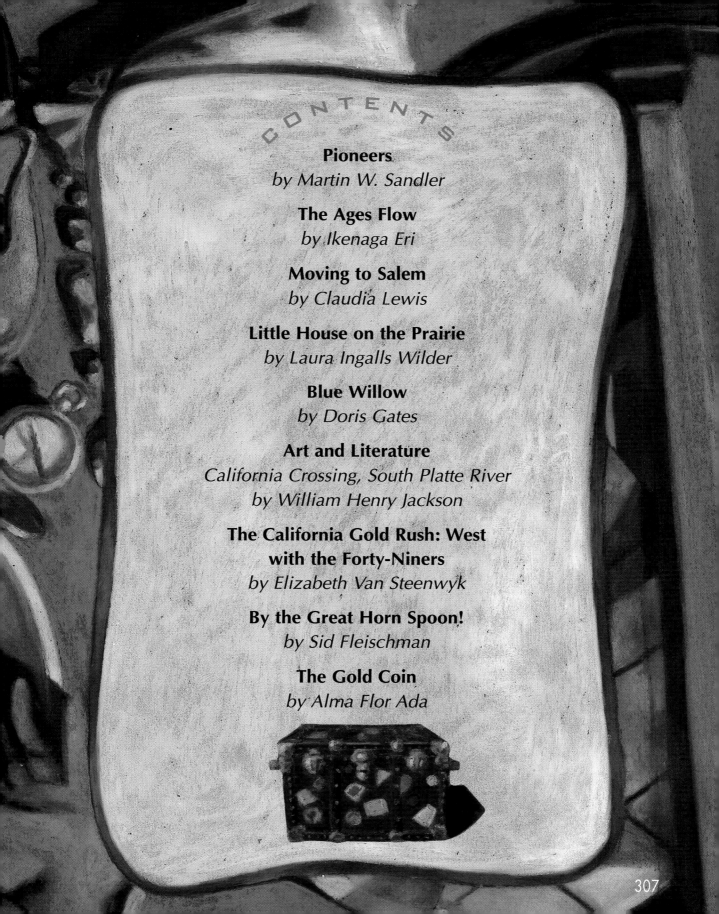

CONTENTS

BOOKSHELF

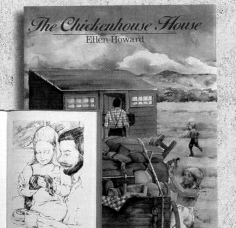

The Chickenhouse House
by Ellen Howard

Alena wonders how a chickenhouse could ever be her home.

Award-Winning Author
Signatures Library

Mr. Blue Jeans: A Story about Levi Strauss
by Maryann N. Weidt
illustrated by Lydia M. Anderson

This is the story of how the man who developed the popular pants threaded his way to success.
Signatures Library

Flight

by Robert Burleigh
illustrated by Mike Wimmer

The story of Charles Lindbergh's famous flight across the Atlantic Ocean is an inspiration to dreamers everywhere.

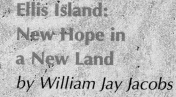

Ellis Island: New Hope in a New Land

by William Jay Jacobs

The experience of arriving in the United States is captured through historical facts and photographs.

Notable Trade Book
in the Field of Social Studies

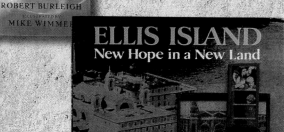

The Violin Man

by Maureen Brett Hooper
illustrated by Gary Undercuffler

When Luigi comes to town in search of a special violin, Antonio joins the hunt and travels outside of his daydreams for a change.

Award-Winning
Author

PIONEERS

BY MARTIN W. SANDLER

WESTWARD HO!

The United States of America in the 1800's is a nation on the move. "We are a people with restlessness in our souls," writes a newspaper editor. He is right. America is a country founded on a love of independence. And for many, independence means the freedom to go after new opportunities wherever they are.

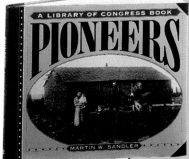

For millions of Americans, the greatest opportunities lie in the vast lands of the West. Into these lands pour hunters and farmers, artists and adventurers, missionaries and shopkeepers. Some hope to strike it rich. Most want to build a new life for themselves and their families. They will include some of the most romantic figures the nation has ever known—mountain men, gold seekers, lumberjacks, and cowboys. They are all pioneers. They will carve a new nation out of the wilderness.

FALLING
CREW
No 1225

313

It will not be easy. The long journey to the West will test the courage and determination of all who attempt it. Once there, the pioneers will encounter a whole new set of hardships and dangers. Out of their great adventure will emerge a simple fact: The great heroes of the West will not be larger-than-life figures like the cowboy or the lumberjack. They will be the pioneer farmer and the pioneer family.

The real story of the American frontier will tell of ordinary people struggling to work the land and build new lives. They will face many dangers and disappointments, but they will succeed. The crops they raise will cover the prairie. They will see towns and cities rise. They will feed the nation and much of the world.

In the early 1800's, most Americans live in cities, towns and farms along the East Coast. But there is a special group of men who live and work in the mountains well beyond the settled areas of the East. They are hunters and trappers, and they play an essential part in the giant fur industry. These mountain men, as they are called, will play a key role in the settlement of the West.

Chasing their main target, the beaver, takes the hunters and trappers through and over the mountains and across the Great Plains, which are filled with streams where the beavers live. It is a hard life. The mountain men live off the land and face danger at every turn. Winters bring bitter cold and fierce snowstorms. Accidents are common. And there is always the threat of attack from a bear or other wild animal that is not about to give up its fur and its life without a fight.

The mountain man's equipment includes his rifle, shot and powder; his traps; a hunting knife and a hatchet. His greatest treasure is his horse.

The hunters and trappers are among the first white men to enter the vast lands known as the Great Plains. There they meet the Native Americans who have lived on the Plains for thousands of years. There aren't many hunters and trappers, and most of these Native Americans do not feel threatened by them. While the mountain men approach each new group of Native Americans cautiously, most develop peaceful relations with these people who have lived on the Plains long before the first white people appeared.

The Native Americans of the Plains become an important part of the American fur trade. Many are skilled and courageous hunters, and in exchange for blankets, guns, and beads, they supply the mountain men with furs of every type and with the hides of buffalo, deer and elk.

In time, the mountain men become more than just hunters and trappers. Because they know the mountain regions so well, the government hires some of them to blaze trails through those areas. These early trails help restless easterners to move westward. The mountain men also find new jobs as guides and scouts for these adventurous early pioneers. Over the years, tales of their courage and daring are spread through story and song. Men like Daniel Boone and Kit Carson become legendary figures.

The men, women and children who follow the trailblazers through the mountain passes will be the first to push the American frontier westward. This first wave of pioneers will settle in the western wilderness areas of established eastern states and in the western wilds of territories such as Kentucky, Tennessee and Ohio. By the 1840's, pioneers will push the frontier westward beyond the Mississippi River. Between the 1850's and the 1890's, the largest of all the waves of pioneers will extend the frontier thousands of miles across the Great Plains, all the way to the Pacific Ocean.

The land between the eastern mountains and the Mississippi River is covered with millions of trees. The forests are so thick, it is said, that a squirrel could spend its entire life moving from tree to tree without ever touching the earth. The early frontier family's first job is to clear enough land to build a house and plant its first crops.

■ 1790 (original colonies)
■ 1820's
■ 1850's
■ 1860's–1890's

Clearing the forest is hard work, but the trees are a blessing. The settlers cut them into logs to build their homes. They keep themselves warm in winter by burning wood from the endless supply that surrounds them. The roots and stumps from the felled trees, along with the rocky soil, make farming difficult, but the woods are filled with wildlife, and the settlers become excellent hunters. Much of the food they eat comes from the animals they track down in the forests.

By the 1840's, American magazines back East feature illustrations of people who have successfully moved into the frontier areas. The early settlers become an inspiration for those who follow them. Yet, for many of these early pioneers, the adventure has just begun. Their restlessness will cause thousands of them to look for more land, richer soil and even greater opportunities much farther to the west.

MARTIN W. SANDLER

◆ ◆ ◆

While writing *Pioneers,* Martin Sandler may have wished he could travel back in time to the 1800s to get a better sense of the nation's movement westward. Instead, he did the next best thing—he researched infor-

mation at the Library of Congress in Washington, D.C. Using many original photographs, Sandler magically re-created one of America's most fascinating time periods.

Before becoming a writer, Sandler played second base for a minor league baseball team. Later, he turned down an offer to play for the Cincinnati Reds and chose instead a career in television, the latest technology of the time. As families sat fascinated before the new invention, Sandler worked behind the scenes as a television producer.

The Library of Congress

His interest in this new form of communication inspired him to create many excellent programs. He has won five Emmy awards for his work.

Now the author of seventeen books, Martin Sandler lives in Massachusetts with his wife, Carol. He is planning more projects and trying to find room in his house for all his prizes and awards.

THE AGES
Flow

by Ikenaga Eri, fifth grade
illustrated by A. Van Mil

The old brown photo album.

Grandfather's pictures tell of

Meiji, Taishō, Shōwa—

all the ages slowly

flowing by.

Smelling a little moldy,

the black-and-white photos

tell sturdily a tale of history.

MOVING
to Salem

by Claudia Lewis
illustrated by A. Van Mil

I grabbed up my little sister,
not quite three.
She mustn't forget!
Around the house we went,
to remember.

"Here's the fireplace
where we hung our stockings
the night before Christmas—
Don't forget!
The bench on this side
for our toys,
and on the other side—
the wood's in there.

"And then the den—
Mamma's fern by the windows,
Papa's desk,
and behind it all our books—
Will you remember?
Here on the wall our telephone,
and now the dining room—"

So we went,
upstairs and down,
our good-bye
to this house
forever.

Glad to move
to the big new home—
Our parents said we'd love
the lawn around
and the great black walnut tree
where we'd have a swing.
And we'd love the city, too, they said,
Salem, full of roses
and forests in the parks,
and orchards on the hills
near town.

Yet, our house here is home
and we are leaving—
Don't forget!
This is forever—
We won't be back.

RESPONSE CORNER

Try to Remember

The child in "Moving to Salem" understands, as did the pioneers, that moving on means leaving parts of your life behind. Make a time capsule of your life today so that if you wanted to remember it in a far-away new home, you could. Gather or list a collection of items and photos for your time capsule.

Frontier Photo Album

Although photography was fairly new when the West was being settled, we have a few photos that show how settlers lived. Draw three pictures for a pioneer "photo" album. Show a pioneer family just reaching their new home, several months later developing their land, and twenty years later, after settling their homestead. Share your album with classmates, and point out the progress shown in the pictures.

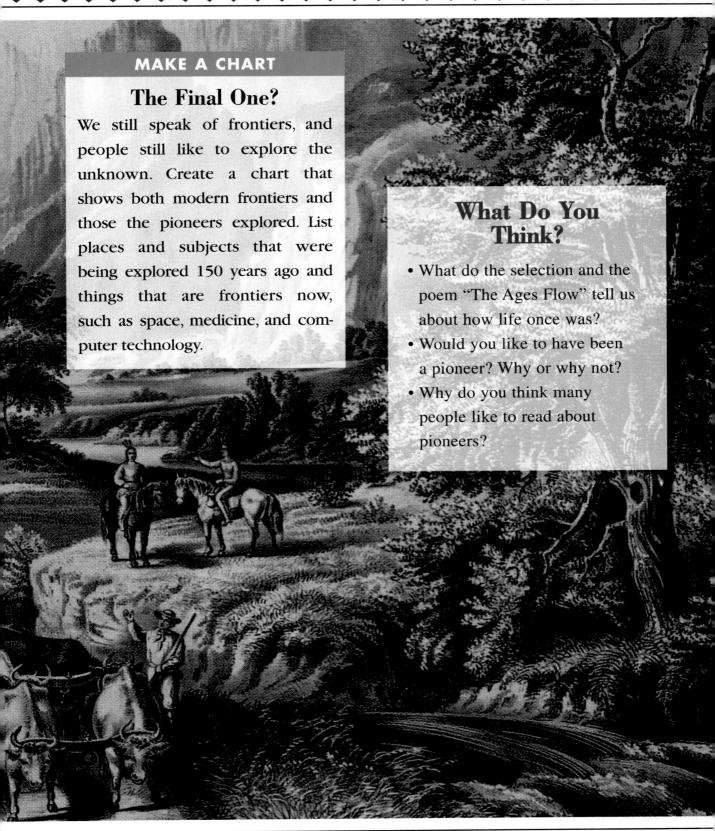

MAKE A CHART

The Final One?

We still speak of frontiers, and people still like to explore the unknown. Create a chart that shows both modern frontiers and those the pioneers explored. List places and subjects that were being explored 150 years ago and things that are frontiers now, such as space, medicine, and computer technology.

What Do You Think?

- What do the selection and the poem "The Ages Flow" tell us about how life once was?
- Would you like to have been a pioneer? Why or why not?
- Why do you think many people like to read about pioneers?

LAURA INGALLS WILDER

Little House
on the Prairie

Little House on the Prairie

by Laura Ingalls Wilder
illustrated by Garth Williams

In the late 1800s, Laura, Mary, and Carrie have moved with their Ma and Pa from the woods of Wisconsin to the prairie of Kansas. After camping out during the entire trip west in their covered wagon, they are eager to begin living in a house again. When the family first moves into the log house Pa has built, they are using the canvas cover from the wagon for a roof and are doing all their cooking outside. Now, Pa begins to make a fireplace.

That afternoon Ma sat sewing in the shade of the house, and Baby Carrie played on the quilt beside her, while Laura and Mary watched Pa build the fireplace.

First he mixed clay and water to a beautiful thick mud, in the mustangs' water bucket. He let Laura stir the mud while he laid a row of rocks around three sides of the space he had cleared by the house-wall. Then with a wooden paddle he spread the mud over the rocks. In the mud he laid another row of rocks, and plastered them over the top and down on the inside with more mud.

He made a box on the ground; three sides of the box were made of rocks and mud, and the other side was the log wall of the house.

With rocks and mud and more rocks and more mud, he built the walls as high as Laura's chin. Then on the walls, close against the house, he laid a log. He plastered the log all over with mud.

After that, he built up rocks and mud on top of that log. He was making the chimney now, and he made it smaller and smaller.

He had to go to the creek for more rocks. Laura and Mary could not go again, because Ma said the damp air might give them a fever. Mary sat beside Ma and sewed another block of her nine-patch quilt, but Laura mixed another bucketful of mud.

Next day Pa built the chimney as high as the house-wall. Then he stood and looked at it. He ran his fingers through his hair.

"You look like a wild man, Charles," Ma said. "You're standing your hair all on end."

"It stands on end, anyway, Caroline," Pa answered. "When I was courting you, it never would lie down, no matter how much I slicked it with bear grease."

He threw himself down on the grass at her feet. "I'm plumb tuckered out, lifting rocks up there."

"You've done well to build that chimney up so high, all by yourself," Ma said. She ran her hand through his hair and stood it up more than ever. "Why don't you make it stick-and-daub the rest of the way?" she asked him.

"Well, it would be easier," he admitted. "I'm blamed if I don't believe I will!"

He jumped up. Ma said, "Oh, stay here in the shade and rest awhile." But he shook his head.

"No use lazing here while there's work to be done, Caroline. The sooner I get the fireplace done, the sooner you can do your cooking inside, out of the wind."

He hauled saplings from the woods, and he cut and notched them and laid them up like the walls of the house, on top of the stone chimney. As he laid them, he plastered them well with mud. And that finished the chimney.

Then he went into the house, and with his ax and saw he cut a hole in the wall. He cut away the logs that had made the fourth wall at the bottom of the chimney. And there was the fireplace.

It was large enough for Laura and Mary and Baby Carrie to sit in. Its bottom was the ground that Pa had cleared of grass, and its front was the space where Pa had cut away the logs. Across the top of that space was the log that Pa had plastered all over with mud.

On each side Pa pegged a thick slab of green oak against the cut ends of the logs. Then by the upper corners of the fireplace he pegged chunks of oak to the wall, and on these he laid an oak slab and pegged it firmly. That was the mantel-shelf.

As soon as it was done, Ma set in the middle of the mantel-shelf the little china woman she had brought from the Big Woods. The little china woman had come all the way and had not been broken. She stood on the mantel-shelf with her little china shoes and her wide china skirts and her tight china bodice, and her pink cheeks and blue eyes and golden hair all made of china.

Then Pa and Ma and Mary and Laura stood and admired that fireplace. Only Carrie did not care about it. She pointed at the little china woman and yelled when Mary and Laura told her that no one but Ma could touch it.

"You'll have to be careful with your fire, Caroline," Pa said. "We don't want sparks going up the chimney to set the roof on fire. That cloth would burn, easy. I'll split out some clapboards as soon as I can, and make a roof you won't have to worry about."

So Ma carefully built a little fire in the new fireplace, and she roasted a prairie hen for supper. And that evening they ate in the house.

They sat at table, by the western window. Pa had quickly made the table of two slabs of oak. One end of the slabs stuck in a crack of the wall, and the other end rested on short, upright logs. Pa had smoothed the slabs with his ax, and the table was very nice when Ma spread a cloth over it.

The chairs were chunks of big logs. The floor was the earth that Ma had swept clean with her willow-bough broom. On the floor, in the corners, the beds were neat under their patchwork quilts. The rays of the setting sun came through the window and filled the house with golden light.

Outside, and far, far away to the pink edge of the sky, the wind went blowing and the wild grasses waved.

Inside, the house was pleasant. The good roast chicken was juicy in Laura's mouth. Her hands and face were washed, her hair was combed, her napkin was tied around her neck. She sat up straight on the round end of log and used her knife and fork nicely, as Ma had taught her. She did not say anything, because children must not speak at table until they are spoken to, but she looked at Pa and Ma and Mary and at Baby Carrie in Ma's lap, and she felt contented. It was nice to be living in a house again.

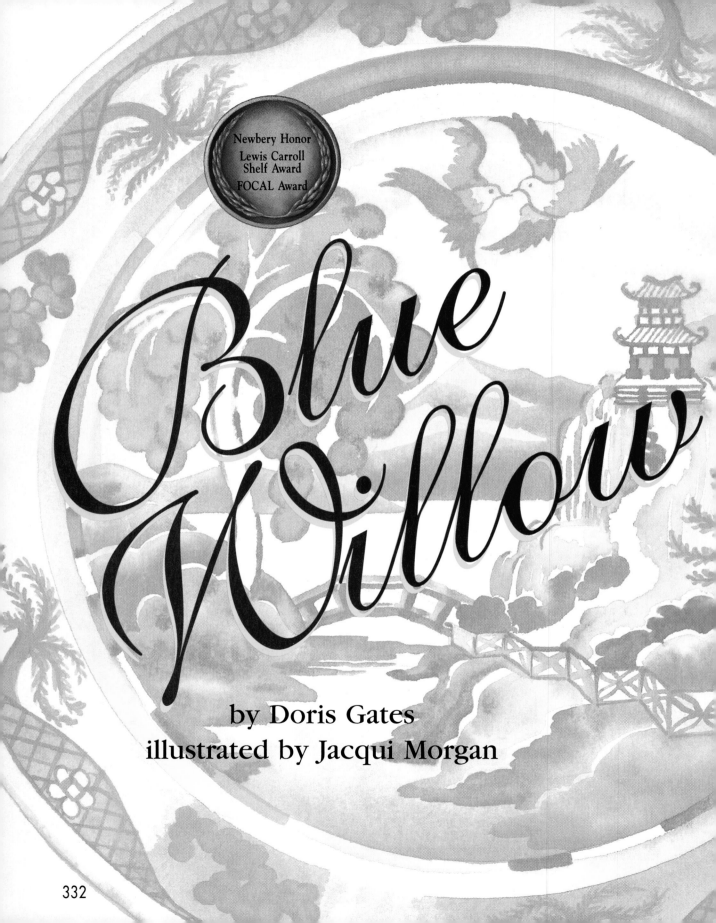

Newbery Honor
Lewis Carroll
Shelf Award
FOCAL Award

Blue Willow

by Doris Gates
illustrated by Jacqui Morgan

*J*aney's father works in the fields, picking crops. His family, and many others like his, must always move on to wherever workers are needed. The family takes only basic necessities with them, except for a blue willow plate that belonged to Janey's great-great-grandmother. To Janey, the plate is a reminder of the time when they had a home. When she discovers a place that reminds her of the picture on the plate and finds a friend, Lupe, she begins to hope that this time they will stay.

Janey and Dad were on their way to the cotton fields. Dad was going to work; Janey was going to school. It was October now. The sun, though bright and warm, was not hot as it had been a month ago, and the mountains, as if rewarding the valley for milder weather, were allowing their blue outlines to be seen. Wild sunflowers turned bright faces to the east, and occasional dust devils went spiraling off across the plain in merry abandon. But Janey, huddled in a corner of the ragged front seat, was sulkily indifferent to the world around her. The corners of her mouth sagged, her lower lip protruded in something close to a pout, and her eyes glowered darkly. She wasn't glad to be going to school, not this school at any rate. If only she were being taken to the town school, the one where Lupe and all the other children of the district went! That is, they did if they belonged to the district. Janey was well aware that actually she herself could have attended that school, too. There was no law forbidding it. But it was a fact, too, that in some communities she would have been extremely unwelcome, and Dad, knowing this, had made his own law in respect to Janey.

"We'll keep with our own kind," he had once said when she had remonstrated with him. "The camp schools are put there for us to use and so we'll use them and be thankful. Besides, a body can learn anywhere if he's a mind to."

Janey hadn't argued further with him on that occasion and she had no desire to do so today. She knew that going to the "regular" school would no longer satisfy her anyway, for just going there couldn't make her really belong. Since she had begun to want to stay in this place, merely going to the district school was no longer enough. What Janey wanted was to belong to this place and to go to the district school because as a member of the community it was her right to go there. The camp school would now be a daily and forceful reminder of the fact that she didn't belong, and so she dreaded it.

She knew what the camp school would be like. No two of the children would have learned the same things, and it would all be a jumble. In some lessons, Janey would find herself way ahead of most of the boys and girls her age, and she would be expected as a matter of course to know other things she had never had a chance to learn. Most of the time she wouldn't know whether she was going or coming and there would be endless questions and much tiresome fussing.

Besides, it was much too early in the day for school to start and she would have to wait around until it did. She would have asked Dad to let her go into the field with him if she had thought it would do any good. But she knew from past experience that it wouldn't. Never had she been allowed to do any field work. Other children did and sometimes Mom, but never Janey. Dad, so easy-going about most things, was firm on this. So Janey sat with a frown on her face as the old car jolted along its way, and came very near to feeling sorry for herself.

She would have known the school house as soon as they came in sight of it even if Dad hadn't bothered to point it out. She had seen many of them before and they all looked alike. Some were newer than others and that was about the only difference. This was one of the newer ones. It was a rather large square building, its unpainted boards gleaming in the bright light. In front of it a flagpole, also unpainted, towered against the morning sky. As yet no flag was in evidence, so Janey knew for sure that school had not yet started. Her father let her off at the front steps, then drove over to park beside a row of cars that looked as if they might all have come from the same junk pile. Janey sat down to wait, her package of lunch beside her.

Across from her were the cottages, row upon row, that comprised the camp. Looking at these little one-room sheds so close together that their eaves almost touched, she was thankful for their own shack and the spreading country around it. Of course there was plenty of country spread around here. But the

camp itself was squeezed into as small a space as possible so as not to use up any more of the cotton ground than was absolutely necessary. The deep green of the cotton plants reached in every direction almost as far as the eye could see. And here and there against the green of every bush a gleam of white showed clearly. That was where a cotton boll had burst open to free the fluffy fibers which would be picked by hand from each boll. There would be thousands, perhaps millions, of these little white bunches and it would take many fingers working many hours a day to pick all the ripening cotton. That is why there was a village of little houses at this place with a school house at hand. During the picking season hundreds of people lived here and worked here until the day should come when all the cotton was harvested. Then they would load their cars with what household goods they owned, and with their boys and girls the cotton pickers would move on to some other part of the country which needed their hands and their heads.

Of course, Janey wasn't thinking of all this while she sat on the steps of the school house. It was so much a part of her life that she didn't bother to think about it any more than she bothered to think about the processes of breathing when she drew fresh air into her lungs.

For perhaps ten minutes, Janey sat there, a blue-overalled figure of gloom, when all at once she caught a movement in the dust in front of her. It was so slight a movement that at first she thought her eyes were playing her tricks. But in the next second, the dust was again stirred, and then she was off the school house steps in one lunge. Flat on the ground she hurled herself, one arm reaching out ahead of her. Slowly she drew in her arm, her hand tightly closed, and gathered herself up. From head to foot she was coated with fine dirt, but she didn't care. She didn't even stop to brush herself off before she slowly began to open her fingers, squinting closely at what she held there. A smile widened across her face, for in the shadowy hollow of her palm was a small horned toad. Its eyes, mere pinheads of glistening black, stared fiercely at her, and its chinless mouth was set grimly. But Janey was not alarmed. She had captured many horned toads before this and knew that for all their fierce expression and spiky covering, they were quite harmless creatures. Slowly she lowered herself onto the school house steps once more to inspect her captive. To most people he would have appeared far from beautiful, but to Janey he seemed an object of delight. His four tiny feet with their minute claws were perfect, and from the fringe of miniature scales outlining what should have been his chin, to the last infinitesimal spike on the end of his brief tail, he was finished and complete. Janey loved him at once and began cautiously to draw her finger across his hard little head.

Suddenly an idea occurred to her. She would use this horned toad to test the new teacher. In every school she had ever been, someone had always solemnly assured her whenever she happened to mention a "horned toad" that she should call them "horned lizards," for they were not really toads at all. Janey had always been entirely willing to accept the fact that they were not, strictly speaking, "horned toads," but to call them anything else just wasn't possible. The minute you said "horned lizard" you turned a perfectly good horned toad into a new and unattractive animal. She would loathe having anyone refer to her new pet as a horned lizard, and if the new teacher did so, Janey's respect for her as a human being would be completely shattered. It would be, she thought, like saying "It is I" instead of "It's me." If you used the former, you would be correct, but you wouldn't be a friend. She was determined to discover whether the new teacher was a friend or merely correct.

She and the horned toad had not long to wait. Janey had hardly got some of the dirt brushed off when a dusty sedan rolled to a halt in the shade of the school house and a fat and smiling woman got out of it. Janey felt hopeful.

"Hello," called the woman. "No ten-o'clock-scholar about you, is there?"

Janey felt increasingly hopeful as she rose to meet this stranger who was undoubtedly the teacher. Surely no one who quoted Mother Goose to you before she had asked your name would call a horned toad a horned lizard. More than that, she would know what to do with you if you were good in reading and poor in arithmetic. Suddenly the whole tone of the day was changed. But the final test was yet to come.

"Look," said Janey, holding out her captive.

"Well, bless my soul," said the woman heartily, bending over Janey's hand, "a horned toad! Did you catch it?"

Janey nodded, too delighted for the moment to speak, then: "But I haven't named him yet."

"Can't let him go without a name. Let's see." The woman thought a moment. Then, "I have it. Let's call him Fafnir. He was a first-class dragon when giants ruled the earth. And this fellow looks a lot like a dragon. A fairy dragon. Does Fafnir appeal to you?"

Janey nodded.

The teacher chuckled. "I suppose the proper thing would be to let the horned toad decide such an important matter for himself. But from the look of him I should say that he wasn't quite on speaking terms with us yet."

She looked at Janey with eyes that were merry and direct. Trustworthy eyes with friendly secrets in their depths.

"I am Miss Peterson," she said.

"I'm Janey Larkin."

A stout arm encircled Janey's narrow shoulders and for a brief moment she felt herself squeezed against Miss Peterson's warm and well-cushioned side.

"Welcome to Camp Miller school, Janey. Come on inside. We'll start the day together."

No questions, no fussing. Just "Come on in," as if she had known you always. Janey slid an arm around Miss Peterson's ample waist and together they entered the building, the small girl walking on tiptoe, to her teacher's secret amusement. Miss Peterson would have been surprised to know she was the innocent cause of that strange behavior. For Janey was thrilling to the certainty that this very morning, unexpectedly and alone, she had discovered the most wonderful teacher in the world. That was enough to make anyone prance on tiptoe! A few minutes ago she had been feeling sorry for herself and all the time there had been Fafnir and Miss Peterson. Not even Lupe going to the "regular" school could possibly have enjoyed such luck as that!

During the next half-hour Janey helped Miss Peterson prepare for the day's work. She cleaned the blackboards and put the tables and benches in order. Some pink petunias were blooming in a window box and Janey watered them from the standing pipe outside the door. Then she picked off the withered blossoms, which left her fingers so sticky she had to return to the water pipe to wash her hands. Soon the boys and girls began to arrive. The school day started at nine o'clock when one of the boys carried the flag out to the unpainted pole and fastened it to the rope neatly secured there.

While the whole school stood grouped at attention, the flag was drawn slowly up into the morning sky until at last it came to rest at the pole's very top and the Stars and Stripes was unfolded above the school and the camp. The little ceremony ended, they all trooped to their lessons.

As the morning advanced, Janey's regard for Miss Peterson increased, if that were possible. Because they were crowded on the benches, and because their legs were not all long enough to reach the floor, she saw to it that the children were given time to move around and rest. And it seemed to be the custom for two or three of the children to tell the others each day which part of the country they had thought the most interesting in their traveling around. Janey, listening to the others this morning, decided, when her turn came, to tell about the place by the river which she had discovered the other day. The place like the willow plate.

*D*oris Gates was raised on a ranch in Mountain View, California. That's where she gained a love of animals, most of all horses. For a while she liked cowboy stories so much that she wanted to be a cowboy herself.

When Gates grew up, she got a job at a library. During the Great Depression, the library went through hard times, and she could work only a few days a week. That's when she started writing children's stories of her own.

Blue Willow is based on her experience teaching children who were living in poverty during Dust Bowl times. Working with these children taught her something important. "There are many kinds of poverty," she said. "Without love, a child is poor; without a feeling of family unity, a child is poor; and without a deep faith in beauty . . . a child is poor indeed."

She thought of life as a long journey. About her own journey through life, she said, "A wise man has said that at the end of every journey, you find what you took there. I have found . . . all the things most important to me as I traveled along the road, . . . love of childhood, love of children, and the conviction that children's books can add . . . to a child's delight in discovering the world."

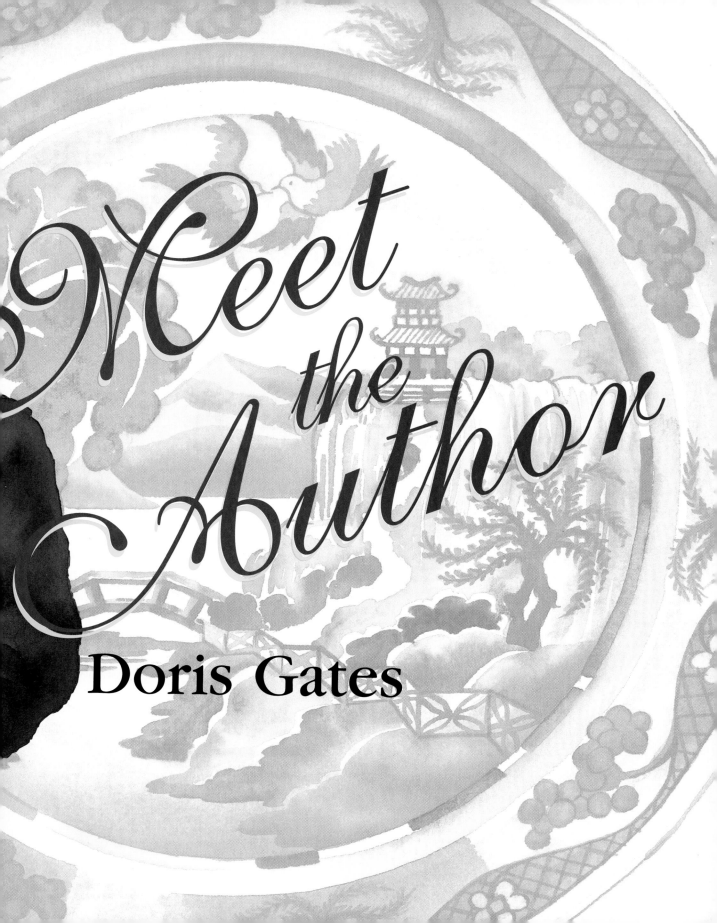

Meet the Author

Doris Gates

Travelogue

Miss Peterson asks her students to tell about the most interesting place they've visited. What is the most interesting place you have visited or read about? Write a short speech about it, and present it to your classmates.

RESPONSE

WRITE AN AD

For Hire

If only all the camp schools could have teachers like Miss Peterson! With a partner, list the traits in Miss Peterson's character that make her right for the job. Then use your list to write a newspaper advertisement for other camp school teachers with the same traits.

MAKE A COLLAGE

100% Cotton

Cotton has many uses—even as art material. Make a collage using cotton balls, pieces of cotton material, cotton yarn or string, and so on. Your collage should show one of your favorite scenes from the selection.

CORNER

What Do You Think?

- What advice might Janey give to someone else who is nervous about going to school?

- Do you agree with Janey that a teacher should be a friend? Explain your answer.

- If you were Janey's father, would you let her choose whether to go to the school in town? Why or why not?

ART AND LITERATURE

The painting *California Crossing, South Platte River* shows a wagon train crossing a river. The artist, William Henry Jackson, was a member of the wagon train. Like many other people in 1866, he was on his way to California. How might the dreams of these pioneers be like those of Janey and her parents?

California Crossing, South Platte River (1867) by William Henry Jackson. Oil on canvas (22" × 34"). The Thomas Gilcrease Institute of American History and Art, Tulsa, Oklahoma.

California Crossing, South Platte River
by William Henry Jackson

William Henry Jackson lived in California but later moved to Nebraska
and became a photographer. Like his paintings, his photographs
capture thrilling moments in history. In 1871 Jackson took the first
photographs of Yellowstone National Park.

THE CALIFORNIA GOLD RUSH

WEST
WITH THE FORTY-NINERS

By Elizabeth Van Steenwyk

THE DRAMA UNFOLDS

IT COULD BE SAID that the story of the gold rush really began on the day in 1839 when John Augustus Sutter first arrived in California. He brought little with him from Switzerland except his dream of creating a farming empire in this sleepy possession of Mexico. Mexico had broken away from Spanish rule in 1821 and claimed California for itself.

Millions of acres in California that once belonged to Spain were now owned by Mexican officials. Thousands of cattle grazed and grew fat on these huge land grants. They became California's leading, and only, product. The time and place seemed to be perfect for making Sutter's dream come true.

Award-Winning Author

Settlers had been traveling to California before the gold rush, but they really started to come in swarms after this precious metal was discovered.

Sutter applied for Mexican citizenship. In 1840 he received a land grant of nearly 50,000 acres (20,235 hectares), in the Sacramento Valley. He built a fort made of adobe near the south bank of the American River. From this fort, he controlled the surrounding land, which he named New Helvetia. (Helvetia is another name for Switzerland.)

Meanwhile, overland emigrants from the United States began to arrive in the valley. They had followed trails established by fur trappers. After 1841, this route through the midsection of the country became known as the California Trail.

Settlers in this period before the gold rush also came by ship. More than 200 Mormons came ashore at Yerba Buena (soon to be called San Francisco). They had sailed around Cape Horn, the southernmost tip of South America, hoping to escape from the religious persecution they had experienced in the East. Many of them found work at Sutter's Fort.

By January 1848, Sutter's Fort was a lively place with a population of nearly 300. More settlers arrived every day, and a sawmill was urgently needed. Sutter appointed a carpenter named James Wilson Marshall to supervise construction of a sawmill

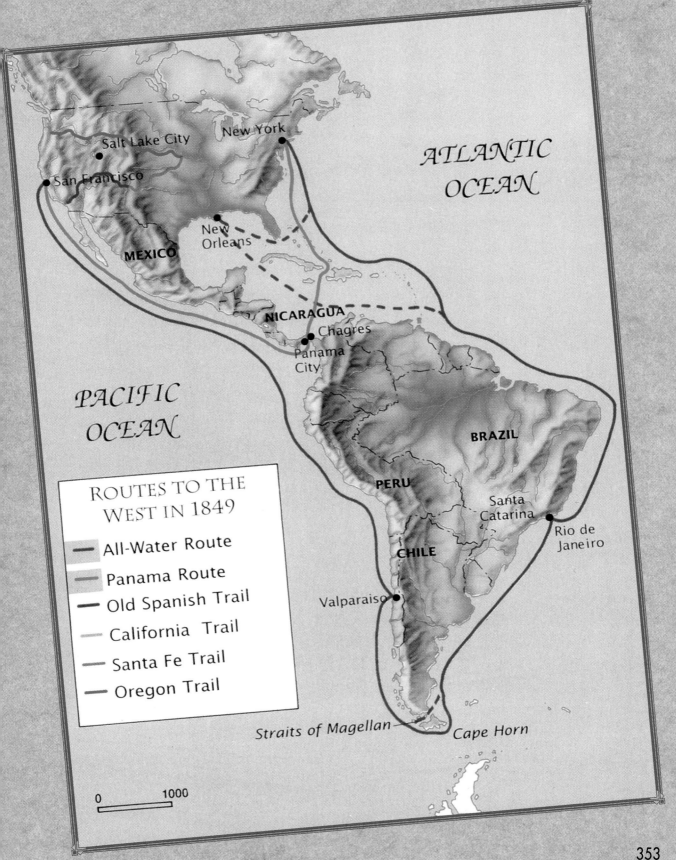

ROUTES TO THE WEST IN 1849

— All-Water Route
— Panama Route
— Old Spanish Trail
— California Trail
— Santa Fe Trail
— Oregon Trail

0   1000

ATLANTIC OCEAN

PACIFIC OCEAN

Salt Lake City

New York

San Francisco

New Orleans

MEXICO

NICARAGUA

Chagres

Panama City

BRAZIL

PERU

Santa Catarina

Rio de Janeiro

CHILE

Valparaiso

Straits of Magellan

Cape Horn

about 45 miles (72.4 km) east of the fort. The location was at a bend in the south fork of the American River in the Coloma Valley.

On the afternoon of January 24, Marshall walked along a ditch that channeled water from the river to the sawmill. Earlier, he thought he had seen some shiny pebbles in the ditch and wanted to examine them more closely. He picked up a pebble about the size of a pea, and his heart began to race. It looked too yellow to be silver but didn't seem bright enough to be gold. He pounded it. It bent but didn't break. Could it be?

Marshall hurried back to some workmen, who were resting at the end of a long day. He announced that he had just found gold. At first, they were unimpressed. Only Henry Bigler, a Mormon from Virginia, thought it might be significant. In his diary, he wrote, "This day some kind of mettle [metal] was found in the tail race that looks like goald [gold]."

The next day, the workmen decided to have a better look at the shiny pebbles. Within minutes, they realized James Marshall knew what he was talking about. He really had discovered gold!

As news of James Marshall's gold discovery at the sawmill reached the Mormons at Sutter's mill, they, too, began to look for gold. They discovered enough to abandon their regular work and begin mining in earnest. This second site became known as Mormon Island.

After Marshall told Sutter of his discovery, Sutter tested the pebbles for himself and became convinced they were gold. He established legal claim to the land, buying it directly from the Indians. Then he asked his workers to say nothing of the discovery for six weeks. But even Sutter himself could not keep quiet. He wrote to his friend, Mariano Vallejo, less than a week later, saying that he had discovered a "mina de oro."[1]

By the second week of March, news of the discovery reached San Francisco. It traveled by word of mouth until the fifteenth, when the news appeared in print for the first time. However, the story appeared on the last page of the San Francisco *Californian* and was only one paragraph long. Even a second story in the other weekly newspaper, the *California Star*, did little to interest the local folks.

---

[1] mē´nä dā ō´rō: gold mine

**Sutter's Mill, in the
Coloma Valley, where James Marshall
discovered gold, and where a nation was changed forever**

The owner of the *Star* was an enterprising man named Sam Brannan. He decided to put out a special edition and send it to the folks in the eastern United States. With this edition, he hoped to persuade people to move to San Francisco and buy the lots he owned. Then he would make a profit for himself.

San Francisco citizens remained skeptical about the gold discovery.

But ranchers near Sutter's Fort began to believe it after they saw the results of the Mormon diggings at a flour mill site. They came and staked out claims for themselves.

Sam Brannan arrived next. After he saw that workers at Sutter's Fort were in a frenzy over the discovery, he bought up future store locations. Those who already had been prospecting displayed their pouches of gold dust as they prepared to dig for more. Sam Brannan realized that something important had happened here. He was determined to be a part of it.

On May 12, Brannan returned to San Francisco, displaying a bottle full of gold dust and shouting, "Gold! Gold! Gold from the American River." Excited people gathered around to ask questions and wonder. But they didn't wonder long. On May 12, there were six hundred men in the city. Three days later, there were two hundred. The others had gone to the gold field. By the end of the month, the city had nearly closed down. Even the newspapers ceased operation —there was no one left to read them. Soon, men from all over California left other jobs and headed for the hills.

Two thousand copies of Sam Brannan's special edition *Star* reached Missouri by the end of July. Many newspapers reprinted stories from it, but most people dismissed the gold discovery idea. It was unimportant, they said, or too good to be true. So, they ignored it.

But the news wouldn't die. Stories continued to trickle back East in letters by private citizens and reports from government officials. Throughout the summer and fall, newspapers featured more stories about the great wealth to be found in the West. What most Americans needed, however, was official support for these tall tales. Finally, on December 5, 1848, President James K. Polk delivered a message to Congress. In it, he said that the news of California's gold discovery had been verified. Those tales weren't fiction; they were fact!

The gold rush was on!

Even though there was no gold to be discovered in San Francisco, it went from a village to a crowded city practically overnight, as travelers passed through on the way to seek their fortunes.

⚒ LIFE IN THE DIGGINGS ⚒

SHIPLOADS OF FORTY-NINERS began arriving in California by the early summer of 1849. They landed at San Francisco, once a sleepy village of less than 900 residents. Now, it had been awakened by thousands of adventurers from all over the world. They stayed only long enough to outfit themselves and find transportation to the "diggings."

The village grew quickly to accommodate the Argonauts.[2] It sprawled along the docks in a collection of wooden huts and tents. Its harbor was crowded with ships abandoned by owners who had gone to the gold fields. Living conditions were crowded and expensive. A small room rented for $50 a month, ten times what it cost in the East. Wood was so expensive that one man paid $100 for a small packing box—to live in!

Some of the newcomers quickly realized that all of the gold wasn't to be found in the hills. They stayed in San Francisco, opening businesses which catered to the needs of the miners. They charged $10 for a hat, $100 for a pair of boots, $100 for a blanket, and $50 for a shovel. The new merchants soon prospered, and so did the village. By 1850, it had grown to a city of 56,000.

The prospectors used any kind of transportation they could afford to get to the mines. Some traveled by riverboat to Sacramento or Stockton. Others journeyed by horse, mule, or foot. Those who arrived via the California Trail had a head start. They hardly paused in Sacramento before pushing on to the gold fields.

At first, everyone wanted to go to the Coloma Valley. Soon, however, mining camps popped up all along the curves of the Sierra foothills. The banks of the American, Feather, and Yuba rivers became populated with settlements as well. Wherever gold was discovered, a camp was soon established. Many of them were given funny, colorful names, such as Bedbug, Total Wreck, and Ten-Cent Gulch.

Prices soared at the tent stores in the diggings. But the miners either had to pay them or go without supplies. A slice of bread cost a dollar, and it took another dollar to butter it. An egg cost from one to three dollars. Nearly all the other basics—flour, sugar, and coffee—sold at ridiculous prices *when* they were available.

The reason was not hard to understand. Local farmers and ranchers had raced off to become miners. They left their crops to die, and no one bothered to replant. Now, food had to be shipped great distances, driving prices nearly out of reach. Since actual money was scarce, gold dust soon became the currency of exchange. A pinch of dust (the amount anyone could pick up between his

---

[2] Argonauts: a group of mythological heroes who traveled by ship in search of treasure. The forty-niners who traveled by ship to California were named for them.

Miners had great
hope that the next pan would yield the
nugget of gold that would make them rich.

thumb and forefinger) was supposed to equal one dollar.

Life was simple, though far from easy, in the mining settlements. The miners rose at dawn, emerging from crudely made shacks, tents, or blankets laid on bare ground under the trees. The weather could be cold and wet at times, and blizzards were not uncommon in the winter. There was no plumbing. The miners bathed in streams. They cooked breakfast over an open fire. Salt pork and bread usually made up both their morning and evening meals. Coffee washed everything down, when they could get it. A real treat, saved for special occasions such as Christmas, was a can of peaches.

Because of their unhealthy diets and harsh living conditions, miners suffered from many ailments. Fevers, chills, and rheumatism were common complaints after weeks of working in icy streams. Scurvy, dysentery, and diarrhea were other discomforts caused by poor diets and food eaten half-raw or spoiled. One miner complained that the bread he bought was full of worms. Even with gold dust in his pockets, however, he could find no decent bread to buy.

Doctors, or men who called themselves that, posted signs reading "Hospital" across their tents and waited for patients to arrive. The only medical weapons against disease at that time were painkilling drugs. Quinine, which could ease malaria, cost four times its weight in gold. It's easy to understand why one out of five miners died in the first year of the gold rush. It's more difficult to understand how so many others survived!

In the evenings, miners sat around their campfires and told stories of home. Sometimes they played card games, but not for long. After a long, hard day of mining, they thought of little else but sleep.

The miners had chosen a back-breaking occupation. They worked alone at first, dressed in dark pants, red flannel shirts, and broad-brimmed hats. In the early days, they would stand knee-deep in icy streams, for ten or twelve hours a day, panning for gold.

Panning was the simplest and easiest way to separate gold from dirt. Gravel and water were mixed together in a pan or any other similar container. The pan was swirled around until the water washed the lighter dirt away. With luck, the heavier material left at the bottom of the pan was gold.

"Cradling" for gold enabled miners to wash through more dirt than panning did, and was even more efficient when two miners worked together.

Miners soon began to use rockers, or cradles, to sift the dirt. A rocker was a rectangular box, mounted on rockers (like a rocking chair) and set on sloping ground. Cleats, wooden or metal spikes, were fastened to the bottom. Dirt was put in the top, and water was added to send the dirt through the box. The heavier gold fell to the bottom, catching on the cleats. More dirt could be washed with a rocker than with a pan. But the individual miner really needed a partner to make the process more efficient.

Hydraulic mining was a successful means of finding gold, but its effects on the land were disastrous. Those who used hydraulic mining left a trail of destruction behind them.

Other methods of mining were invented as the supply of placer, or surface, gold dwindled. Sluice boxes—used to wash out the gold— were larger versions of rockers, requiring many miners working together. Later, hydraulic mining came into use. It turned out to be the most efficient method, but it was also the most destructive. Water, applied under great pressure to banks of gravel, caused the ground to disintegrate. Once the gold was taken from the gravel, the miners moved on, leaving ruined hillsides behind.

Eventually, dredging and quartz mining developed. These methods required more complicated tools, more money, and more miners working together. Gold mining then ceased to be an adventure and became a business.

Most miners rested on Sunday. That was the day they chopped wood for the following week's campfires, repaired their tools, and washed clothes in nearby streams. They also wrote letters to their families and put down their thoughts in journals. The gold rush was one of the most written-about events in United States history.

About the Author

ELIZABETH VAN STEENWYK

When Elizabeth Van Steenwyk was a young girl in Galesburg, Illinois, she would sometimes spend all day at the town library. Little by little, Elizabeth read just about every book in that library. She also discovered its collection of old newspapers. She especially enjoyed learning about great historical figures from the part of Illinois where she lived. She had a favorite seat by a window in the library where she would read and watch students going to their classes at Knox College.

Many years later, after she herself had been to Knox College, the old library burned down. Her own children could not understand why she cried. They didn't know how important the library had been to her when she was their age.

Van Steenwyk says she writes books for children because there are so many things to write about. She adds, "I can sum it up in the words of a child who wrote to me after reading one of my books. She said, 'Happiness must be writing children's books.' I wonder how she knew."

148. Mormon Island Emporium, Excelsior Tent

RESPONSE

MAP OUT A ROUTE

Westward Wagons

When people on the east coast of the United States heard about the discovery of gold, they couldn't get to California quickly. They had to travel slowly by ship or by wagon. Using a map of North and South America, trace the routes someone could have traveled by wagon from Washington, D.C., to San Francisco, California. How many miles long is each trip? Share your findings with the class.

WRITE AN AD

Come One, Come All!

Sam Brannan used the newspaper to advertise Marshall's gold discovery to the eastern states. Think of a discovery that might bring visitors to your area. Then write and illustrate a full-page newspaper advertisement encouraging people to come. Remember to use vivid words and eye-catching pictures to get readers' attention.

CORNER

Get Rich Quick?

During the gold rush, many who tried to "get rich quick" took chances with their health and gave up their farms back home, even though they knew they might not find the precious metal. Hold a debate about whether it is better to try to get rich quickly or to stick with slower but surer ways of making money. Support your viewpoint with examples. After the debate, ask classmates to vote for the point of view they agree with.

What Do You Think?

- How did the gold rush change California between 1848 and 1850?
- If you had been an adult living in Boston in 1850, do you think you would have gone west to search for gold? Why or why not?
- How do you think the history of California might have been different if gold had not been discovered there?

365

By The Great Horn Spoon!

By Sid Fleischman   Illustrated by Gary Head

By the Great Horn Spoon!

SID FLEISCHMAN

In 1849, young Jack Flagg and his butler, Praiseworthy, leave their home with Jack's Aunt Arabella in Boston to search for gold in California. Along the way, they meet Quartz Jackson, a prospector who teaches them how to pan for gold. At one dig site, a rough character named Pitch-pine Billy Pierce first accuses them of stealing his pan and then invites them to join him for coffee.

Pitch-pine Billy led them to his weathered canvas tent pitched along the slope. The coffee pot was boiling merrily. He filled three tin cans—black. Black as paint, it looked to Jack. He had never tasted coffee in his life. Aunt Arabella would be furious. He looked at Praiseworthy. And Praiseworthy gave him a nod, as if to make up for having Jack wash his ears back at the hotel.

The tin cans were so hot they felt as if they had just been forged. Jack sat on a rock to let the brew cool. Although Praiseworthy's coat and bowler hat had fallen by the wayside, he clung to the

black umbrella as a last badge of his calling.

"A butler, a butler," mused Pitch-pine Billy. He drank his coffee down, steam and all. "You any relative to Hemp Butler over at Muletown?"

"The name is Praiseworthy— not Butler, sir."

The miner crimped an eye. "You don't say? Well, he calls himself Butler, ol' Hemp does. Never knowed his name was Praiseworthy. But I always figured him for the shifty type. How about Ten-spot Butler over at Poker Flat. He your folks?"

There seemed no point in trying to make himself clear and Praiseworthy let it go. "Tell me, Mr. Pierce—"

"Just call me Pitch-pine Billy."

"How do we stake a claim?"

"Easy. Find yourself a piece of real estate nobody's workin' and pound four pegs in the corners. Put tin cans on 'em so folks can see. Rags'll do. And you got yourself a legal claim. That's miners' law. As long as you work it at least one day a month, it stays yours." He laughed and stroked his beard. "Of course, the other thirty days you got to stand around shootin' off squatters and claim jumpers." He refilled his tin can. "Why, there are places along the river where the claims is only four-foot square and the boys is diggin' out a fortune, back to back."

Jack finally picked up his tin can. The steam alone was like a dragon's breath. Now he was almost sorry Praiseworthy had given him a nod. At the first taste, the coffee bit his tongue.

"Drink up, Jack. Jamoka Jack, that's what we'll call you. A man ain't really accepted around here until he's won himself a nickname."

"Best coffee I ever tasted," Jack said hoarsely.

"Plenty more in the pot. I ground in a few acorns for flavor."

Jack winced inwardly. Jamoka Jack—the name pleased him, but he wasn't sure he could win it. The coffee stung and burned and tasted poisonous. He forced down another mouthful. He was afraid the miner would take back the name if he didn't drain the can. He tried another swig—but it wouldn't go down.

Praiseworthy, catching Jack's distress out of the corner of his eye, shifted his position. The tip of his umbrella jiggled Jack's elbow and the tin can jumped. The coffee spilled.

"It's no account," said Pitch-pine Billy. He lifted the pot and refilled Jack's can. "We don't stand on table manners out here."

Jack gulped and stared at the fresh, steaming black potion of coffee. He had to begin all over again. Praiseworthy gave him a compassionate glance. He considered it his duty to look out for Jack, but now he had only made matters worse.

"Lemme show you how to wash out gold without water," Pitch-pine Billy was saying. "Take your horn spoon,[1] boy, and scrape me some dirt from the crack in that rock. It's places like that the spangles like to hide, if there is any."

Jack was glad to set the coffee aside to cool. He slipped the horn spoon from his belt and turned eagerly to the crack in the rocks.

"Just a handful, boy."

Jack scraped away, gathering up river sand and bits of dead pine needles. The horn spoon worked fine.

---

[1] horn spoon: a mining tool carved from ox horn

It got in the cracks. He filled the miner's outstretched hand and sat on his heels to watch.

"This is a trick the Sonorians use," said Pitch-pine Billy. "They come from Sonora down Mexico way. Water must be scarcer than gold around there. We call this dry washin'."

He poured the dirt in a small stream from fist to hand, like sand in an hour glass, while at the same time blowing on it. Sand and pine needles scattered under the force of his breath. He poured again and again and each time the handful of dirt grew smaller.

"Grain for grain, gold is eight times heavier than sand. If you blow just right, the spangles fall and the lighter stuff goes flyin'."

Jack bent closer. Finally Pitch-pine Billy had nothing left to blow. He held out the rough palm of his hand and laughed. "Boy, you struck it rich already. Look there!"

Resting in his hand were two gleaming pinheads of gold. But to Jack they looked as large as jewels.

"Put 'em in your pouch, boy!" said Pitch-pine Billy. "Easy—don't knock over your coffee."

"Thank you, sir," Jack smiled, whipping out his brand new buckskin pouch. "But—they're yours."

The miner grinned. "Anything that small, I throw back in. You and your pa can squat on my claim."

"But Praiseworthy's not—"

"There's more yeller underfoot than I can dig out. I'd be obliged if you'd clear some of it away. You got any idea how to work that tin pan of yours, boy?"

"Mr. Quartz Jackson—"

"You a friend of ol' Quartz! Why didn't you say so? Stay for dinner, hear. We'll have sowbelly-and-beans! I won't take no for an answer, hear! Now let's get our boots wet and I'll learn you how to pan. Bring your coffee."

Jack exchanged a glance with Praiseworthy. Sowbelly-and-beans! "We'd be delighted to join you for dinner," Praiseworthy said, since Pitch-pine Billy had left them no choice.

They moved to the edge of the stream and Jack took a swallow of coffee. The miner pulled a few weeds and threw them in the pan. Jack got down another mouthful of coffee.

"Around runnin' water," explained Pitch-pine Billy, "gold has a way of gettin' tangled in the roots of weeds and grass." He dipped water in the pan and washed the roots clean. He added more dirt until the washbasin was better than half full. Then he began to pan, using the same circular motion Quartz Jackson had shown them.

"You get rid of the rocks and slickens, little by little."

"Slickens?" said Jack.

"Mud with the gold worked out of it. Keep the pan workin' and dippin' and workin' until the spangles reach bottom. Fish out the rocks. See how I'm lettin' the slickens spill over the edge of the pan? It takes practice, boy. At first, you'll lose more color over the side than you'll save in the bottom. But you'll get the hang of it. Ain't you drinkin' your coffee, boy? Why, look there. We struck it rich again. Lemme have your pouch."

Jack took two hard swallows of coffee. Then he pulled off his shoes,

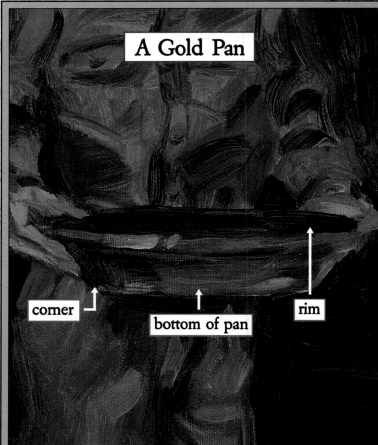

A Gold Pan

corner

bottom of pan

rim

rolled up his trousers, and tried his hand with the gold pan. The mountain water was icy, but he hardly noticed it at first. He hunted grass and weeds. Five minutes later he could no longer feel his feet.

"You're standin' in melted snow off the high peaks," Pitch-pine Billy chuckled. "Wash out enough color and you can buy yourself some boots." Then he turned to

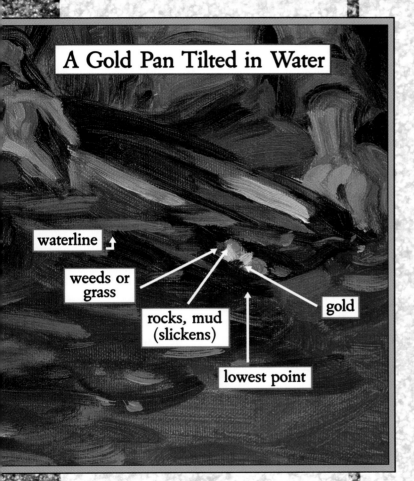

A Gold Pan Tilted in Water

waterline

weeds or grass

rocks, mud (slickens)

gold

lowest point

Praiseworthy. "You ain't exactly dressed for prospectin' yourself. You and your boy will be needin' a tent and a mountain canary."

"A mountain canary?" Praiseworthy asked.

"Mule or burro. There goes one hee-hawin' now. Got a fine singin' voice, don't he? What's that umbrella for?"

"A matter of habit."

"Well, it ain't goin' to rain around here for some time. But seein' as how I punctured your gold pan I don't see any reason why an umbrella won't work just as well. Lemme show you."

"But—"

Pitch-pine Billy lifted it off Praiseworthy's arm and opened the umbrella wide. He stuck it in the ground, upside down.

"If you don't mind, sir," said Praiseworthy, with a flash of impatience. "I happen to treasure that—"

"Yes, sir," the miner was saying to himself. "It oughta work fine—just fine."

Then he began shoveling dirt into the open umbrella. Praiseworthy watched with a kind of quiet horror. He'd carried that black umbrella for years and now it was being ruined before his eyes. "I'll thank you, sir—"

But by then Pitch-pine Billy had lifted the dirt-filled umbrella into the water and was dunking it. He began to twirl it by the handle. He dunked and twirled and twirled and dunked. "Why, I've panned gold in a pocket handkerchief," the miner said. "The dirt dissolves and washes through and leaves the spangles behind."

Jack, meanwhile, was working the slickens out of his pan. He'd step out of the water to warm his feet and take a sip of coffee and then return. He worked two pans of dirt without finding a speck of color, but then he didn't have the hang of it. He was losing the gold with the slickens. But he stayed with it and his feet turned blue.

Finally Pitch-pine Billy was no longer plunging the umbrella, but working with a deft, gentle, washing movement. He fingered out the rocks and after another moment returned the umbrella to Praiseworthy.

"Best gold pan along the river," he grinned. "I might buy me one of these myself."

The mud was gone. In its place along the black fabric of the umbrella lay a bright dusting of gold and spangles.

Praiseworthy crimped an eye and smiled at the hospitable miner. "I think I can get the hang of it, sir."

He removed his shoes, rolled up his trousers and set to work. All through the afternoon Jack could be seen panning and taking a sip of cold coffee, and Praiseworthy cut an elegant figure plunging a muddy umbrella in the stream.

Finally Jack reached the bottom of the tin can and that was that. "Yes sir, first-rate coffee, Pitch-pine Billy," he said. "First-rate."

"Glad you liked it," answered the miner with a bushy-faced grin, "—Jamoka Jack."

THE GOLD COIN

by Alma Flor Ada
illustrated by Neil Waldman

Notable
Trade Book
in Social Studies

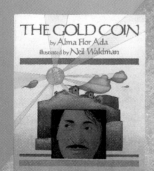

Juan had been a thief for many years. Because he did his stealing by night, his skin had become pale and sickly. Because he spent his time either hiding or sneaking about, his body had become shriveled and bent. And because he had neither friend nor relative to make him smile, his face was always twisted into an angry frown.

One night, drawn by a light shining through the trees, Juan came upon a hut. He crept up to the door and through a crack saw an old woman sitting at a plain, wooden table.

What was that shining in her hand? Juan wondered. He could not believe his eyes: It was a gold coin. Then he heard the woman say to herself, "I must be the richest person in the world."

Juan decided instantly that all the woman's gold must be his. He thought that the easiest thing to do was to watch until the woman left. Juan hid in the bushes and huddled under his poncho, waiting for the right moment to enter the hut.

Juan was half asleep when he heard knocking at the door and the sound of insistent voices. A few minutes later, he saw the woman, wrapped in a black cloak, leave the hut with two men at her side.

Here's my chance! Juan thought. And, forcing open a window, he climbed into the empty hut.

He looked about eagerly for the gold. He looked under the bed. It wasn't there. He looked in the cupboard. It wasn't there, either. Where could it be? Close to despair, Juan tore away some beams supporting the thatch roof.

Finally, he gave up. There was simply no gold in the hut.

All I can do, he thought, is to find the old woman and make her tell me where she's hidden it.

So he set out along the path that she and her two companions had taken.

It was daylight by the time Juan reached the river. The countryside had been deserted, but here, along the riverbank, were two huts. Nearby, a man and his son were hard at work, hoeing potatoes.

It had been a long, long time since Juan had spoken to another human being. Yet his desire to find the woman was so strong that he went up to the farmers and asked, in a hoarse, raspy voice, "Have you seen a short, gray-haired woman, wearing a black cloak?"

"Oh, you must be looking for Doña Josefa," the young boy said. "Yes, we've seen her. We went to fetch her this morning, because my grandfather had another attack of—"

"Where is she now?" Juan broke in.

"She is long gone," said the father with a smile. "Some people from across the river came looking for her, because someone in their family is sick."

"How can I get across the river?" Juan asked anxiously.

"Only by boat," the boy answered. "We'll row you across later, if you'd like." Then turning back to his work, he added, "But first we must finish digging up the potatoes."

The thief muttered, "Thanks." But he quickly grew impatient. He grabbed a hoe and began to help the pair of farmers. The sooner we finish, the sooner we'll get across the river, he thought. And the sooner I'll get to my gold!

It was dusk when they finally laid down their hoes. The soil had been turned, and the wicker baskets were brimming with potatoes.

"Now can you row me across?" Juan asked the father anxiously.

"Certainly," the man said. "But let's eat supper first."

Juan had forgotten the taste of a home-cooked meal and the pleasure that comes from sharing it with others. As he sopped up the last of the stew with a chunk of dark bread, memories of other meals came back to him from far away and long ago.

By the light of the moon, father and son guided their boat across the river.

"What a wonderful healer Doña Josefa is!" the boy told Juan. "All she had to do to make Abuelo better was give him a cup of her special tea."

"Yes, and not only that," his father added, "she brought him a gold coin."

Juan was stunned. It was one thing for Doña Josefa to go around helping people. But how could she go around handing out gold coins—*his gold coins*?

When the threesome finally reached the other side of the river, they saw a young man sitting outside his hut.

"This fellow is looking for Doña Josefa," the father said, pointing to Juan.

"Oh, she left some time ago," the young man said.

"Where to?" Juan asked tensely.

"Over to the other side of the mountain," the young man replied, pointing to the vague outline of mountains in the night sky.

"How did she get there?" Juan asked, trying to hide his impatience.

"By horse," the young man answered. "They came on horseback to get her because someone had broken his leg."

"Well, then, I need a horse, too," Juan said urgently.

"Tomorrow," the young man replied softly. "Perhaps I can take you tomorrow, maybe the next day. First I must finish harvesting the corn."

So Juan spent the next day in the fields, bathed in sweat from sunup to sundown.

Yet each ear of corn that he picked seemed to bring him closer to his treasure. And later that evening, when he helped the young man husk several ears so they could boil them for supper, the yellow kernels glittered like gold coins.

While they were eating, Juan thought about Doña Josefa. Why, he wondered, would someone who said she was the world's richest woman spend her time taking care of every sick person for miles around?

The following day, the two set off at dawn. Juan could not recall when he last had noticed the beauty of the sunrise. He felt strangely moved by the sight of the mountains, barely lit by the faint rays of the morning sun.

As they neared the foothills, the young man said, "I'm not surprised you're looking for Doña Josefa. The whole countryside needs her. I went for her because my wife had been running a high fever. In no time at all, Doña Josefa had her on the road to recovery. And what's more, my friend, she brought her a gold coin!"

Juan groaned inwardly. To think that someone could hand out gold so freely! What a strange woman Doña Josefa is, Juan thought. Not only is she willing to help one person after another, but she doesn't mind traveling all over the countryside to do it!

"Well, my friend," said the young man finally, "this is where I must leave you. But you don't have far to walk. See that house over there? It belongs to the man who broke his leg."

The young man stretched out his hand to say good-bye. Juan stared at it for a moment. It had been a long, long time since the thief had shaken hands with anyone. Slowly, he pulled out a hand from under his poncho. When his companion grasped it firmly in his own, Juan felt suddenly warmed, as if by the rays of the sun.

But after he thanked the young man, Juan ran down the road. He was still eager to catch up with Doña Josefa. When he reached the house, a woman and a child were stepping down from a wagon.

"Have you seen Doña Josefa?" Juan asked.

"We've just taken her to Don Teodosio's," the woman said. "His wife is sick, you know—"

"How do I get there?" Juan broke in. "I've got to see her."

"It's too far to walk," the woman said amiably. "If you'd like, I'll take you there tomorrow. But first I must gather my squash and beans."

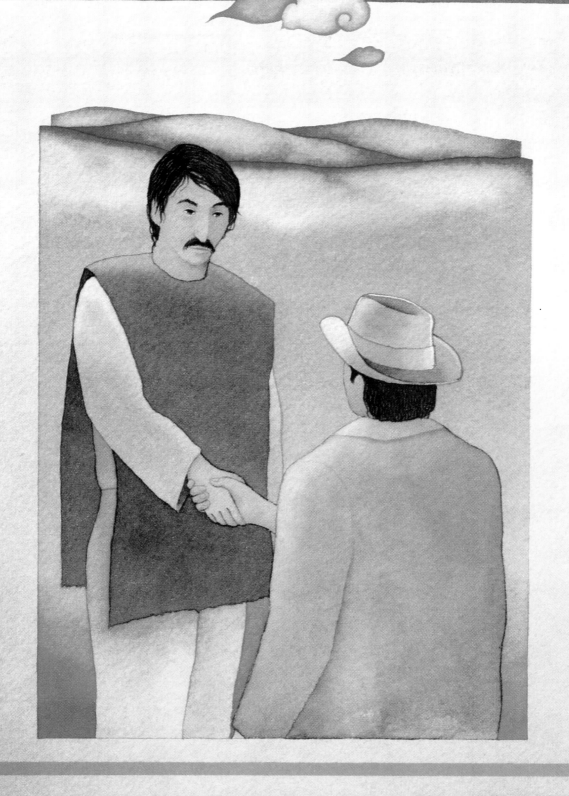

So Juan spent yet another long day in the fields. Working beneath the summer sun, Juan noticed that his skin had begun to tan. And although he had to stoop down to pick the squash, he found that he could now stretch his body. His back had begun to straighten, too.

Later, when the little girl took him by the hand to show him a family of rabbits burrowed under a fallen tree, Juan's face broke into a smile. It had been a long, long time since Juan had smiled.

Yet his thoughts kept coming back to the gold.

The following day, the wagon carrying Juan and the woman lumbered along a road lined with coffee fields.

The woman said, "I don't know what we would have done without Doña Josefa. I sent my daughter to our neighbor's house, who then brought Doña Josefa on horseback. She set my husband's leg and then showed me how to brew a special tea to lessen the pain."

Getting no reply, she went on. "And, as if that weren't enough, she brought him a gold coin. Can you imagine such a thing?"

Juan could only sigh. No doubt about it, he thought, Doña Josefa is someone special. But Juan didn't know whether to be happy that Doña Josefa had so much gold she could freely hand it out, or angry for her having already given so much of it away.

When they finally reached Don Teodosio's house, Doña Josefa was already gone. But here, too, there was work that needed to be done. . . .

Juan stayed to help with the coffee harvest. As he picked the red berries, he gazed up from time to time at the trees that grew, row upon row, along the hillsides. What a calm, peaceful place this is! he thought.

The next morning, Juan was up at daybreak. Bathed in the soft, dawn light, the mountains seemed to smile at him. When Don Teodosio offered him a lift on horseback, Juan found it difficult to have to say good-bye.

"What a good woman Doña Josefa is!" Don Teodosio said, as they rode down the hill toward the sugarcane fields. "The minute she heard about my wife being sick, she came with her special herbs. And as if that weren't enough, she brought my wife a gold coin!"

In the stifling heat, the kind that often signals the approach of a storm, Juan simply sighed and mopped his brow. The pair continued riding for several hours in silence.

Juan then realized he was back in familiar territory, for they were now on the stretch of road he had traveled only a week ago—though how much longer it now seemed to him. He jumped off Don Teodosio's horse and broke into a run.

This time the gold would not escape him! But he had to move quickly, so he could find shelter before the storm broke.

Out of breath, Juan finally reached Doña Josefa's hut. She was standing by the door, shaking her head slowly as she surveyed the ransacked house.

"So I've caught up with you at last!" Juan shouted, startling the old woman. "Where's the gold?"

"The gold coin?" Doña Josefa said, surprised and looking at Juan intently. "Have you come for the gold coin? I've been trying hard to give it to someone who might need it," Doña Josefa said. "First to an old man who had just gotten over a bad attack. Then to a young woman who had been running a fever. Then to a man with a broken leg. And finally to Don Teodosio's wife. But none of them would take it. They all said, 'Keep it. There must be someone who needs it more.'"

Juan did not say a word.

"You must be the one who needs it," Doña Josefa said.

She took the coin out of her pocket and handed it to him. Juan stared at the coin, speechless.

At that moment a young girl appeared, her long braid bouncing as she ran. "Hurry, Doña Josefa, please!" she said breathlessly. "My mother is all alone, and the baby is due any minute."

"Of course, dear," Doña Josefa replied. But as she glanced up at the sky, she saw nothing but black clouds. The storm was nearly upon them. Doña Josefa sighed deeply.

"But how can I leave now? Look at my house! I don't know what has happened to the roof. The storm will wash the whole place away!"

And there was a deep sadness in her voice.

Juan took in the child's frightened eyes, Doña Josefa's sad, distressed face, and the ransacked hut.

"Go ahead, Doña Josefa," he said. "Don't worry about your house. I'll see that the roof is back in shape, good as new."

The woman nodded gratefully, drew her cloak about her shoulders, and took the child by the hand. As she turned to leave, Juan held out his hand.

"Here, take this," he said, giving her the gold coin. "I'm sure the newborn will need it more than I."

AN INTERVIEW WITH

Alma Flor Ada

Alma Flor Ada has written many popular stories and poems for young people. Here interviewer Ilene Cooper asks her about ways she gets her ideas.

Cooper: *Where did you get the idea for "The Gold Coin"?*

Ada: For many years I have worked with migrant farm workers. One summer night about midnight, I was driving home after a meeting, and I was thinking how moved I was by these people—by the hard work they do in the fields, but also by their generosity and support of each other.

As I was driving along, the story came to me, full-blown. I cried all the way home, and then I went to my study and wrote it all down. When I awoke, I was sure the whole experience was a dream, and I was surprised when the story was there waiting for me. I have always said that the story of the Gold Coin was just floating along the California fields waiting for someone to listen to it and pick it up.

Cooper: *In what other ways have stories come to you?*

Ada: Every book is different. Sometimes it is the shortest books that take the longest time to write. Sometimes revising is the difficult part. I don't have one writing style the way some authors do. I never know what I'm going to write next. It's always a response to something that comes from inside.

Cooper: *What kind of response have you gotten to "The Gold Coin"?*

Ada: This is a story that young people really seem touched by. Children from the Latin American community like it because the illustrations show people that resemble people they know.

Sometimes children write and say that they know someone like Doña Josefa, who is good to others. Some write and say they are thinking of Juan and wonder why he has gone astray. What has happened in his life to make him so unhappy? Did he have bad friends? The children say it is important not to start doing things that are wrong, but it makes them glad to know that someone like Juan can change.

Cooper: *How did you begin writing?*

Ada: When I was a child in Cuba, in the fourth grade, I thought the textbooks we used were very ugly. So I told myself that when I grew up, I would write books that were fun to look at. Then, as an adult, I did write high school textbooks, but I had forgotten my promise.

One day when my daughter was about five, she said, "I am making a book. Do you know why?" I replied, "No, why?" And she said, "Because the books you make are so ugly!" That brought everything back to me. I decided to collect the poems and stories of my childhood, and that was my first project, which became a reading series. When I began, I thought of myself as a collector of stories. I didn't know that I was also a writer, but that is what I became.

RESPONSE CORNER

X Marks the Spot

Juan traveled the countryside in his week of searching for Doña Josefa. Make up a map of where he may have gone. Show rivers, mountains, farms, and roads. Make up a scale of miles and a compass rose. If you wish, make up a name for the land he traveled through and for the landforms. Share your map with your classmates.

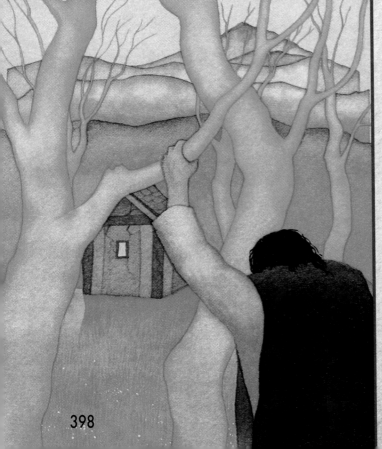

Fan Club

If movie stars and singers can have fan clubs, why not a good person like Doña Josefa? Work with a group to plan and organize the club. List Doña Josefa's character traits. Then write membership rules for club members based on your list. You may want to create a flag or T-shirts for club members, too. Finally, plan a club project.

Looking Back and Ahead

Juan was not always a thief, and we are given the idea that he will not be a thief after his week's experiences. Prepare a chart contrasting Juan's way of looking at the world at the beginning of the story and at the end. Show how he feels about gold, friendship, work, hurrying, and daylight.

What Do You Think?

In what way was Doña Josefa rich?

What would you like to see Juan do next? Why?

How did the author make the ending of the story believable?

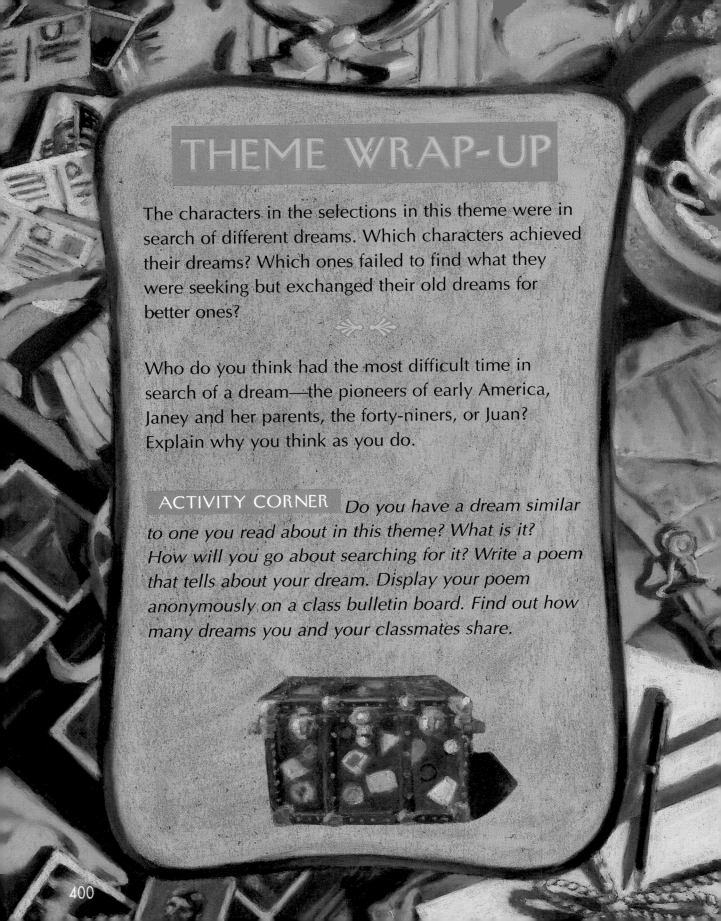

THEME WRAP-UP

The characters in the selections in this theme were in search of different dreams. Which characters achieved their dreams? Which ones failed to find what they were seeking but exchanged their old dreams for better ones?

Who do you think had the most difficult time in search of a dream—the pioneers of early America, Janey and her parents, the forty-niners, or Juan? Explain why you think as you do.

ACTIVITY CORNER *Do you have a dream similar to one you read about in this theme? What is it? How will you go about searching for it? Write a poem that tells about your dream. Display your poem anonymously on a class bulletin board. Find out how many dreams you and your classmates share.*

MAKING PROGRESS

How does progress help us? How does it hurt us? The selections in this theme describe how technological changes and other forms of progress have made our lives better. They also describe how progress sometimes harms us and what can be done to try to keep this from happening.

CONTENTS

BOOKSHELF

June 29, 1999
written and illustrated by David Wiesner

Holly Evans' science experiment is out of this world!

Award-Winning Author and Illustrator

Signatures Library

Garbage and Recycling
by Judith Woodburn

Garbage, garbage everywhere! How can we show that we care?

Signatures Library

At last the almonds were ready. Papa hitched the horses to the wagon, piled high with the heavy sacks. My brother and I rode along as he drove the wagon to the train station. Later we watched the train chug off to the city with our almonds.

Papa sold the crop to a man in the city who bought almonds from many growers. The selling price changed from year to year, but Papa usually got about five cents a pound for the almonds. Our eight-acre orchard produced four thousand pounds in an average year.

The city man who bought our almonds sent them to store-keepers in different parts of the country. Customers scooped the almonds from a burlap sack, and the storekeeper weighed them, charging by the pound.

In the almond orchard, new buds already had formed on the branches, although they would not begin to grow for many weeks. The weather cooled, and soon the leaves changed color and fell to the ground. It was time to prune the trees.

In the early hours before his store opened, Papa worked in the orchard. He removed a few branches from each tree so that when summer came more sunlight would reach the almonds. My brother gathered the fallen branches into piles to be hauled away and burned.

Toward the end of autumn, Papa lined the orchard with smudge pots, which he had filled with fuel oil. In the cold months ahead, he would light the smudge pots. Their smoky fires would protect the trees from frost.

Soon the winter rains came, soaking the orchard floor. Some years we had a drought, and Papa worried that the crop would be poor. But with normal rainfall, the soil absorbed enough water to nourish the trees throughout the coming summer.

The weeks passed, and as spring drew near the days became slightly warmer. We saw the tips of flower petals emerging from the tiny buds.

Here and there, the buds began to open. Then one morning I woke to find the orchard white with blossoms. Their sweet smell filled the air.

Bees moved busily from one flower to another, gathering nectar and pollen. At the same time, they pollinated the trees. This ensured that the inside of each flower would grow to become a soft nutlet.

Rain or freezing temperatures would ruin the flowers, so we hoped for dry weather during blossom time. And if frost seemed likely, Papa lit the smudge pots.

The blossoms soon faded, and the delicate petals floated to the ground. Leaves sprouted and the nutlets started to grow, beginning a new cycle of seasons.

But even in spring, the nights were sometimes cold, and frost would harm the soft nutlets. Papa kept the smudge pots in the orchard until late spring, when the nutlets had hardened into young almonds.

Over the years, I saw many springtimes come and go. And although I moved away when I grew up, I always thought of the house in the valley as home. When Papa was very old, he gave part of the almond orchard to me. By that time he had planted over seventy acres of trees.

I hired a caretaker to handle the seasonal chores and manage the harvest. He put in a well and an electric pump to bring more water to the orchard. If a tree became too old to produce a good yield, he cut it down, dug out the stump, and helped me plant a seedling.

Today, at blossom time, he rents hives from a beekeeper to make certain that pollination occurs. And instead of lighting smudge pots, he turns on wind machines. These keep the air moving so that frost cannot form on the trees.

Many other changes have come about since Papa first planted the orchard. Tractors and trailers have replaced horses and wagons. During harvest, a mechanical shaker knocks the almonds. It grips each tree trunk and vibrates, bringing a shower of almonds to the ground. Spinning brushes clear the way so that the wheels of the shaker do not crush the nuts.

Then a mechanical sweeper pushes the almonds into rows. A pickup machine follows, blowing out leaves and dirt as it scoops the almonds into a trailer bin. Finally, a mechanical huller removes the hulls, which are saved and fed to livestock.

A conveyor belt transfers the almonds to bins on the back of a truck. Then a driver delivers the crop to an almond processing plant. He turns a crank, opening a panel beneath each bin. The almonds fall through a funnel, past a grate, and into an underground chamber.

Samples are checked for quality. Then the almonds are stored in silos, where cool temperatures keep them from spoiling. Later machines remove the almond shells, gently cracking them without damaging the nuts. The shells are burned, creating electricity to power the processing plant.

Inside the plant, almonds from many orchards are slivered, sliced, chopped, diced, blanched, roasted, salted, toasted, seasoned, and ground into powder and paste. They are packaged in bags, jars, cans, and boxes, then labeled and shipped all over the world.

Many of the almonds are sent to companies that make ice cream, candies, and cookies. Others go to restaurants, where chefs prepare trout amandine and almond tarts and soufflés.

Researchers have perfected age-old methods of making almond oil, almond butter, and almond soaps and lotions. And they continue to develop ideas for new almond products.

But not everything has changed. I worry about the crop, just as Papa did, when the weather is too cold or too dry. Although I can no longer help with the work, I still make sure that the trees are well cared for. And I always go home when the almond orchard is in bloom.

LAURA JANE COATS

When Laura Jane Coats wrote *The Almond Orchard*, she wrote from experience. Growing up among the farms of Sacramento, California, Coats became familiar with the growing, harvesting, and processing of many crops, including almonds.

After graduating from college, Coats worked as an artist. However, she soon combined her drawing and writing talents to create her first book, *Marcella and the Moon*. The book was a big hit. It left young people hungry for more books filled with her lively characters and beautiful illustrations. Coats went on to write and illustrate *Mr. Jordan in the Park, Ten Little Animals, The Oak Tree, Goodyear the City Cat,* and *The Almond Orchard.*

Occasionally, Coats can be found at her design table, but most of the time she's busy writing. Today she lives in San Francisco, California, with her husband and family.

Laura Jane Coats

RESPONSE

Aah! Almonds

Almonds are a special taste treat.
Look in a cookbook for some
recipes that use almonds. Copy
the ones you like and make an
almond cookbook of your own.
Then you may want to work
with a few classmates to make
an almond snack that everyone
can enjoy.

That Was Then . . . This Is Now

The old way of harvesting almonds
is different from the new way.
Prepare a chart with the headings
Then and *Now*. Compare the
steps for each way. Then write
a paragraph explaining which
way you think is better.

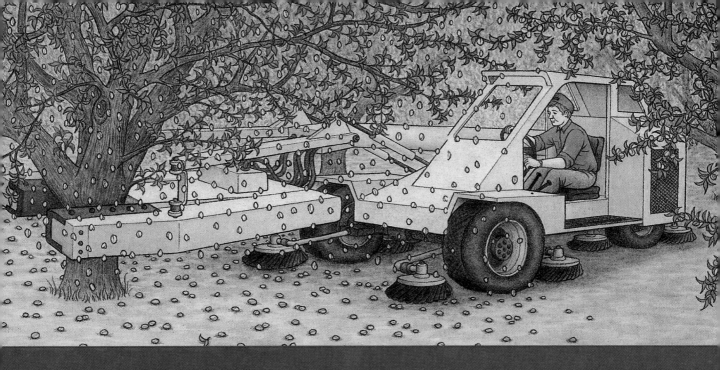

CORNER

It's Raining Almonds

Imagine that you are a weather reporter in the valley where the almond orchard is located. Write a forecast for freezing weather, rain, or a dry spell. Add information about what the almond growers should do to save their crops.

What Do You Think?

- What do almond trees need to stay healthy?
- What was the most interesting thing you learned about almond orchards?
- Do you think that harvesting almonds was more fun in the past? Why or why not?

419

EXTRAORDINARY
BLACK

Frederick
McKinley
Jones

Elijah McCoy

Jan Ernst Matzeliger

AMERICANS

by Susan Altman
illustrated by Colin Bootman

Madame
C. J. Walker

Lewis Howard Latimer

JAN ERNST MATZELIGER

Inventor
1852–1889

"If the shoe fits," it's partly because a man named Jan Matzeliger invented a wonderful machine that knocked shoe manufacturers right off their feet.

Jan Matzeliger was born in Paramaribo, Suriname (then called Dutch Guiana), in South America. His mother was a native black from Suriname and his father was a wealthy Dutch engineer from Holland. At age ten, Jan went to work in a machine shop. When he was nineteen, he got a job on an East Indian merchant ship and spent the next two years at sea. When the ship docked in Philadelphia, he decided to give life in the United States a try.

After working at various jobs in Philadelphia, Matzeliger moved to Boston in 1876 and, a year later, settled in Lynn, Massachusetts, where he got a job with a shoe manufacturing company. Meanwhile, he started night school to study physics and improve his English. In his spare time, he painted and gave art lessons.

As Matzeliger worked in the shoe manufacturing company, he noticed that production was slow because workers had to attach the bottom of the shoe to the top by hand. So he decided to invent a machine that could perform that task. Within six months, he had built his first model from wood, wire, and cigar boxes. Although it was far from perfect, it was impressive enough to attract a $50 offer, which he rejected.

In 1880 Matzeliger completed a more advanced model. This one got him a $1,500 offer. Although he needed the money, he turned down the offer again and began work on a third model. He soon realized, however, that he would need financial help. He got it from Melville S. Nichols and Charles H. Delnow, in exchange for a two-thirds interest in his machines.

On March 20, 1883, Matzeliger received patent no. 274, 207 for a "Lasting Machine" that would rapidly stitch the leather of a shoe to the sole. The drawings of it were so complicated that a scientist from the patent office in Washington, D.C., had to travel to Lynn to observe the machine in action before he could understand it. But it was worth the trip. Jan Matzeliger's lasting machine made it possible to turn out 150 to 700 pairs of shoes a day, instead of only fifty pairs a day previously. It also cut the manufacturing costs in half.

Anticipating success, Matzeliger, Nichols, and Delnow established the Union Lasting Machine Company and went into business. Soon, they sold out to a larger company. Matzeliger sold all his patents (five by this time) in return for stock in the company.

Union Lasting Machine Company

No. 274,207.

In 1886 Matzeliger became ill with tuberculosis and died three years later at the age of thirty-seven. He left his stock in the Union Lasting Machine Company to the North Congregational Church, the one church in Lynn that had not rejected him because of race. As for the company that owned his patents, it became the United Shoe Machinery Corporation. Sixty-five years later, it was worth over a billion dollars.

So, the next time you go for a walk, you might remember that it was the skill and inventiveness of Jan Ernst Matzeliger that enabled the entire U.S. shoe manufacturing industry to step out in front and put its best foot forward.

FREDERICK McKINLEY JONES
Inventor
1893–1961

When it comes to being cool, nobody can beat Frederick McKinley Jones, the man who put the freeze on the entire food industry and changed the eating habits of everyone in America. The whole thing came about when Jones overheard his boss, Joseph A. Numero, discussing the problem of developing an air-conditioner that would work in a truck.

Earlier truck refrigeration units took up too much space and tended to fall apart from vibrations caused by the movement of the truck on the road.

After much experimentation, Frederick Jones designed a small, light, shockproof refrigeration unit. But when he installed it under a truck, it became mud-clogged and broke down. His second unit, which he installed on top of the truck, worked just fine. Realizing the potential of his invention, Jones and his boss formed the U.S. Thermo Control Company, later called The Thermo King Corporation. Soon, they were manufacturing air-conditioners and refrigeration units for trucks, trains, airplanes, and ships.

Up until this time, many foods could be shipped only short distances before they spoiled. Thanks to Frederick Jones, fruit, vegetables, meat, and dairy products could be refrigerated and shipped all over the country. Refrigeration also made it possible to transport blood and medicines safely—a procedure that became very important during World War II.

But solving problems was nothing new to Frederick McKinley Jones. Born in 1893, in Cincinnati, Ohio, he was orphaned at age nine and sent to live with a Catholic priest in Kentucky.

In 1912 he moved to Hallock, Minnesota, where he got a job fixing farm machinery. When he wasn't working, he studied the fundamentals of electricity and mechanical engineering. After he returned from fighting in World War I, he began working with race cars and built the first radio station transmitter in Hallock and a soundtrack device for motion pictures.

It was at this time that Joseph Numero hired Frederick Jones to work for him, and it was the smartest move he ever made.

Frederick McKinley Jones received more than sixty patents for his inventions—forty for refrigeration alone. His work made it possible to transport food and medicines all over the world. Brilliant, creative, and hardworking, Frederick McKinley Jones was a cool guy in more ways than one.

ELIJAH McCOY

Inventor

1843–1929

When Elijah McCoy's parents escaped from slavery in Kentucky via the Underground Railroad, they didn't know that one day they would have a son whose inventions would affect railroad transportation all over the world.

Born in Canada in 1843, Elijah McCoy was the third of twelve children. After he attended school near his home, his parents sent him to Edinburgh, Scotland, where he studied mechanical

engineering. Moving to Detroit to find work, he was forced to take a job as a fireman on the Michigan Central Railroad, when prejudice kept him from being hired as an engineer.

In those days, trains and other machinery were stopped every day to be oiled. Recognizing that this was a great waste of time and money, McCoy started the Elijah McCoy Manufacturing Company in Detroit, Michigan, and developed a device that would lubricate machinery automatically while it was still in operation. In 1872 he received a U.S. government patent for his steam engine lubricator, the "lubricator cup."

But McCoy didn't stop there. He kept improving his device and developing variations of it. In time, he received forty-two patents for inventions and saved millions of dollars. Soon his systems were in use all over the world.

Although others tried to copy his work, people continued to demand the original. Using a phrase that has now become part of the American language, people said they wanted the "Real McCoy."

MADAME C. J. WALKER

Cosmetics Manufacturer, Humanitarian

1867–1919

"I am a woman who came from the cotton fields of the South. . . . I promoted myself into the business of manufacturing hair goods and preparations. . . . I have built my own factory on my own ground."

—Madame C. J. Walker

Most people's dreams are forgotten quickly; Madame C. J. Walker turned hers into a million dollars.

Born Sarah Breedlove to former slaves in Louisiana in 1867, she was orphaned at age five. At fourteen, she married a man named McWilliams. But six years later, he died, leaving her alone to raise their daughter A'Lelia.

After moving to St. Louis, Missouri, Sarah McWilliams, as she was known then, found work as a washerwoman. While working hard to educate her daughter, Ms. McWilliams's hair began falling out. Although she tried various remedies, nothing seemed to help. Then one night, she dreamed about an old man who showed her things to mix up for her hair. When she awoke, she gave the formula a try. After combining the various ingredients, she tested

the mixture on herself. The result: "My hair was coming in faster than it had ever fallen out," she said. "I tried it on my friends; it helped them. I made up my mind that I would sell it."

In July 1905, Sarah McWilliams moved to Denver, Colorado. Six months later, she married a newspaperman named Charles Walker and began calling herself Madame C. J. Walker, the name by which she is known today. She began to travel widely, demonstrating her beauty preparations, and in 1908 opened a second office in Pittsburgh. Walker advertised extensively in black newspapers and, in 1910, was able to establish her own factory in Indianapolis. By then her company was earning $7,000 a week.

During this time, black women were among the lowest paid workers in America. Victimized by both race and sex discrimination, those not working as sharecroppers or on farms were employed mainly as domestic workers and washerwomen. For the approximately 5,000 black women working for Madame Walker, there was better pay, greater opportunity, and more dignity. She insisted that "loveliness" was linked to "cleanliness" rather than race. In a society where white skin and Caucasian features were the standard for beauty, Walker's assertion, that black women were beautiful, helped many change their self-image.

Always concerned about the black community, Madame Walker organized her women agents into "Walker Clubs" and provided cash prizes for outstanding community service. She contributed generously for scholarships to Tuskegee, to the National Association for the Advancement of Colored People, and to other black charities both in the United States and abroad. She helped direct a fund-raising drive to establish Mary McLeod Bethune's school in Daytona and donated the money needed to pay off the mortgage on Frederick Douglass's home.

A woman of determination, energy, and vision, Madame C. J. Walker became America's first black woman millionaire when she followed her dream to become a hair restorer and came out ahead.

LEWIS HOWARD LATIMER

Inventor

1848–1928

When Alexander Graham Bell applied for a patent on his telephone in 1876, the blueprints he submitted to illustrate his invention were drawn by Lewis Howard Latimer, a young black draftsman.

Born in Chelsea, Massachusetts, in 1848, Lewis Howard Latimer was raised in Boston. When he was only ten his father deserted the family, and Lewis was forced to quit school and go to work.

After the Civil War, he got a job as an office boy for Crosby and Gould, a legal firm specializing in patent law. Investors, hoping to acquire patents protecting the rights to their inventions, paid Crosby and Gould to provide drawings of the inventions. As a result, Crosby and Gould employed a number of draftsmen—artists who specialize in drawing inventions.

Drafting fascinated Latimer. He bought a set of secondhand drafting tools and, with the help of library books and advice from other draftsmen, learned the trade. Feeling confident in his ability, he submitted some of his drawings to Crosby and Gould. They were impressed, and in a short time, Lewis had progressed from junior draftsman to chief draftsman.

One day Lewis met Alexander Graham Bell. A friendship developed, and Bell asked Latimer to make the drawings for his telephone. Then in 1880 Latimer became a draftsman for the United States Electric Lighting Company in Bridgeport, Connecticut. In addition to illustrating the work of others, he began working on inventions of his own.

Lewis Latimer became fascinated with the new electric light process, and, in 1881, along with Joseph V. Nichols, he received a patent for the Latimer Lamp. It utilized a greatly improved method of manufacturing the carbon filaments that give off the light in a light bulb. As a result of Latimer's invention, he was called upon to supervise the installation of electric light plants in New York City and the creation of an incandescent light division for the Maxim-Weston Electric Company in London, England.

In 1884 Latimer became a member of the Edison Pioneers— a small, select group of scientists who worked closely with Thomas Edison. When Lewis Latimer died in 1928, they said of him, "We hardly mourn his inevitable going so much as we rejoice in pleasant memory at having been associated with him in a great work for all people."

Meet the Author
SUSAN ALTMAN

"Curiosity and the willingness to explore are the qualities that all the inventors I wrote about had in common," says Susan Altman, author of *Extraordinary Black Americans*. "Writers need these same qualities."

Altman says that she knows writing can sometimes seem difficult, especially getting started. She says that some young people may have great ideas but get stuck when they go to write about them. What is her advice?

"If you feel stuck, don't start at the beginning. Start in the middle and then go back and add the beginning. If you don't like what you've written, put away your writing for a while. Everything will look different the next day, and you will be able to revise your writing more easily."

When Altman is not writing, she works as a television producer for the Emmy Award–winning program "It's Academic." She is also the author of two other books. She lives in Washington, D.C., where she grew up.

A revised page from "Extraordinary Black Americans"

MECHANICAL MENAGERIE

SQUAWK!

My Uncle Ike's an engineer.
He has the nutty habit
Of building beasts from wheels and wire.
He's built a robot rabbit

That hides in manholes in the street
And lives on tinfoil lettuce.
His brand new chrome-trimmed crocodile
Keeps trying hard to get us.

He has lightning bugs that come with plugs,
Electric eels that boil,
A bat that flies on batteries,
An oyster that you oil,

A forty-four-seat elephant
With a trunk so you can pack her,
And a parrot that says, "Polly want
A lighted cannon cracker!"

BY X. J. KENNEDY

Award-Winning
Poet

BATTERY

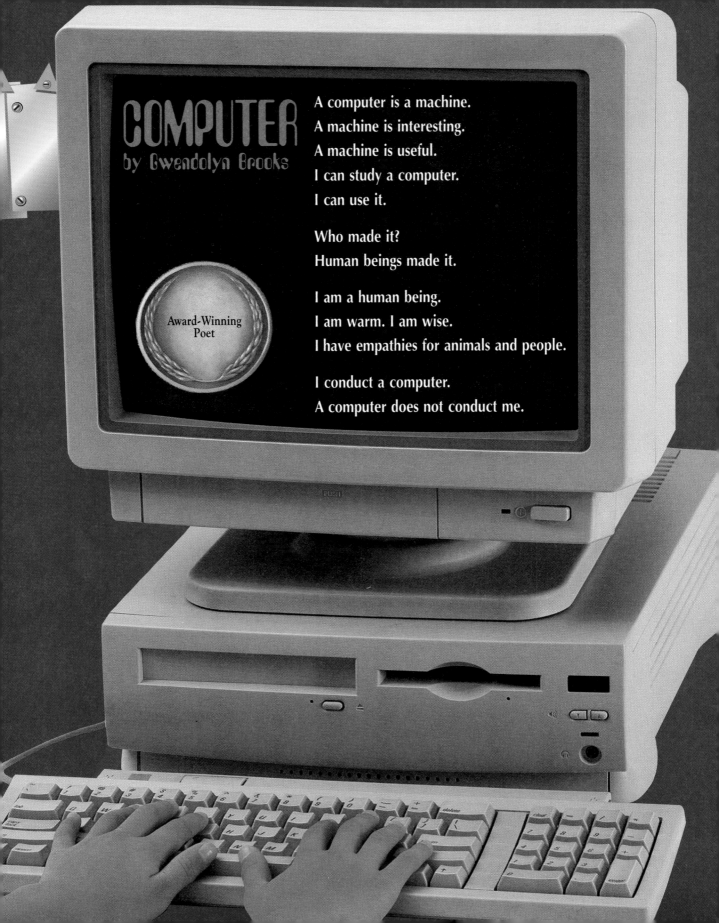

COMPUTER
by Gwendolyn Brooks

Award-Winning Poet

A computer is a machine.
A machine is interesting.
A machine is useful.
I can study a computer.
I can use it.

Who made it?
Human beings made it.

I am a human being.
I am warm. I am wise.
I have empathies for animals and people.

I conduct a computer.
A computer does not conduct me.

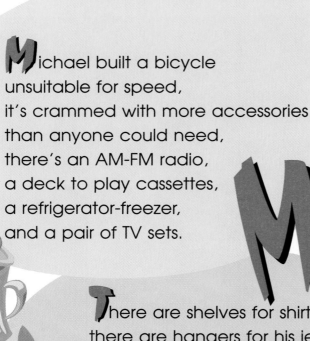

Michael built a bicycle
unsuitable for speed,
it's crammed with more accessories
than anyone could need,
there's an AM-FM radio,
a deck to play cassettes,
a refrigerator-freezer,
and a pair of TV sets.

Michael

There are shelves for shirts and sweaters,
there are hangers for his jeans,
a drawer for socks and underwear,
a rack for magazines,
there's a fishtank and a birdcage
perched upon the handlebars,
a bookcase, and a telescope
to watch the moon and stars.

There's a telephone, a blender,
and a stove to cook his meals,
there's a sink to do the dishes
somehow fastened to the wheels,
there's a portable piano,
and a set of model trains,
an automatic bumbershoot
that opens when it rains.

Built a Bicycle

by Jack Prelutsky

Award-Winning
Poet

There's a desk for typing letters
on his fabulous machine,
a stall for taking showers,
and a broom to keep things clean,
but you'll never see him ride it,
for it isn't quite complete,
Michael left no room for pedals,
and there isn't any seat.

437

RESPONSE

A Meeting of the Minds

What might the inventors in "Extraordinary Black Americans" say to each other if they could meet and talk? With a partner, write and perform a scene in which two of the inventors meet each other. They can discuss their lives and work, including problems they faced, their feelings about their work, and their achievements.

A Place in History

Make a time line to show the time period in which the five "extraordinary black Americans" lived. Show the years in which important events occurred in each person's life. Also, show important historical events, such as World War I. Your time line needs to begin with the year 1840 and end with 1970. You might want to use a different colored pencil to mark the dates for each inventor.

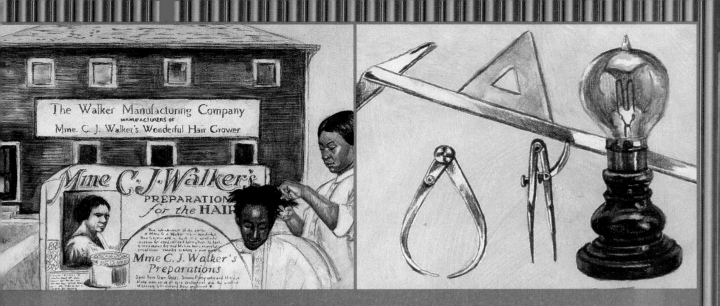

CORNER

WRITE A LETTER

I'm Going to Try

Suppose you were lucky enough to visit the office or workplace of one of the inventors in "Extraordinary Black Americans" or the poems that follow it. Write a letter thanking the inventor for letting you visit and telling what you admire about his or her achievements. You might also tell about a goal you have for yourself and some things you can begin doing to achieve it.

What Do You Think?

- How did each inventor in "Extraordinary Black Americans" make the most of an opportunity?

- Which of the inventors in "Extraordinary Black Americans" would you especially like to know more about? Tell why.

- Do you think the inventors in the poems and those in "Extraordinary Black Americans" have anything in common? Explain your response.

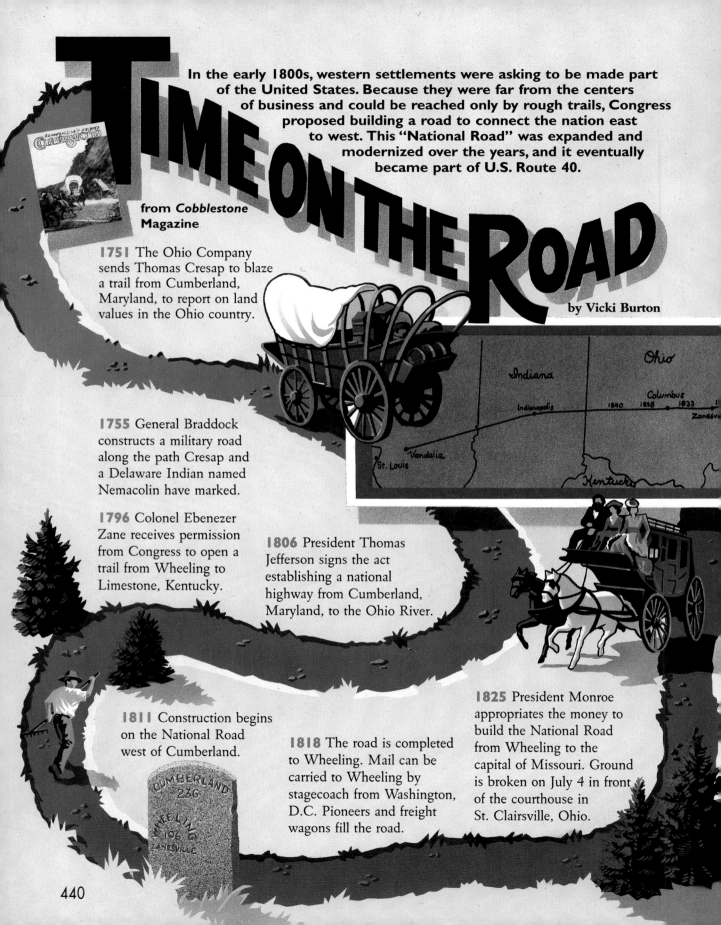

TIME ON THE ROAD

In the early 1800s, western settlements were asking to be made part of the United States. Because they were far from the centers of business and could be reached only by rough trails, Congress proposed building a road to connect the nation east to west. This "National Road" was expanded and modernized over the years, and it eventually became part of U.S. Route 40.

from *Cobblestone* Magazine

by Vicki Burton

1751 The Ohio Company sends Thomas Cresap to blaze a trail from Cumberland, Maryland, to report on land values in the Ohio country.

1755 General Braddock constructs a military road along the path Cresap and a Delaware Indian named Nemacolin have marked.

1796 Colonel Ebenezer Zane receives permission from Congress to open a trail from Wheeling to Limestone, Kentucky.

1806 President Thomas Jefferson signs the act establishing a national highway from Cumberland, Maryland, to the Ohio River.

1811 Construction begins on the National Road west of Cumberland.

1818 The road is completed to Wheeling. Mail can be carried to Wheeling by stagecoach from Washington, D.C. Pioneers and freight wagons fill the road.

1825 President Monroe appropriates the money to build the National Road from Wheeling to the capital of Missouri. Ground is broken on July 4 in front of the courthouse in St. Clairsville, Ohio.

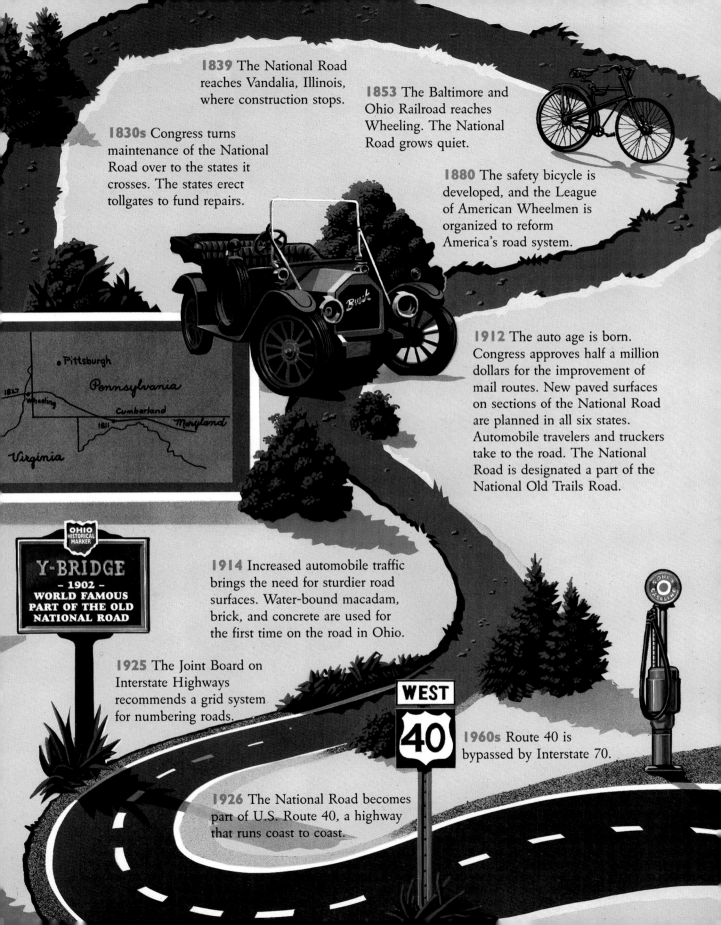

1839 The National Road reaches Vandalia, Illinois, where construction stops.

1830s Congress turns maintenance of the National Road over to the states it crosses. The states erect tollgates to fund repairs.

1853 The Baltimore and Ohio Railroad reaches Wheeling. The National Road grows quiet.

1880 The safety bicycle is developed, and the League of American Wheelmen is organized to reform America's road system.

1912 The auto age is born. Congress approves half a million dollars for the improvement of mail routes. New paved surfaces on sections of the National Road are planned in all six states. Automobile travelers and truckers take to the road. The National Road is designated a part of the National Old Trails Road.

1914 Increased automobile traffic brings the need for sturdier road surfaces. Water-bound macadam, brick, and concrete are used for the first time on the road in Ohio.

1925 The Joint Board on Interstate Highways recommends a grid system for numbering roads.

1960s Route 40 is bypassed by Interstate 70.

1926 The National Road becomes part of U.S. Route 40, a highway that runs coast to coast.

OHIO HISTORICAL MARKER

Y-BRIDGE
– 1902 –
WORLD FAMOUS
PART OF THE OLD
NATIONAL ROAD

WEST
40

Pittsburgh
Pennsylvania
Wheeling
Cumberland
Maryland
Virginia

ART AND LITERATURE

Look at the painting *Builders #1*, by Jacob Lawrence. How is the message of this painting similar to the messages in "The Almond Orchard" and in "Extraordinary Black Americans"?

BUILDERS #1
by Jacob Lawrence

In 1930, when Jacob Lawrence was about twelve, he moved to New York City with his mother. They spent a lot of time at a community center called Utopia House. There, Lawrence met older African American artists who encouraged him in his drawing and painting. When he grew up, Lawrence often painted scenes of African American life.

Builders #1 (1972) by Jacob Lawrence.
Watercolor and gouache over pencil (22 1/2″ × 30 3/4″).
The Saint Louis Art Museum, Purchase, Eliza McMillan Fund.

A RIVER RAN WILD

By Lynne Cherry

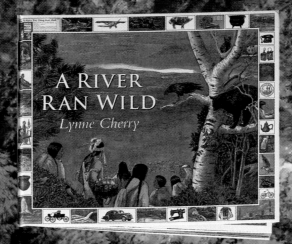

A RIVER
RAN WILD
Lynne Cherry

LONG AGO a river
ran wild through a
land of towering
forests. Bears, moose, and
herds of deer, hawks, and
owls all made their homes
in the peaceful river valley.
Geese paused on their
long migration and rested
on its banks. Beavers,
turtles, and schools of fish
swam in its clear waters.

Teachers'
Choice

Outstanding
Science Trade Book

Notable Trade Book
in Social Studies

One day a group of native people, searching for a place to settle, came upon the river valley. From atop the highest mountain, known today as Mt. Wachusett, they saw the river nestled in its valley, a silver sliver in the sun.

They came down from the mountain, and at the river's edge they knelt to quench their thirst with its clear water. Pebbles shone up from the bottom.

"Let us settle by this river," said the chief of the native people. He named the river Nash-a-way — River with the Pebbled Bottom.

446

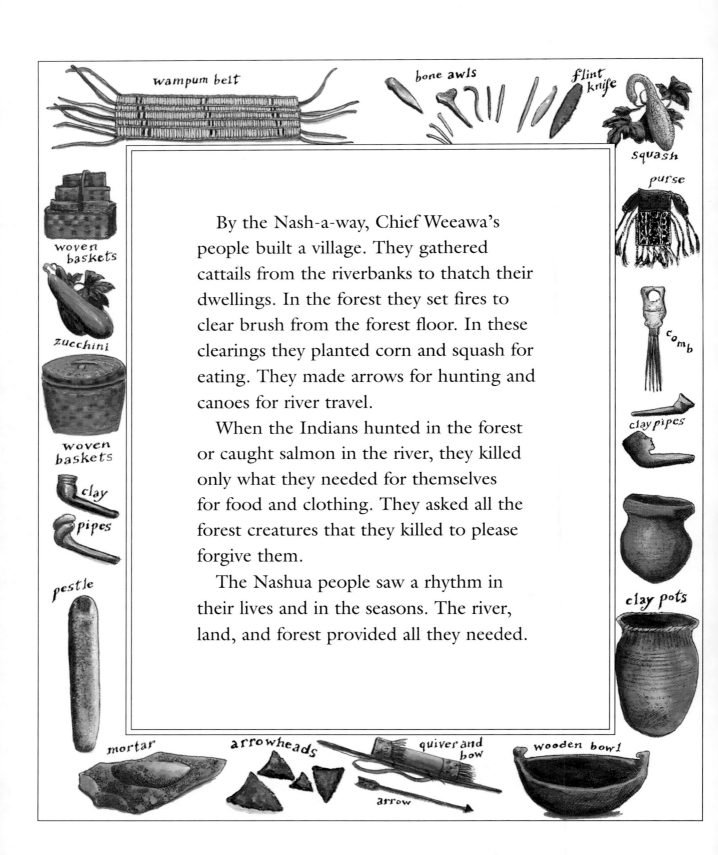

By the Nash-a-way, Chief Weeawa's people built a village. They gathered cattails from the riverbanks to thatch their dwellings. In the forest they set fires to clear brush from the forest floor. In these clearings they planted corn and squash for eating. They made arrows for hunting and canoes for river travel.

When the Indians hunted in the forest or caught salmon in the river, they killed only what they needed for themselves for food and clothing. They asked all the forest creatures that they killed to please forgive them.

The Nashua people saw a rhythm in their lives and in the seasons. The river, land, and forest provided all they needed.

wampum belt

bone awls

flint knife

squash

purse

comb

clay pipes

clay pots

woven baskets

zucchini

woven baskets

clay pipes

pestle

mortar

arrowheads

quiver and bow

arrow

wooden bowl

The Nashua had lived for generations by the clear, clean, flowing river when one day a pale-skinned trader came with a boatload full of treasures. He brought shiny metal knives, colored beads, and cooking kettles, mirrors, tools, and bolts of bright cloth. His wares seemed like magic. The Nashua welcomed him, traded furs, and soon a trading post was built.

In the many years that followed, the settlers' village and others like it grew and the Nash-a-way became the Nashua. The settlers worked together to clear land by cutting down the forests, which they thought were full of danger — wilderness that they would conquer. They hunted wolves and beaver, killing much more than they needed. Extra pelts were sent to England in return for goods and money.

The settlers built sawmills along the river, which the Nashua's current powered. They built dams to make the millponds that were used to store the water. They cut down the towering forest and floated tree trunks down the river. The logs were cut up into lumber, which was used for building houses.

rake

razorback hog

spinning

sheep

turkey

fireplace implements

well bucket

candlemaking

spinning wheel

guinea hen

cider press

butter churn

rooster

wagon

plow

horse

spinning wheel

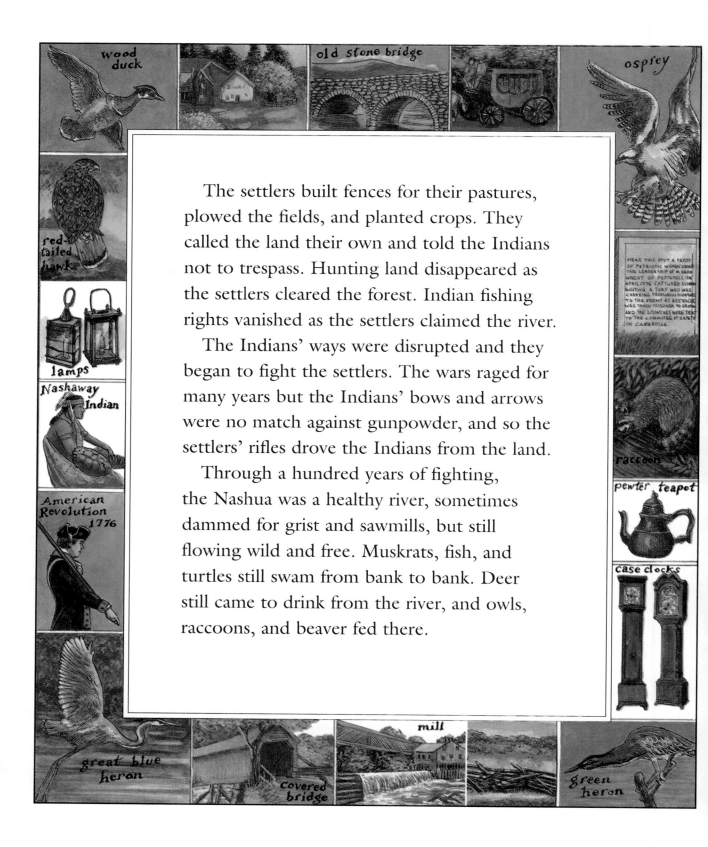

The settlers built fences for their pastures, plowed the fields, and planted crops. They called the land their own and told the Indians not to trespass. Hunting land disappeared as the settlers cleared the forest. Indian fishing rights vanished as the settlers claimed the river.

The Indians' ways were disrupted and they began to fight the settlers. The wars raged for many years but the Indians' bows and arrows were no match against gunpowder, and so the settlers' rifles drove the Indians from the land.

Through a hundred years of fighting, the Nashua was a healthy river, sometimes dammed for grist and sawmills, but still flowing wild and free. Muskrats, fish, and turtles still swam from bank to bank. Deer still came to drink from the river, and owls, raccoons, and beaver fed there.

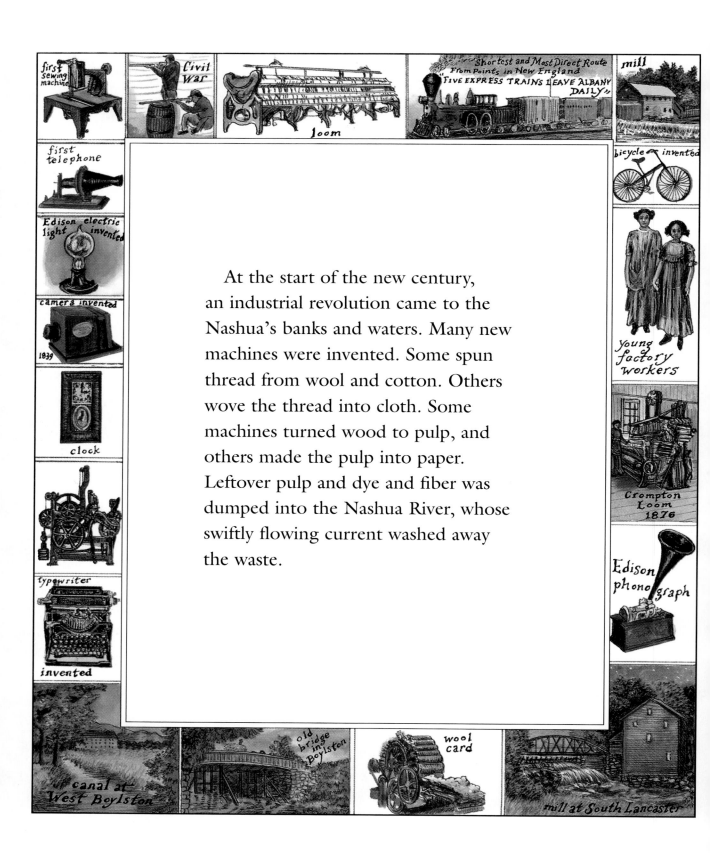

At the start of the new century, an industrial revolution came to the Nashua's banks and waters. Many new machines were invented. Some spun thread from wool and cotton. Others wove the thread into cloth. Some machines turned wood to pulp, and others made the pulp into paper. Leftover pulp and dye and fiber was dumped into the Nashua River, whose swiftly flowing current washed away the waste.

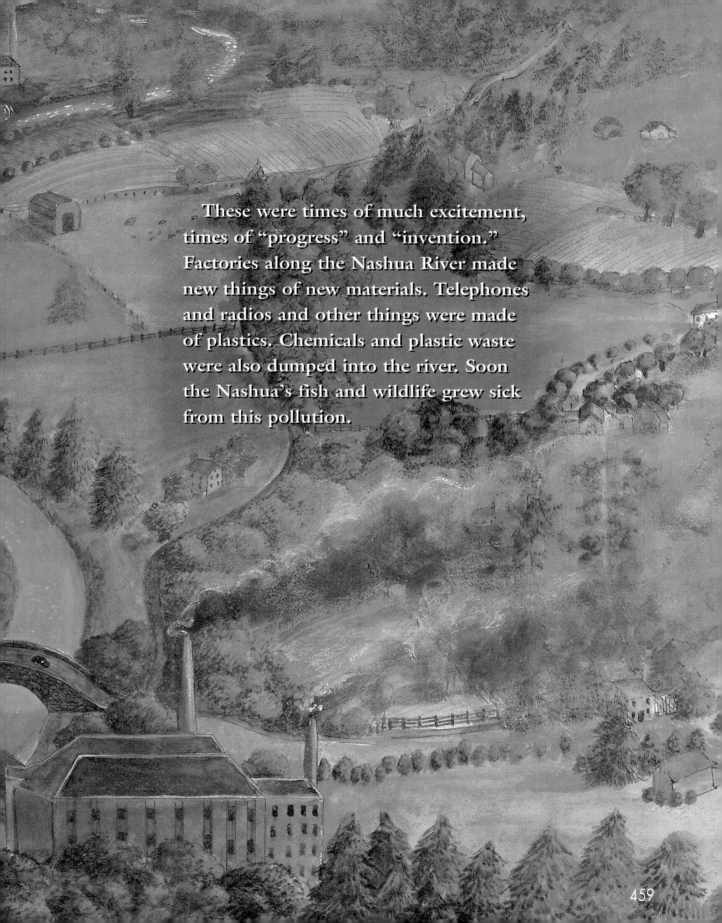

These were times of much excitement, times of "progress" and "invention." Factories along the Nashua River made new things of new materials. Telephones and radios and other things were made of plastics. Chemicals and plastic waste were also dumped into the river. Soon the Nashua's fish and wildlife grew sick from this pollution.

Wright biplane-
first airplane

1927 Charles Lindbergh-first
solo nonstop transatlantic flight

radio invented

Model-T Ford

plastic eyeglass frames

plastic hoola hoops

camera

I WANT YOU

U.S. ARMY
World War II poster

adding machine

T.V.

rubber band

plastic paintbrush

1st nuclear explosion

camera

plastic telephone

Sewing machine

airplane

1955 Cadillac

movie projector

The paper mills continued to pollute the Nashua's waters. Every day for many decades pulp was dumped into the Nashua, and as the pulp clogged up the river, it began to run more slowly.

As the pulp decomposed, bad smells welled up from the river. People who lived near the river smelled its stench and stayed far from it. Each day as the mills dyed paper red, green, blue, and yellow, the Nashua ran whatever color the paper was dyed.

Soon no fish lived in the river. No birds stopped on their migration. No one could see pebbles shining up through murky water. The Nashua was dark and dirty. The Nashua was slowly dying.

461

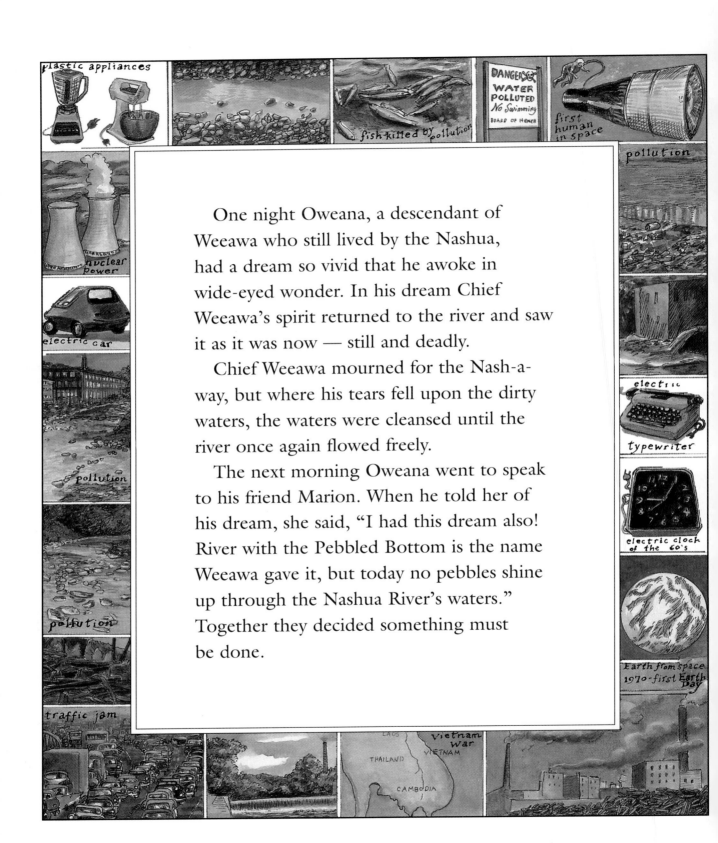

One night Oweana, a descendant of Weeawa who still lived by the Nashua, had a dream so vivid that he awoke in wide-eyed wonder. In his dream Chief Weeawa's spirit returned to the river and saw it as it was now — still and deadly.

Chief Weeawa mourned for the Nash-a-way, but where his tears fell upon the dirty waters, the waters were cleansed until the river once again flowed freely.

The next morning Oweana went to speak to his friend Marion. When he told her of his dream, she said, "I had this dream also! River with the Pebbled Bottom is the name Weeawa gave it, but today no pebbles shine up through the Nashua River's waters." Together they decided something must be done.

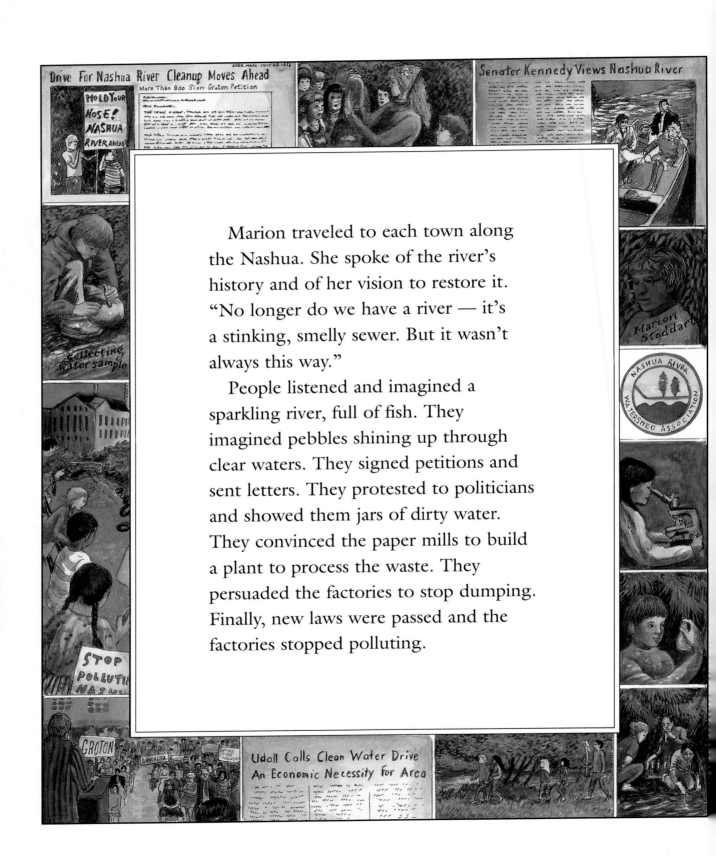

Marion traveled to each town along the Nashua. She spoke of the river's history and of her vision to restore it. "No longer do we have a river — it's a stinking, smelly sewer. But it wasn't always this way."

People listened and imagined a sparkling river, full of fish. They imagined pebbles shining up through clear waters. They signed petitions and sent letters. They protested to politicians and showed them jars of dirty water. They convinced the paper mills to build a plant to process the waste. They persuaded the factories to stop dumping. Finally, new laws were passed and the factories stopped polluting.

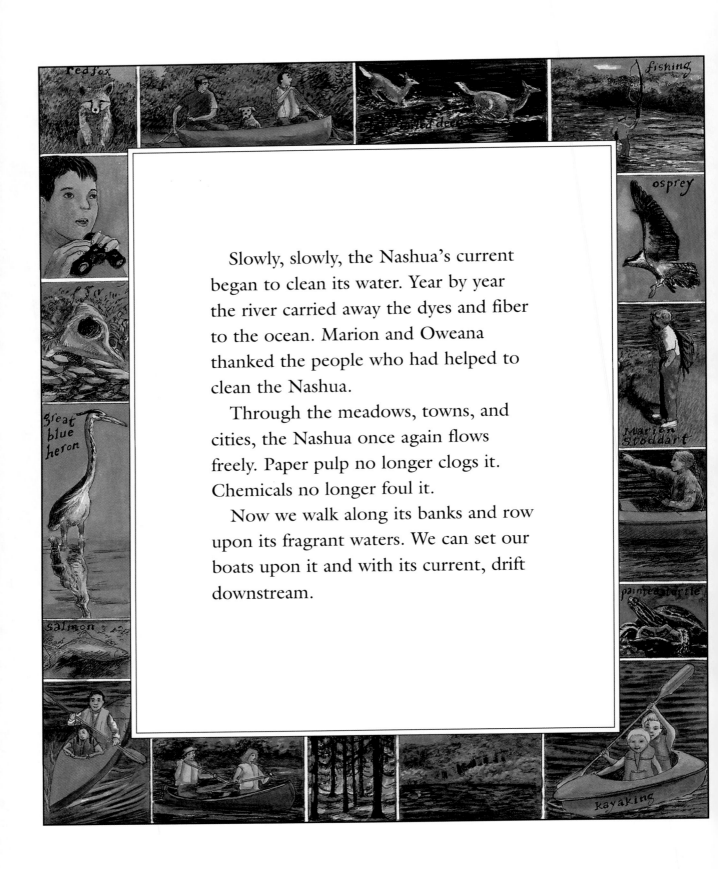

Slowly, slowly, the Nashua's current began to clean its water. Year by year the river carried away the dyes and fiber to the ocean. Marion and Oweana thanked the people who had helped to clean the Nashua.

Through the meadows, towns, and cities, the Nashua once again flows freely. Paper pulp no longer clogs it. Chemicals no longer foul it.

Now we walk along its banks and row upon its fragrant waters. We can set our boats upon it and with its current, drift downstream.

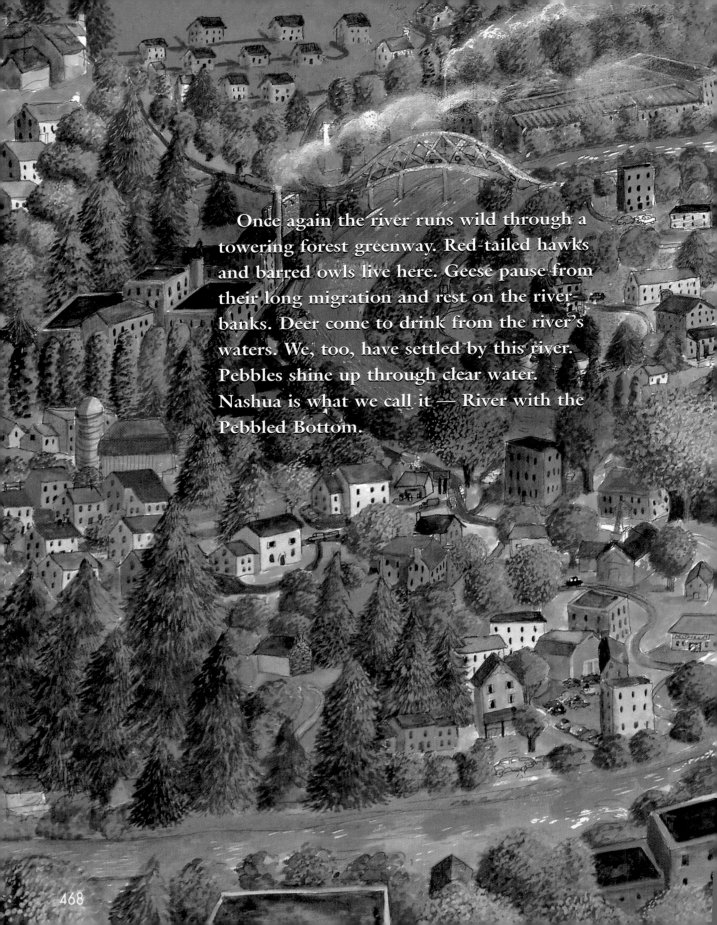

Once again the river runs wild through a towering forest greenway. Red-tailed hawks and barred owls live here. Geese pause from their long migration and rest on the riverbanks. Deer come to drink from the river's waters. We, too, have settled by this river. Pebbles shine up through clear water. Nashua is what we call it — River with the Pebbled Bottom.

LYNNE CHERRY
AUTHOR AND ILLUSTRATOR

Like any other writer, Lynne Cherry has to come up with topics that interest her readers. Interviewer Ilene Cooper asked her where she gets her ideas.

Cooper: *Where did you get the idea for* A River Ran Wild *?*

Cherry: From two books I read. One was called *Changes in the Land* and the other was *Restoring the Earth.* The book *Changes in the Land* was about the contrasting views of nature held by the Indians and the Colonists. The Indians didn't take more than they needed from the land. The Colonists wanted to conquer nature. As I read this book, it struck me that we are still living by that value system.

Cooper: *Why did you pick the Nashua River to write about?*

Cherry: I want kids to realize they have a choice in how they live with the natural world. *Restoring the Earth* was a series of success stories about places that had been devastated by pollution or other problems. Then individuals decided this was not the way they wanted things to be. One chapter talked about the Nashua River. I decided that I wanted to bring this story to children.

Lynne Cherry

RESPONSE

Ode to Nature

Imagine that you are one of Chief Weeawa's people. Write a poem that tells how you feel about the animals and plants around you and about your place among them. You may want to read your poem aloud to your classmates.

How You Look at It

Role-play a debate between the Indians and the settlers. Each side should give its point of view about how humans should interact with nature. Remember to support opinions with good arguments based on facts. Present your debate in a news-show format for your classmates. You could even take "call-in" questions.

CORNER

The Best Is Yet to Come

Plan, write, and illustrate a magazine advertisement to get people to take care of the land along the Nashua River. List some ways they can still use the river, and describe how plentiful the wildlife, lumber, and other natural resources are.

What Do You Think?

- In what ways has the Nashua River changed over the years?
- What time period or topic in the selection interests you the most? Explain your response.
- What do you think we can learn from the Nashua people?

BE KIND TO YOUR MOTHER (EARTH)

by Douglas Love
illustrated by Obadinah Heavner

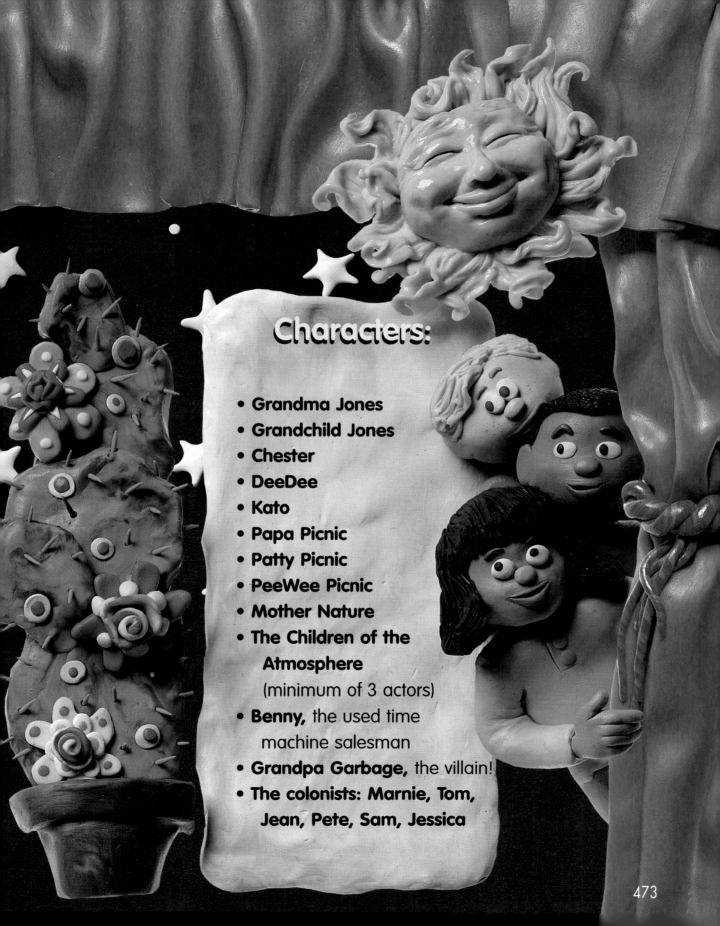

Characters:

- Grandma Jones
- Grandchild Jones
- Chester
- DeeDee
- Kato
- Papa Picnic
- Patty Picnic
- PeeWee Picnic
- Mother Nature
- The Children of the Atmosphere
  (minimum of 3 actors)
- **Benny,** the used time machine salesman
- **Grandpa Garbage,** the villain!
- The colonists: Marnie, Tom, Jean, Pete, Sam, Jessica

Scene 1
Time: Year 2053

GRANDMA JONES *is getting* GRANDCHILD JONES *ready for bed. There is one single bed stage left. Just right of the bed is a rocking chair. There is a window upstage right that can open and close.*

GRANDCHILD: Grandma, I don't want to go to bed yet. I'm not tired! Let me stay up and demoleculize something.

GRANDMA: You're not tired? You've been running around here all day! Not only that, we went to the planetarium and the jet propulsion center and we toured the meteorite! I'm worn out!

GRANDCHILD: I'm not! I want to hear a story!

GRANDMA: A story! Goldilocks and the Three Androids? Or Little Red Shooting Star?

GRANDCHILD: That's kid's stuff! I want to hear a real story! *(At that moment, debris flies in the window. It is pollution.)*

GRANDMA: Oh, dear! *(She crosses to shut the window.)* The pollution level is so high today!

GRANDCHILD: They finally plowed a path through the old park. Before that we couldn't even walk through it, there was so much garbage! It smelled really bad too! P.U.! Were things this polluted when you were a kid, Grandma?

GRANDMA: There was pollution. That's for sure. But not this bad. We used to be able to look out the window of a four-story building and see the ground when we looked down. Now all you see is smog, and if you could see the ground, you'd see that it's covered with garbage.

GRANDCHILD: Why does the sun shine only twelve minutes a day?

GRANDMA: That's air pollution, dear. It's caused a haze all around the planet.

GRANDCHILD: Yuck.

GRANDMA: Yuck is right. If we didn't have air purifying systems in our homes, we'd never breathe clean air. *(Thinking it over)* You want to hear a story? I've got a story for you. It's a true story too! When I was your age, back in 1993 . . .

GRANDCHILD: 1993! Wow, you're old! Did they have dinosaurs back then?

GRANDMA: No, dear. Listen to Grandma's story. Back in 1993, I knew three kids who were very upset about the condition of the environment.

GRANDCHILD: So there *was* pollution back in the dark ages.

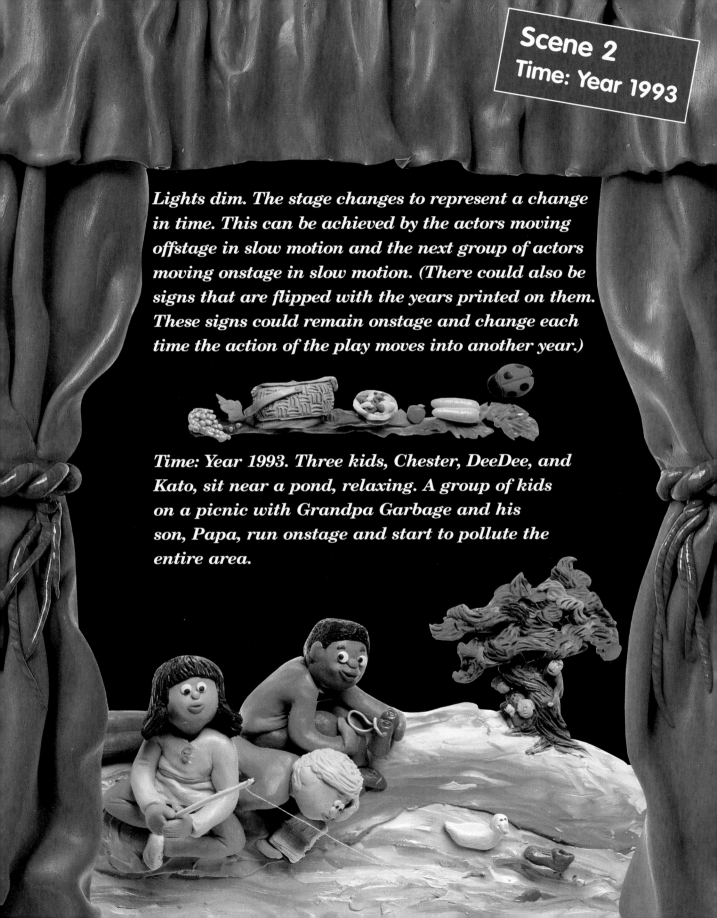

Lights dim. The stage changes to represent a change in time. This can be achieved by the actors moving offstage in slow motion and the next group of actors moving onstage in slow motion. (There could also be signs that are flipped with the years printed on them. These signs could remain onstage and change each time the action of the play moves into another year.)

Time: Year 1993. Three kids, Chester, DeeDee, and Kato, sit near a pond, relaxing. A group of kids on a picnic with Grandpa Garbage and his son, Papa, run onstage and start to pollute the entire area.

GRANDPA GARBAGE: Come on! Come on over here! I found a great spot for us to picnic!

PAPA: Come on, kids! Patty! PeeWee! This way! Grandpa's found us a spot. *(He begins to stretch out a picnic blanket.)*

PATTY: I don't like this spot! Yuck! You're not going to lay that blanket on the yuckie ground! In the dirt!

PAPA: Ah! A little dirt never hurt anybody! Besides, I'm hungry! I didn't want to go on this picnic! It was all your grandpa's idea.

GRANDPA GARBAGE: Come on, kids! We have some good food here! Here *(handing some sandwiches to PeeWee)*, pass these out.

PEEWEE: Goodie, goodie, goodie!

PATTY: What should I do with the wrapper?

PAPA: Just throw it in the water. It doesn't matter. Just look around. There's so much pollution, a few more wrappers aren't going to make any difference. *(They proceed to eat things and throw their garbage all over the stage.)*

PATTY: I'm done!

PAPA: I'm done!

PEEWEE: I'm done!

GRANDPA GARBAGE: You all run along and play. I'll catch up to you. *(Papa, Patty, and PeeWee exit. Grandpa Garbage hides in the corner and listens to Chester, DeeDee, and Kato's conversation.)*

CHESTER: Did you see that? They just threw all of their garbage all over the place.

KATO: Some of it went into our pond!

DEEDEE: Wait a minute! I think I've got something!

KATO: Pull it in! *(DeeDee has been fishing in the pond all this time. She reels in her catch. It is an old shoe.)*

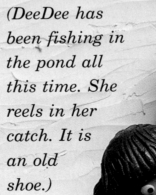

CHESTER: That's it! I'm going to complain to someone!

KATO: To whom?

CHESTER: I don't know! To our congressperson!

KATO: We're just kids! They're not going to listen to us. We have to find someone with power! With experience! With the ability to get the job done!

DEEDEE (looking offstage): Someone's coming! (Mother Nature enters with The Children of the Atmosphere.)

MOTHER NATURE: Children! Try to stay in line! Don't get lost! Here, here. Let's stop and rest a moment! Dip your tiny toes in the pond.

DEEDEE: Who are you?

MOTHER NATURE: Who are you!?

DEEDEE: I asked you first.

MOTHER NATURE: What does that have to do with the price of potatoes?

DEEDEE: The price of what?

MOTHER NATURE: Potatoes!

DEEDEE: I don't know. What DOES it have to do with the price of potatoes?

MOTHER NATURE: I asked you first.

DEEDEE: I'm so confused!

MOTHER NATURE: I was just fooling, dear! That was just an expression.

DEEDEE: Oh, well, then I was just fooling too. (There is a clap of thunder and some lightning.)

MOTHER NATURE: It's not nice to fool Mother Nature!

DEEDEE: I'm still confused!

CHESTER: You're Mother Nature? Wow! Am I glad that you came along. We need to talk! There is far too much littering and polluting going on around here!

KATO: Just look around! There is garbage everywhere! And this is from only one family!

MOTHER NATURE: You don't have to tell me about pollution. Pollution has been around for centuries! I do fear that it will stick around for centuries more.

CHESTER: If it sticks around there won't be more centuries. Soon all the garbage will take over, and we'll all be in it up to our eyebrows!

MOTHER NATURE: You can't change the past! People are used to littering! They don't understand that when they throw their trash on the ground or in the water, it hurts our environment. And they're cutting down trees, not to mention the number of endangered species there are now.

DEEDEE: What can we do?

MOTHER NATURE: I wish I knew. The condition of the earth is making my Children of the Atmosphere quite ill. Every time someone throws garbage on the ground, or out their car window or into our rivers, lakes, and oceans, my Children of the Atmosphere get very, very sick. (*The Children of the Atmosphere cough and moan.*)

MOTHER NATURE: Well, we must be running along. This so-called fresh air isn't good for my children. (*They exit.*)

KATO: I don't get it. Why did people start littering and cutting down trees?

CHESTER: You heard what Mother Nature said. They're used to it. They've been doing it for centuries.

KATO: If only we could go back and tell them not to start!

DEEDEE: We'd need some kind of time machine to do that. (*Used time machine salesman Benny enters with a* boing!)

BENNY: Did someone say that they needed a time machine?

DEEDEE: Who are you?

BENNY: Benny! I sell time machines—new and used. I've also got watches. (*Benny rolls up his jacket sleeve to show watches strapped all the way up his arm.*)

KATO: We need a time machine!

BENNY: You're in luck. I got my last one—still available.

CHESTER: New or used?

BENNY: Used—but only by a little old lady who used to take it to the seventeenth century on Sundays.

KATO: How much? *(Benny whispers a figure into Kato's ear. Kato whispers into Chester's ear. Chester whispers into DeeDee's ear.)*

DEEDEE: What?!

CHESTER and KATO *(covering her mouth)*: Shh!

CHESTER *(to Benny)*: We have to talk it over. *(They huddle.)*

KATO: We can't afford that! All I've got on me is 37 cents.

CHESTER: I only have $2.53 at home, and I was saving it for a rainy day.

DEEDEE: Don't look at me! I don't have any money.

CHESTER: We only need it for one day! *(He gets a bright idea and turns to Benny.)* We thought it over, and we would like it, but we'd have to take it for a test drive first.

BENNY: Well . . .

DEEDEE: I thought we only needed it for one . . . *(Kato stops her before she spills the beans.)*

BENNY: What . . . ?

KATO: Umm. . . . We only need one test drive and then we'll decide!

CHESTER: We'll be back soon.

KATO: Just once around the millennium, you know.

BENNY: All right. Don't be long! *(He exits. The kids go over to the machine.)*

DEEDEE: Wow! A real time machine.

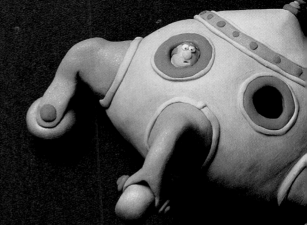

KATO: What do we do now?

DEEDEE: Simple! Don't you see? If we can go back in time and convince people to stop littering and cutting down trees, then their children won't ... and their children won't ... and their children won't ... and their children won't either.

CHESTER: That's a great idea, DeeDee!

DEEDEE: It is?

KATO: Sure! But we don't have much time.

DEEDEE: Where should we go first?

CHESTER: Let's do something to clean up the harbors, rivers, oceans, and ponds!

KATO: Let's see. Who were the first people to pollute the water?

CHESTER: I've got it! (*The three of them pop into the time machine and it takes off. Grandpa Garbage emerges from*

the corner where he has been hiding all along.)

GRANDPA GARBAGE: So, they think that they can clean up the past, do they? They want to get rid of all my beautiful garbage, do they? They think they're the only ones who can get a time machine, do they? Well, do they? (*Benny enters.*)

BENNY: Did someone say that they needed a time machine?

GRANDPA GARBAGE: What?

BENNY: Benny's the name. I sell time machines—new and used. I also got watches. (*Benny rolls up his jacket sleeve to show his watches.*)

GRANDPA GARBAGE: I need a time machine!

BENNY: You're in luck. I got my last one—still available. Step this way. I'll show it to ya! (*They exit.*)

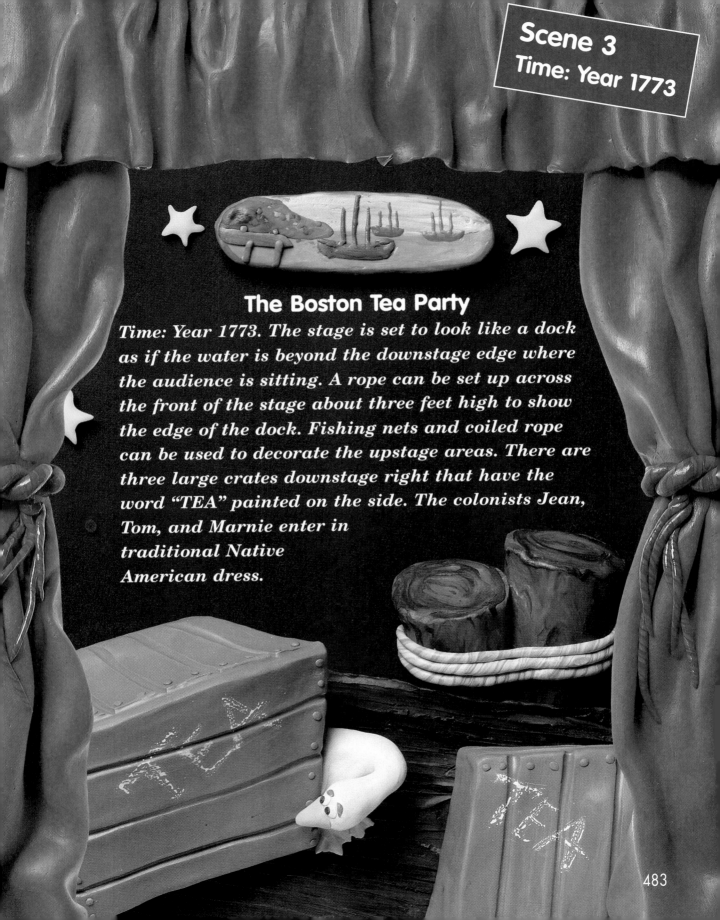

The Boston Tea Party

Time: Year 1773. The stage is set to look like a dock as if the water is beyond the downstage edge where the audience is sitting. A rope can be set up across the front of the stage about three feet high to show the edge of the dock. Fishing nets and coiled rope can be used to decorate the upstage areas. There are three large crates downstage right that have the word "TEA" painted on the side. The colonists Jean, Tom, and Marnie enter in traditional Native American dress.

JEAN: This new land promises great freedoms for all colonists.

TOM: I see great happiness here. We shall overcome the oppression of the King! *(Pete runs on. He is dressed in traditional Native American dress. He has a headband without a feather.)*

PETE: We are almost ready for you. Do you have the feathers?

JEAN: Yes, here they are. *(She hands him some feathers.)*

TOM: Is all of the tea loaded on the boat?

PETE: Oh, yes! The boat is full of tea! *(Sam and Jessica enter.)*

SAM: Pete, we are ready!

JESSICA: Those redcoats will be surprised when we toss their tea in the harbor!

PETE: We will show them that our freedom will not be threatened by taxes on tea.

SAM: We will gladly go without tea for a year rather than pay their tax!

JESSICA: We will go without tea for ten years!

MARNIE: I will gladly give up tea for fifteen years.

JEAN: I like tea. I have six cups a day—very hot with cream and sugar. I especially like it in the morning with a biscuit and orange marmalade.

JESSICA: Don't you want to put an end to the oppression of the King?

PETE: We have to make a statement!

JEAN: Couldn't we just send him a letter?

MARNIE *(pointing offstage)*: Look!

TOM: Where?

JEAN: Look at that house that has fallen from the sky . . . next to the ship. *(Chester,*

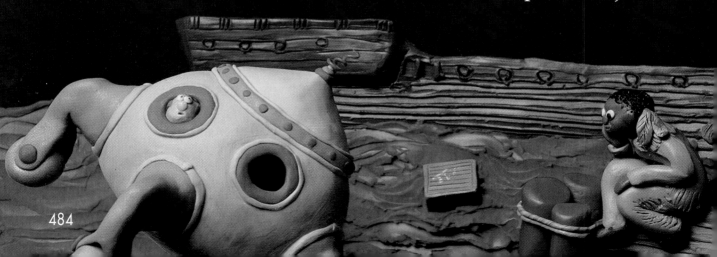

484

DeeDee, and Kato enter.)

CHESTER: Hello!

DEEDEE and KATO: Hi!

PETE: Who are you?

CHESTER: My name is Chester.

KATO: We've come to convince you not to spill the tea into the harbor.

MARNIE: They must be redcoats!

TOM: But how would the redcoats know that we were going to spill the tea?

JEAN: Spies!

DEEDEE: No! We are Americans!

PETE: You don't look like anyone I know.

KATO: That's not important. We don't have much time.

CHESTER: You can't put all that tea in the water. You'll pollute it!

JESSICA: But we have to make a statement.

PETE: We are being taxed unfairly.

KATO: Boycott the tax. Refuse to pay it! If you dump all that tea into the water, where will it go? Who will clean it up? Think of the fish.

DEEDEE: The fish might not even be thirsty!

KATO: What if everyone just went around dumping things into the water?

CHESTER: Think how dirty it would become.

TOM: I like to swim in the water. I wouldn't like to swim in a place full of garbage.

MARNIE: I wash my clothes with the same water. I would not like to wash clothes with dirty water.

JEAN: And I like tea! Why waste it? We thank you for your guidance.

CHESTER: We're glad to help. Come on. *(He exits with the other kids.)*

JEAN: Well, now what should we do?

TOM: Let's go over to my house. Maybe we'll see Paul Revere.

JEAN: Did you hear his latest? Last night he opened his window and yelled, "The British are humming! The British are humming!"

TOM: Humming? What were they humming?

JEAN: "God Save the King" no doubt! *(They all laugh and exit. Grandpa Garbage sneaks on and dumps the tea into the harbor himself.)*

GRANDPA GARBAGE: Little cleanies!

The Pond

The pond is still in the same mess that the kids left it in. The work that they did in the time machine did nothing to help the environment.

487

KATO (running on): Here we are, back at the great, big, beautiful . . . (looking around) polluted, dirty, garbage pond!

CHESTER: I don't understand it. I thought that we could make a difference! All of our hard work and traveling was for nothing!

DEEDEE: I don't get it. Why didn't it help? I thought that we were coming back to a brand new and improved 1993. Instead, it is just as dirty and polluted as we left it.

CHESTER: So much for time travel chain reactions.

KATO: I can't believe that we did all that for nothing. (They all sit in despair amidst the pollution. Grandma and Grandchild enter in their own time machine.)

GRANDCHILD: Look, Grandma. There they are!

KATO: Who are you?

GRANDMA: We're from the future. We came to help.

GRANDCHILD: We know about your travels.

GRANDMA: We just wanted to tell you that you are wasting your time.

CHESTER: We know!

DEEDEE: We tried to go back and change things but it didn't work.

KATO: I guess that some things never change.

GRANDMA: Well, some things DO!

DEEDEE: What do you mean?

GRANDMA: You are concentrating on changing the wrong thing. You have to do something in your own time.

GRANDCHILD: Don't try to change things in somebody else's time!

GRANDMA: The future is yours. You must make of it what you will. Act today to clean the world for tomorrow.

CHESTER: I get it! We can only make changes today for tomorrow!

KATO: Don't change yesterday for today!

CHESTER: What is past is past! We can't fix it.

KATO: We are in charge of what happens today!

DEEDEE: I don't get it!

GRANDCHILD: We have to pick up trash and recycle and save trees and animals today so we can enjoy them tomorrow and the day after and the day after and all the days after that.

DEEDEE: Wow! You're so smart! It sometimes takes me a while to catch on to things. I guess that will never change.

CHESTER: Hey, everybody, let's clean up! *(Grandpa Garbage enters.)*

GRANDPA GARBAGE: No! Don't clean up! Don't clean up my beautiful garbage! If you clean up the earth, you'll destroy me! *(No one listens to him and they continue to clean.)*

KATO: Hey, this place is looking better already.

CHESTER: There's just one big piece of garbage to get rid of. *(DeeDee wheels on a big garbage can with a phony lid made of paper so the actor can later break through it.)*

DEEDEE: Ready! *(Chester, DeeDee, and Kato help Grandpa Garbage into the trash can.)*

GRANDPA GARBAGE: No! Not my beautiful garbage! Not the can! Anything but the can! *(The kids put on the lid.)*

CHESTER, DEEDEE, KATO: Done! *(At that moment the actor playing Grandpa Garbage breaks through the top of the trash can. He has taken off his outer coat of garbage and is dressed like a regular kid.)*

KATO: Who are you?

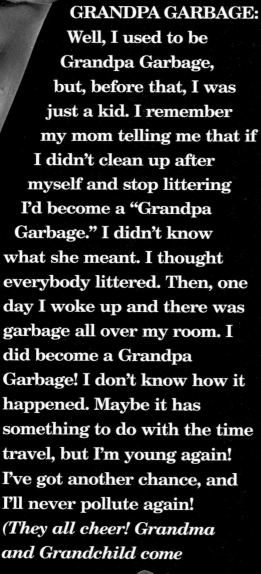

GRANDPA GARBAGE:
Well, I used to be
Grandpa Garbage,
but, before that, I was
just a kid. I remember
my mom telling me that if
I didn't clean up after
myself and stop littering
I'd become a "Grandpa
Garbage." I didn't know
what she meant. I thought
everybody littered. Then, one
day I woke up and there was
garbage all over my room. I
did become a Grandpa
Garbage! I don't know how it
happened. Maybe it has
something to do with the time
travel, but I'm young again!
I've got another chance, and
I'll never pollute again!
*(They all cheer! Grandma
and Grandchild come*

*downstage away from the
group.)*
GRANDCHILD: Where are
you, Grandma?
GRANDMA: What do you
mean?
GRANDCHILD: You said
that you knew these kids
in 1993. Here we are in
1993. Where are you? We
want to see what you
looked like when you were
a kid. *(realizing)* Your first
name is Deirdre, isn't it?
GRANDMA: Oh, yes. But
when I was young, they
used to call me DeeDee.
GRANDCHILD: Wow!
Things can change,
Grandma! Things can
change!
(Curtain)

The End

Meet the Author
Douglas Love

Douglas Love enjoys show business. He began acting as a child, and since then he has appeared in more than fifty shows. He has also become a producer himself, putting on five shows that traveled to cities all over the United States.

Love is a playwright, too. Besides *Be Kind to Your Mother (Earth)*, he wrote the folktale *The Emperor's New Clothes* as a Kabuki play. A Kabuki is a type of traditional Japanese play. That experience taught him that a good story can be enjoyed by people from many different cultures. He was also one of the authors of the stage play *Free to Be . . . You and Me.*

Today, Love is the artistic director of the Broadway Children's Theater in New York City. He also visits schools throughout the country, talking to teachers about using theater in the classroom. He's proof of the old saying that once you get show business in your blood, you just can't get enough!

Douglas Love

Jellies

by Ruth Heller

Like ice cream on a summer day
jellyfish will melt away
as the sun grows hot and hotter
if they're stranded out of water.

These fascinating blobs of gel
have no bones and have no shell.
They pulsate as they jet propel,
or at the mercy of the tide,
hitch a ride.

Let's have healthy, wholesome seas
for living treasures such as these
translucent purple, milky blue
jellies you can see right through.
Some are so clear they disappear,
but like a crystal chandelier,
they more or less . . .

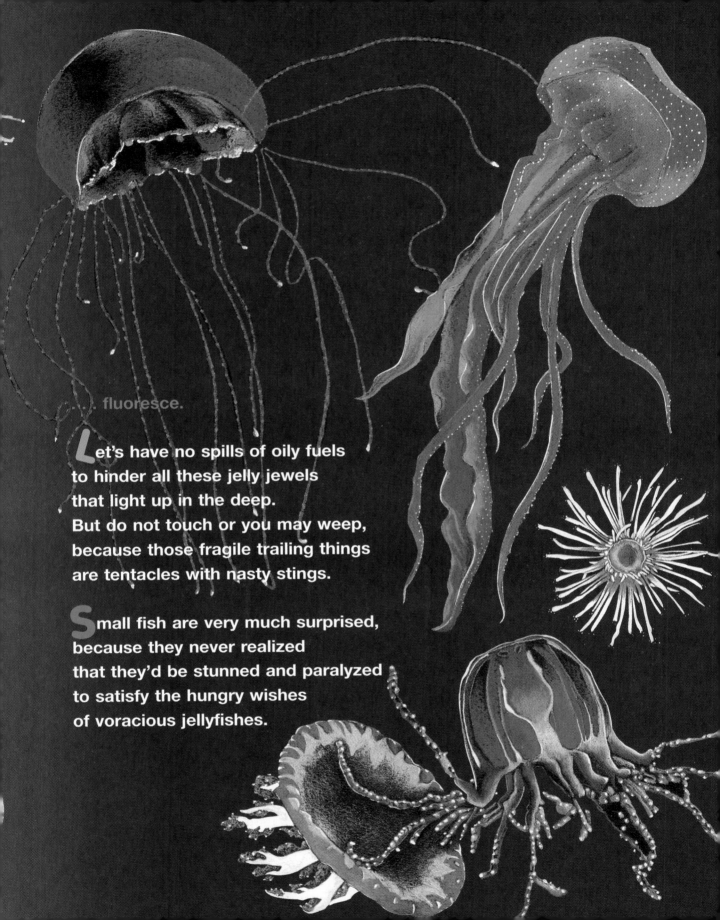

. . . . fluoresce.

Let's have no spills of oily fuels
to hinder all these jelly jewels
that light up in the deep.
But do not touch or you may weep,
because those fragile trailing things
are tentacles with nasty stings.

Small fish are very much surprised,
because they never realized
that they'd be stunned and paralyzed
to satisfy the hungry wishes
of voracious jellyfishes.

Response Corner

CREATE A SLOGAN
Give a Hoot!

Work with a group to create catchy slogans that will make people want to stop littering or polluting in your community. Hold an election in which your classmates will vote for the best slogans. Then send your slogans to your congressperson or to an organization that fights pollution.

MAKE A POSTER
See the Difference

Turn your litter into great art. Use a small paper bag to collect pencil shavings, small scraps of paper, and any other litter for a day or two. Then use these materials to create a three-dimensional travel poster for Anycity, 2053. List on the poster some of the wonderful things travelers will find there in their 12 daily minutes of sunlight.

WRITE A PARAGRAPH

Plan Ahead

Write a paragraph explaining how "Be Kind to Your Mother (Earth)" and "Jellies" have helped you look at your own habits of littering or recycling. Describe two or three ways you can begin to help make your own community better.

What Do You Think?

- How did traveling back to the past help the three children understand pollution problems?

- Did you like the play? Why or why not?

- What might the world of the jellyfish be like in 2053 if people keep treating nature in the way described in the play?

495

THEME WRAP-UP

After reading the selections in this theme, what thoughts do you have about progress and how it affects people and the environment? What are some things you can begin to do to make sure the changes around us improve our lives?

Suppose that Elijah McCoy had invented a machine that helped clean up water pollution. If he were alive today, how do you think Elijah McCoy could persuade other people that his invention was necessary?

ACTIVITY CORNER

Think about the different ways that making progress was described in this theme. How have you made progress since you were in third grade? Have you improved your grades or helped your family in some way? Write a "progress report" for yourself. Rate yourself on three or four different accomplishments, and explain why you rated yourself as you did. List some areas you would like to improve.

GREAT INSPIRATIONS

Do you like to paint, sculpt, sing, dance, or write stories and poems? All of these creative activities can help you express your feelings. In this theme, you will read about some of the talented people who have shared their inspirations with others.

GREAT INSPIRATIONS

CONTENTS

BOOKSHELF

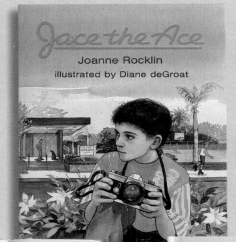

Jace the Ace
by Joanne Rocklin
illustrated by Diane deGroat

Ten-year-old Jason Caputo, who prefers to be called "Jace the Ace, junior photo-journalist," learns to focus on just being himself.
Signatures Library

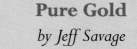

Kristi Yamaguchi: Pure Gold
by Jeff Savage

Kristi's girlhood dream of becoming an Olympic champion inspires her to go for the gold.
Signatures Library

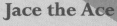

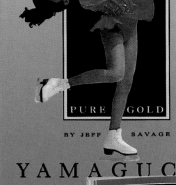

Totem Pole

by Diane Hoyt-Goldsmith
photographs by Lawrence Migdale

David's proud heritage is carved out for him with the help of his father's skill.

Teachers' Choice,
Notable Trade Book in the Field of Social Studies

Zora Hurston and the Chinaberry Tree

by William Miller
illustrated by
Cornelius Van Wright
and Ying-Hwa Hu

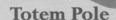

Writer Zora Neale Hurston dreams as a child from a chinaberry tree and shares scenes from her life.

Notable Trade Book in the
Field of Social Studies

Paint and Painting

Explore the history of art with this colorful, hands-on picture book.

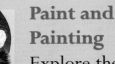

The Nightingale

BY HANS CHRISTIAN ANDERSEN
ILLUSTRATED BY DEMI

HE PALACE of the Emperor of China was the most splendid in the world. It was made of priceless porcelain that was both brittle and delicate. Anyone who touched it, therefore, had to be very careful.

The garden was filled with beautiful flowers, and on the loveliest of them were tied silver bells. Their tinkling made a wonderful sound, and anyone who passed by could not help admiring the flowers.

Everything was arranged to please the eye, and the garden was so large that even the gardener did not know where it ended.

New York Times
Best Illustrated Book

Notable Trade Book
in Social Studies

Beyond it, however, lay a stately forest with great trees and deep lakes. The forest sloped down to the sea, which was a clear blue. Large ships could sail under the branches of the trees, and in the trees lived a nightingale. She sang so beautifully that even a poor fisherman, who had too much to do, stood and listened when he came at night to cast his nets. "How beautiful!" he said, but then he had to go back to his work. He forgot about the bird, but when he came back the next night and heard her sing, he said again, "How beautiful!"

Travelers from many countries came to admire the palace and the garden, but when they heard the nightingale sing, they all said, "This is the finest thing in all the kingdom."

When they returned home, they told about all they had seen, and scholars wrote books about the city, the palace, and garden, praising the nightingale above everything else. Poets also composed splendid verses about the nightingale in the forest by the sea.

Eventually some of the books reached the Emperor. He sat on his golden chair and read and read. He nodded his head from time to time, for he enjoyed reading about the city, the palace, and the garden. But when he came to the words, "But the nightingale is best of all," he was amazed.

"What is that?" said the Emperor. "I don't know anything about such a bird in my kingdom. I have never heard it! Fancy learning about it for the first time in a book!"

He called his First Lord. "There is a most remarkable bird called a nightingale in the forest," he said. "The book says it is the most glorious thing in my kingdom. Why has no one ever said anything to me about it?"

"I have never heard it mentioned," said the First Lord. "I will look for it and find it."

But where was it to be found? The First Lord ran upstairs and downstairs, through the halls and corridors, but no one he met had ever heard of the nightingale. He eventually went back to the Emperor and told him it must be an invention on the part of those who had written the books.

"But the book in which I read this," said the Emperor, "was sent to me by the Emperor of Japan. It cannot be untrue, and I will hear this nightingale. She has my gracious permission to appear this evening, and if she does not, the whole court shall be beaten."

The First Lord and half the court searched and searched. At last they met a poor kitchen maid who said, "Oh, I know the nightingale. I am allowed to carry food left over from the court meals to my sick mother. When I go home at night, tired and weary, and stop to rest in the woods, I hear the nightingale singing. She brings tears to my eyes, and I feel as if my mother were kissing me."

"Little kitchen maid," said the First Lord. "I will give you a good place in the kitchen and permission to see the Emperor at dinner if you can lead us to the nightingale. She is invited to the court this evening."

And so they set out for the forest, and half the court went too.

On the way they heard a cow mooing.

"Oh," said one of the courtiers, "we have found her. What a wonderful voice for such a small creature!"

"No, that is a cow mooing," said the kitchen maid. "We still have a long way to go."

Then the frogs began to croak in the marsh. "Splendid," said the chaplain. "Her voice sounds like church bells."

"No, no, those are frogs," said the kitchen maid. "But I think we shall soon hear her."

507

Then the nightingale began to sing. "There she is!" cried the little kitchen maid. "Listen! She is sitting there." And she pointed to a little gray bird up in the branches.

"Is it possible?" said the First Lord. "How ordinary she looks! Seeing so many distinguished people around must have made her lose her color."

"Little nightingale," called the kitchen maid. "Our Gracious Emperor wants you to sing for him."

"With the greatest pleasure!" said the nightingale, and she sang so gloriously that it was a pleasure to listen.

"It sounds like glass bells!" said the First Lord. "And look how her little throat works. She will be a great success at court."

"Shall I sing once more for the Emperor?" asked the nightingale, thinking that the Emperor was there.

"My esteemed little nightingale," said the First Lord. "I have the great pleasure of inviting you to the court this evening, where His Gracious Imperial Highness will be enchanted with your song."

"It sounds best in the green woods," said the nightingale, but she came willingly when she heard the Emperor wished it.

At the palace everything was in readiness. The porcelain walls and floors glittered in the light of thousands of gold lamps, and there was such a hustle and bustle that the silver bells placed on the flowers in the corridors jingled constantly.

In the center of the great hall where the Emperor sat, a golden perch had been set up for the nightingale. The whole court was in attendance, including the little kitchen maid, who had been promoted to a cook. Everyone was looking at the little gray bird.

When the Emperor nodded, the nightingale began her song. She sang so gloriously that tears came into the Emperor's eyes and ran down his cheeks. Then she sang even more beautifully, touching the hearts of all who heard her. The Emperor was so delighted that he suggested she wear his golden slipper around her neck.

The nightingale thanked him but said she had had enough reward already. "I have seen tears in the Emperor's eyes."

She was a great success. All the court ladies tried to imitate the nightingale by holding water in their mouths to make a gurgling sound whenever someone spoke to them. Eleven grocers' children were named after her, even though not one of them could sing a note.

Now the nightingale had to stay at court. She had her own cage and was allowed to take a walk twice a day and once at night. She could not enjoy flying, however, because the twelve servants she had been given each held a silken string fastened around her leg.

One day the Emperor received a large parcel on which was written: *The Nightingale*.

"Here is another book about our famous bird," said the Emperor. It was not a book, however, but a mechanical toy lying in a box—an artificial nightingale that looked like the real one but was covered with diamonds, rubies, and sapphires. When the artificial bird was wound up, it could sing as sweetly as the real nightingale and could move its glittering silver and gold tail up and down, as well.

Round its neck was a little collar on which was written: *The nightingale of the Emperor of Japan is nothing compared to that of the Emperor of China*.

"Now they must sing together," ordered the Emperor. "What a duet we shall have!"

511

Their voices did not blend, however. The real nightingale sang in her own way, and the artificial bird sang only waltzes.

"The new bird is not at fault," said the music master. "It keeps very good time and does its job well."

Then the artificial bird sang alone. It gave as much pleasure as the real nightingale and was much prettier to look at with its sparkling jewels. Three and thirty times it sang the same piece without tiring. People would have liked to hear it again, but the Emperor thought it was time for the real nightingale to sing again. But she was nowhere to be found. No one had noticed that she had flown out the open window.

"What shall we do?" asked the Emperor.

The members of the court called the real nightingale ungrateful and said, "But we still have the best songbird!"

Then for the thirty-fourth time they heard the same piece, but they still did not know it because it was much too difficult. The music master assured them that the artificial bird was better than the real nightingale. "My lords and ladies and your Imperial Majesty, with the real nightingale one can never tell what song will come out, but everything is in perfect order with the artificial bird. You can examine its mechanism and see how it operates."

"That is just what we think," said all the courtiers.

The music master was then given permission to show the bird to the people the next Sunday. When they heard it, they were enchanted and nodded time with their forefingers. But the poor fisherman who had heard the real nightingale said, "This one sings well enough. The tunes glide out, but there is something wanting—I don't know what."

The real nightingale was banished from the kingdom.

513

The artificial bird was put on silken cushions near the Emperor's bed, and all the presents it received, gold and precious stones, lay around it. It was given the title of Imperial Night Singer.

The music master wrote twenty-five volumes about the artificial bird. They were so learned and long that all the people pretended they had read and understood them, for they did not want to appear stupid and be flogged for it as had happened in the past.

A whole year passed. The Emperor, the court, and the people knew every note of the artificial bird's songs. They preferred it that way because they could sing along with the bird.

But one evening, while the artificial bird was singing for the Emperor, something snapped. The music ceased. The Emperor sprang up and summoned his physician, but what could *he* do? Then the clockmaker came, and he managed to put the bird somewhat back in order. He said, however, that it must be used very seldom since the works were nearly worn out and it was impossible to put in new ones.

Only once a year was the artificial bird allowed to sing, and even that one performance was almost too much for it. Five years passed, and then a great sorrow befell the country. The Emperor became ill, and it was reported that he was unlikely to recover. Already a new Emperor had been chosen.

Cold and pale, the Emperor lay on his bed. The whole court believed him dead, and everyone went to pay respects to the new Emperor. Cloth was laid down in the corridors so that no footstep could be heard, and everything was very still.

The Emperor longed for something to relieve the monotony of the deathlike silence. If only someone would speak to him or sing to him! Music would break the spell that enveloped him. Moonlight was streaming in the open window, but that, too, was quite silent.

515

"Music! Music!" cried the Emperor. "You bright golden bird, sing! I gave you gold and jewels and hung my gold slipper around your neck. Sing, do sing!" But the bird was silent. There was no one to wind it up, and so it could not sing. All was silent, so terribly silent!

All at once there came through the window the most glorious burst of song. It was the real nightingale, who was sitting in the tree outside his window. She had heard of the Emperor's illness and had come to sing to him of comfort and hope. As she sang, the blood flowed more and more quickly through the Emperor's body and life began to return.

"Thank you, thank you!" said the Emperor. "You divine little bird! I know you. I chased you from my kingdom, and you have given me life again. How can I reward you?"

"You have done that already," said the nightingale. "I brought tears to your eyes the first time I sang. I shall never forget that. They are the jewels that gladden a singer's heart. But now sleep and get strong again; I will sing you a lullaby." And the Emperor fell into a deep, calm sleep as she sang.

The sun was shining through the window when he awoke, strong and well. None of his servants had come back yet, for they thought he was dead. But the nightingale sat and sang to him.

"You must stay with me always," said the Emperor. "You shall sing whenever you like, and I will break the artificial bird into a thousand pieces."

"Don't do that!" said the nightingale. "He did his work as long as he could. Keep him. I cannot build my nest in the palace and live here, but let me come whenever I like. In the evening I will sit outside your window and sing you something that will make you feel happy and grateful.

"I will sing of joy and of sorrow, of the evil and the good that lies hidden from you. A singing bird flies all over, to the poor fisherman's hut, to the farmer's cottage, to all those who are far away from you and your court. I love your heart more than your crown, though that has about it a brightness as of something holy. Now I will sing to you again, but you must promise me one thing—"

"Anything!" said the Emperor, standing up in his imperial robes, which he himself had put on, and fastening on his sword richly embossed with gold.

"One thing I beg of you. Don't tell anyone that you have a little bird who tells you everything. It will be much better not to." Then the nightingale flew away.

Later that morning everyone was astonished to see the Emperor step out on his balcony and with his great deep voice firmly greet one and all with a grand "Good morning!"

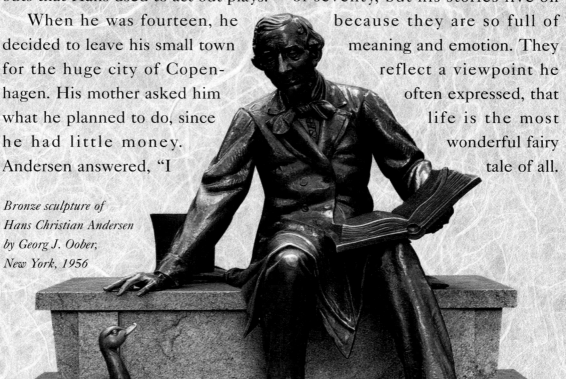

Words About the Author
Hans Christian Andersen

Hans Christian Andersen was born in Denmark in 1805 and was the son of a shoemaker and a washerwoman. His interest in story-telling began when he was young. His father read him wonderful books, and his mother told him entertaining Danish folktales. His father also made him a puppet theater and paper cut-outs that Hans used to act out plays.

When he was fourteen, he decided to leave his small town for the huge city of Copen-hagen. His mother asked him what he planned to do, since he had little money. Andersen answered, "I

Bronze sculpture of Hans Christian Andersen by Georg J. Oober, New York, 1956

shall be famous. First, you suffer terrible things. Then you get to be famous." As if he were a character in a fairy tale, Andersen did go through hard times. Then he started writing fairy tales like "The Little Mermaid," which became popular throughout the world.

Andersen died in 1875 at the age of seventy, but his stories live on because they are so full of meaning and emotion. They reflect a viewpoint he often expressed, that life is the most wonderful fairy tale of all.

Response Corner

A Little Bird Told Me

The nightingale and the Emperor like different things. With whom do you agree? Write a theme song for one of these characters that shows how he or she feels about life. Begin by making a list of what the character thinks is important. Sing the song for your classmates.

ACT OUT A SCENE

A Bird You Can Dance To

With a group, create a scene that shows the nightingale trying to sing with the mechanical bird. The characters will be the nightingale, the machine, the Emperor, and the members of the court. Write and practice your play. You may want to add some simple costumes and props. Then treat your classmates to a wonderful performance.

What Do You Think?

- How does the nightingale's relationship with the Emperor change from the beginning to the end of the story?
- What would you do if the nightingale from the story visited you at your house? Why?
- Do you think the nightingale was smart to return to the Emperor's palace? Why or why not?

WRITE INSTRUCTIONS

Say "Aah!"

Do you like music? Do you think music could make someone well? Write some instructions to the Emperor for taking care of his health. Don't forget to list a healthy dose of music!

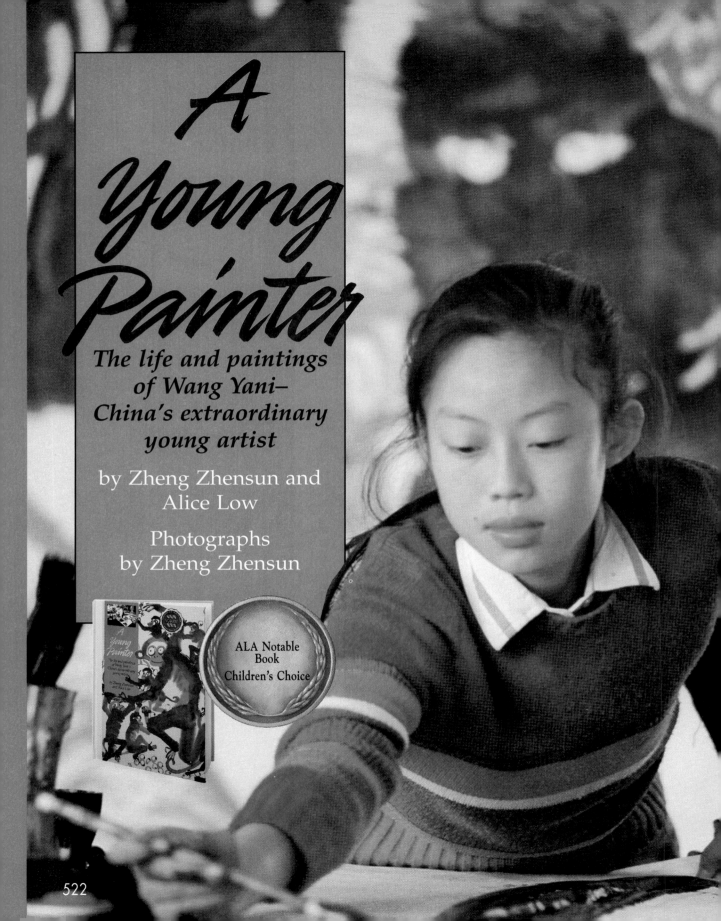

A Young Painter

The life and paintings of Wang Yani— China's extraordinary young artist

by Zheng Zhensun and Alice Low

Photographs by Zheng Zhensun

ALA Notable Book
Children's Choice

Little Monkeys
and Mummy
Age 5
1 ft. 3 in. × 1 ft. 9 in.
Yani spent a lot of time watching monkeys closely. In this painting Yani has captured the lively antics of the monkeys.

Wang Yani started painting as a way of playing and using her imagination while she watched her father, a well-known Chinese artist, work in his studio. By the time she was three years old, she was painting hundreds of recognizable pictures of the monkeys at the zoo and other subjects that interested her. She had her first major exhibition in China at age four, and since age ten has held solo exhibitions around the world. Yani uses painting to communicate her impressions of things around her, such as the beautiful Guilin mountains near her home. For this reason she is sometimes called "the Picasso of China."

How Yani Paints

Like many other people, Yani started to draw by doodling dots and lines. But in less than a year, she passed that stage of early childhood drawing, a stage that most children take years to get through. Yani also mastered the art of using brush and ink when she was a very young child. At the age of three, while other children could barely draw recognizable figures, she was painting her pictures of lively cats and monkeys.

Yani's paintings are fresh, vigorous, and bold. A Japanese artist, Yikuo Hiyayama, commented on the works Yani painted at this early age. He said they were "solid in structure, with smooth brushwork, and clear lines." He said they did not have any unnecessary polishing, for Yani had known just what to omit, and he also stated that she knew how to use the paper in a way that would bring out its ability to soak up paint.

Above:
On her twelfth birthday Yani painted a huge picture and poured some ink on the painting. She wanted to see the effect of the natural flow of ink on paper.

Yani holds her brush in different ways according to the size of the brush and the way she thinks is best for her. Once, when Yani's schoolteacher wanted her to hold the brush in a way that was unnatural to her, Yani's father interfered. He encouraged Yani to go back to holding the brush in her own way.

Yani's father has also advised her never to fix her eyes on the tip of the brush as she paints, but to scan the whole sheet of paper and even beyond it so as to have a wide field of vision. As time has gone by, Yani's brushstrokes have become more powerful. Now, with a few rapid sweeps of the brush and a soft twist of her wrist, Yani swiftly paints an old green tree and adds a tail to a monkey.

Yani handles the brush with ease, sometimes painting swiftly, sometimes slowly, sometimes cleverly, sometimes bluntly, and sometimes unevenly. She also uses ink in different ways—dry, moist, strong and light—to create different effects.

When Yani was very young, she could not concentrate on her painting as deeply as she does now. She used to leave her painting to play after doing only a few brushstrokes. Sometimes while painting she sang, danced, chatted, made faces, and even imitated other people and animals.

Now that Yani is older, she approaches her painting a little differently. Before she paints, she calms herself to clear her mind and then waits for inspiration. But when she starts painting, she does not know exactly what she will paint. The idea develops as she works. Yani likes to listen to music on her Walkman while she paints. She believes that music stimulates her feelings. Her favorite music is Beethoven's Fifth Symphony and works by Schubert and Mozart, as well as Chinese music.

Yani's father never comments on his daughter's work in her presence, for he doesn't want her to paint according to *his* likes and dislikes. Nor does he expect her to do perfect work. In his opinion, if he were to consider her work to be perfect, her imaginative ideas would probably dry up. He wants Yani, the child artist, to keep searching for ways to push her experiences and knowledge forward.

Yani never does any copying, nor does she paint from life. She remembers everything she sees, and she paints her lively pictures completely from memory. One example of her amazing visual memory occurred when, as a young child, Yani asked her father to write some words for her to copy. Yani's father did not want her to copy his way of writing Chinese characters, so he wrote them in the air with his fingers. Yani watched

Below top:
Listening to music on her Walkman helps Yani paint.

Below bottom:
Careful brushwork.

Above:
Animals'
Autumn
Age 14
3 ft. 2 in. ×
5 ft. 10½ in.
(Painted in
Washington,
D.C.)
Yani's inscrip-
tion tells how
autumn is a
time when trees
wither, but when
animals are
happy because
there is plenty
of food for them
to eat.

his movements very carefully and proceeded to write the characters on paper, just as her father had drawn them.

Yani's father encourages Yani to remember what she has seen during the day and to paint what has affected her the most. He has always stressed that Yani should paint her impressions of the things she has seen, rather than concentrating on the details and special features. That is why there are no peaks in Yani's paintings of beautiful Guilin. Instead, she has painted her overall impressions that the Guilin landscape has left in her mind.

Likewise, though Yani's monkeys are very lively and have all the traits of these mischievous animals, none of them is painted true to form. They are the products of her impressions after her many trips to the zoo. Some of their gestures are simply from Yani's imagination. Instead of reproducing their actual behavior, Yani lets her monkeys reflect her own feelings about them.

Her first monkeys were without hair or toes, but her father did not point this out to her because he knew that his small daughter had to pass through a certain process before becoming familiar with her subject. He knew that Yani would make changes in the way she painted the monkeys within the natural course of time. Though Yani did give her monkeys hair and toes as she grew older, her monkeys were still not painted in great detail. They were Yani's overall impression of monkeys.

When Yani was eight years old, her father made a painful personal decision in order to further protect his daughter's originality and creativity. He quit painting altogether, even though he was rising to the peak of his career. His oil paintings were shown at every art exhibition in Guangxi, and the largest one, *Liberate Guangxi*, was in the collection of the regional museum.

Why did he cut short his painting career? The reason was that he was afraid his style of painting, using oils rather than Chinese brush and ink, would have a poor effect on Yani, who painted with traditional Chinese materials and used many of the traditional Chinese brushstrokes.

Wang Shiqiang's friends have asked him if he feels sad about giving up his oil painting.

"Yes," he said, "but I see in Yani a more promising artist than Wang Shiqiang. I have a duty to help and protect her so that she will use her artistic talents fully." He added that he hopes to go back to his own painting when Yani turns eighteen.

Above:
Yani and her father at home.

Opposite:
Let Me Get to the Bank
Age 6
1 ft. 1 in. ×
4 ft. 4 in.
Yani's paintings are full of life. In this painting she captures the movement of fish swimming and of a monkey swinging on branches above the water.

Yani and Her Father

Though Wang Shiqiang has protected Yani's creativity and freedom to express herself, he has also furnished her with guidance and stimulation, and he has done everything possible to create an atmosphere that would lead to her artistic growth.

Not only did he introduce her to the beauties of nature while she was very young, but he also took her to interesting places, which stimulated her mind.

After Yani was four, she went with her father to many cities where her work was exhibited, and so she had many wonderful experiences. She climbed the Taishan Mountains and the Great Wall, visited the Palace Museum in Beijing and the Confucian temple in

Qufu, Shandong Province. In recent years she has toured many countries, and these trips have expanded her knowledge and broadened her artistic approach.

And though Yani's father has been cautious about giving advice to Yani, he has helped to strengthen her understanding of the things she has seen.

For instance, one day a botanist visited the Wang family, and Yani's father asked him to talk about the function of leaves, for Yani had painted trees without leaves. Yani listened to the botanist speak, and the next day, Yani's painting showed leaves on a tree. On the tip of each leaf hung a fruit. Yani also said, "Monkeys eat fruit, and fruit eat leaves." This was *her* understanding of the botanist's explanation of how leaves get their food. Though she could not absorb all of the facts, she was making progress. Soon after that, Wang Shiqiang took Yani to an orchard, where she saw that fruit grew on twigs.

Since then, Yani has painted many paintings of trees and fruit, and the fruit hangs from twigs, not from leaves!

Yani's father has helped her to see pictures in her mind by encouraging her to make up stories. When Yani was five, he took her to Guangzhou on a ship. Wang Shiqiang started telling Yani a story, then Yani responded with one of her own. To the astonishment of the passengers, the two of them told each other stories for seven hours!

Yani's father has also encouraged her to think independently and to solve problems by herself. In the Wangs' courtyard there is a hibiscus tree, which bears white flowers in the morning and red in the evening. Yani painted a picture and called it *Hibiscus Flowers*

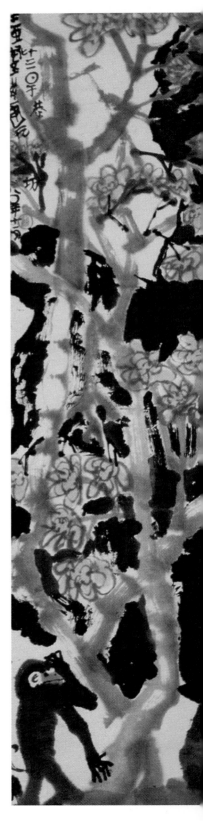

Are White in the Morning. She painted the petals in a very light color and showed the painting to her father. "Doesn't this look beautiful?" she asked.

"Is this white?" asked Wang Shiqiang, for the petals looked quite gray.

Yani thought for a moment. Then she took her brush, dipped it in thick black ink, and painted the background dark. In contrast, the petals now looked white. Yani's father thought so, too, and nodded his head in approval.

Wang Shiqiang frequently created problems for Yani while she was painting, in order to sharpen her mind and make her more visually sensitive. One day, Yani drew a horizontal line across a sheet of paper. When her father asked her what she was going to paint, she answered, "A bridge."

"A bridge is not pleasing to the eye," said her father. "Why not paint something else?"

Yani thought for a few moments. Then quickly, she transformed the line into a shoulder pole with a basket of fruit hanging from either end. She added a little monkey carrying it and hurrying along.

Yani and her father have made it a rule that she should never say, "I don't know," when he asks her a question, for there is always an answer to be found.

"When Yani was painting, I would pretend not to know anything about what she was after," said Wang Shiqiang. "Every time she would finish a painting, I would ask her why it was painted in that certain way; for example, why there was so much space left in the painting. Yani would never say, 'I don't know.' Instead, she would think about what I had asked." He added that if their views differed because of the difference in their ages, he would just say, "I don't necessarily agree with you." Sometimes, when Yani's painting didn't seem to make sense to him, he would praise her on purpose and even say, "It's wonderful." Then Yani would keep on painting enthusiastically, until she herself realized what a mess she had made.

When Yani's father treated her this way, his aim was to build up her thinking and creativity, rather than to let her mind drift. "Inspiration and guidance, when given in an appropriate way, are essential to protect and develop a child's ability to imagine and create," he says. He adds that it is important to keep that guidance within the boundaries of the child's stage of development.

Yani's father loves her very much, but he can be strict with her when necessary. He feels that a good artist must have a strong character; therefore, discipline is important.

As Yani became famous, she became proud, too, and sometimes she lost her temper. Her father and his friends were concerned about this.

When Yani was four and a half years old, she put on a painting demonstration in the city of Yangzhou. Somebody overturned a cup by accident and wet the table on which she was working. She went into a rage, flung her brush away, and sat fuming, tight-lipped. Soon she started to paint again, but she did it half-heartedly.

Afterwards, Yani and her father returned to the hotel room, and her father told her that if she wanted to continue to be a painter she must be serious, not temperamental and arrogant.

Above:
Painting the first monkey using light brushstrokes.

Below:
Cat
Age 3
4½ × 8½ in.
In this painting, Yani captures the feeling of the way a cat moves.

Yani promised to paint seriously, saying, "Papa, I love painting. I want to paint." But her father insisted that she stop. Yani broke into tears and told her father that more than anything she wanted to keep on painting. Just then, he was called out of the room.

When her father returned with a friend, he was surprised to see that the whole floor was covered with Yani's paintings, each done in all seriousness. Yani looked up with tears in her eyes and said, "I can never paint again. These are my last works."

Her father said, "You have already apologized by words. And the paintings on the floor show you realize the mistake you have made." He told Yani that now she could continue to paint.

Wang Shiqiang's friend said to him, "You are really too strict with your daughter. But you are right. We must be strict with child prodigies who have won a name for themselves."

In 1985, when Yani was ten years old, she was interviewed by some sixty reporters in a big Tokyo hotel. One reporter asked, "We in Japan regard you as a great talent. How do you feel about that?"

"I feel nothing special," answered Yani, amid the flashes and clicks of cameras.

"Are your paintings the best in the world?"

"No," answered Yani. "If mine are, what about the works of other famous artists?"

Above:
Rabbits and Butterfly
Age 13
1 ft. 3 in. ×
1 ft. 7 in.
Rabbits mean something special to Yani because according to the Chinese calendar of years, she was born in the Year of the Rabbit.

Opposite:
Who Picked the Fruit?
Age 4
1 ft. 1 in. ×
4 ft. 3 in.

Interview with Photojournalist
Zheng Zhensun

Zheng Zhensun worked closely with Wang Yani to write about her and photograph her paintings. Here is what he had to say about his experiences from his home in Beijing, China.

Interviewer: How did you come to write about Wang Yani?

Wang Yani with
Zheng Zhensun

Zheng: I am a writer and a photographer, but mostly I'm a photographer—a photojournalist. I was asked to write about Wang Yani when I worked as a photojournalist with the Xinhau News Agency in Beijing.

Interviewer: When did you start your career as a photojournalist?

Zheng: When I was young, I studied photo-journalism in Shanghai, China. I am retired now, but I still take photographs. My favorite topic is children. They are so interesting! I have a daughter of my own, but she is an adult now—an engineer.

Interviewer: What advice would you give to young people who want to be photojournalists like yourself?

Zheng: I would tell them to do as Wang Yani did and paint. Studying painting will help them learn to see and then to paint with words. Studying painting will also help them learn to be a good photographer. Tell the children in the United States that I wish them the best of luck—every one of them!

RESPONSE

Everyone's a Critic

With a group, look through the collection of Yani's art in the selection and talk about pieces you like and don't like. Then write an art review as if you were a reporter visiting one of Yani's shows.

Museum Store

Some well-known museums take photographs of their best paintings to sell as posters. Choose one of Yani's paintings that you think would make a good poster. Create a design for the poster that tells about Yani's work and will make people want to find out more about her.

536

CORNER

The Power of Observation

Yani's dad invited a botanist to visit the family to teach Yani about leaves. Carefully observe a plant, a class pet, or a food. Touch it, smell it (if possible), and look at it through a magnifying glass. Then draw it. Share your work with your classmates and describe how closely observing the object helped you draw it.

What Do You Think?

- How might you describe Yani's paintings to someone who has not seen them?
- Would you like to be a child prodigy like Yani? Why or why not?
- Do you think Yani's father was right when he said that discipline is important for an artist? Explain your answer.

The Case of the Painting Contest

Encyclopedia Brown helps his father, the Idaville Chief of Police, solve cases. In the summer he runs a detective agency from the family's garage with the help of his friend Sally Kimball. True to his nickname, Encyclopedia has the answers, even to problems that stump everyone else.

from Encyclopedia Brown and the Case of the Treasure Hunt
by Donald J. Sobol
Illustrated by
Mary Beth Schwark

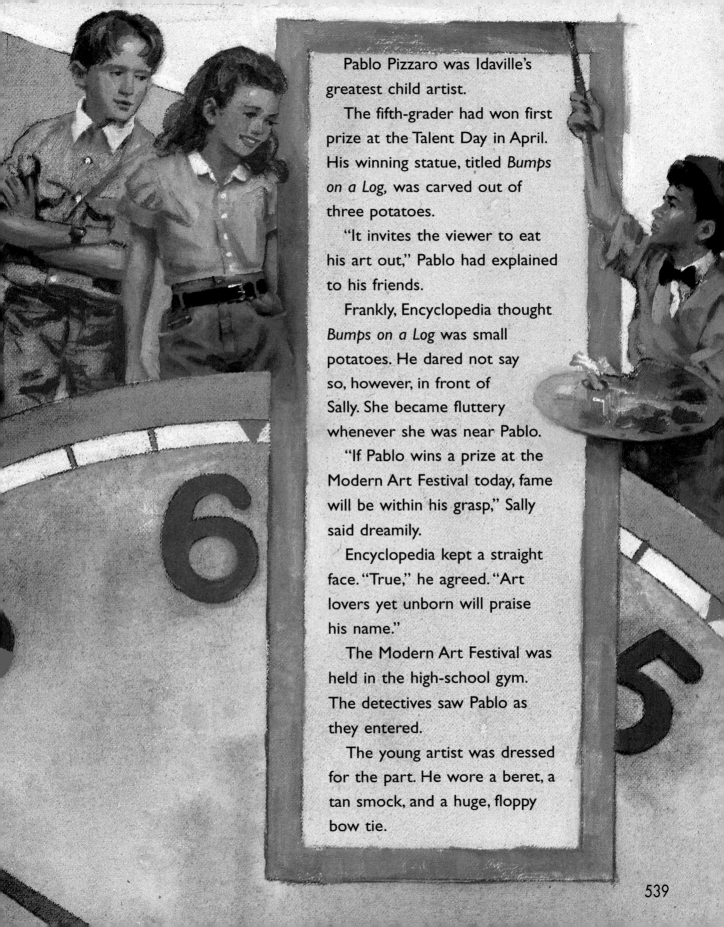

Pablo Pizzaro was Idaville's greatest child artist.

The fifth-grader had won first prize at the Talent Day in April. His winning statue, titled *Bumps on a Log,* was carved out of three potatoes.

"It invites the viewer to eat his art out," Pablo had explained to his friends.

Frankly, Encyclopedia thought *Bumps on a Log* was small potatoes. He dared not say so, however, in front of Sally. She became fluttery whenever she was near Pablo.

"If Pablo wins a prize at the Modern Art Festival today, fame will be within his grasp," Sally said dreamily.

Encyclopedia kept a straight face. "True," he agreed. "Art lovers yet unborn will praise his name."

The Modern Art Festival was held in the high-school gym. The detectives saw Pablo as they entered.

The young artist was dressed for the part. He wore a beret, a tan smock, and a huge, floppy bow tie.

"He looks gift-wrapped," Encyclopedia thought.

"What have you in the show, Pablo?" Sally asked.

"Nothing," replied Pablo. "No other kid would enter a painting or a sculpture against me. So the children's division was dropped this year."

"Oh, that's unfair," Sally said.

"I've entered the speed-painting contest," Pablo said. "It's open to any amateur artist in the state. How fast you paint counts more than how well you paint."

He led the detectives to a corner of the gym. A group of modern art lovers gazed at a white canvas set upon an easel. "What soul—superb!" a woman gushed. "A major breakthrough!"

"The canvas is white because it hasn't been painted on yet," Pablo whispered disgustedly.

A man with a judge's badge moved the onlookers back. "Our first speed-painter," he announced, "is John Helmsly, a sea captain."

"Here and ready!" responded a bearded man. He strode to the canvas. In one hand, he carried a board with blobs of paint. In the other hand, he held a square-tipped knife.

The judge gazed at his stopwatch. "On your mark, get set, go!"

John Helmsly began whacking paint wildly against the canvas with the knife.

"I don't use brushes," he said, panting. "They take too long to clean."

The knife flew . . . *whack, whack, whack.* Soon a boat, water, and sky were visible to onlookers with a helpful imagination.

"The boat is moving at about only four knots an hour," John Helmsly said. "So we need just a touch of foam where the front cuts the water, and a little behind. And here's the skipper at the back looking at a map of where he's going. There—done! I shall call it *Sailboat in Motion.*"

"Two minutes and fifty-eight seconds," the judge announced.

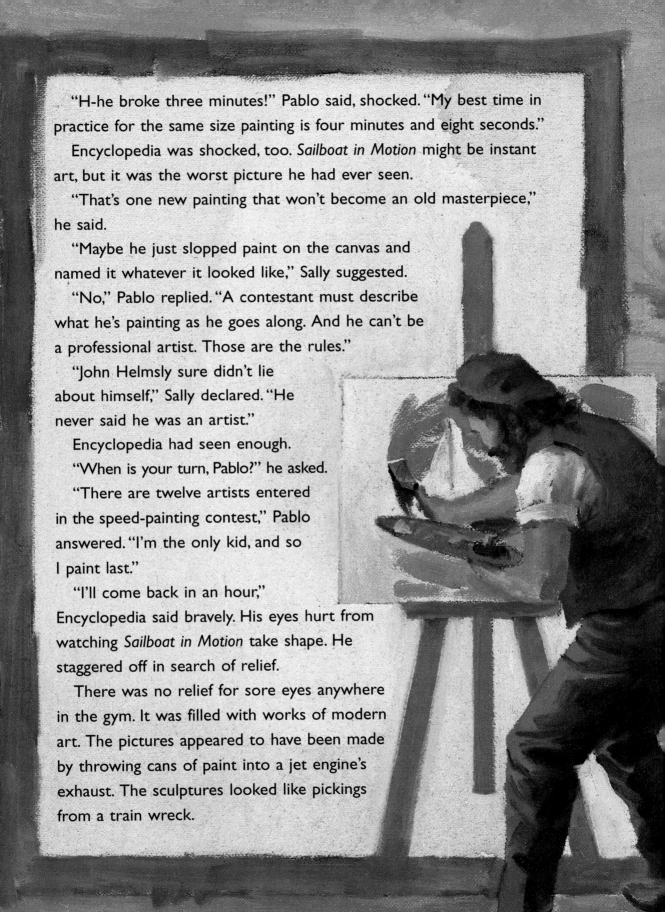

"H-he broke three minutes!" Pablo said, shocked. "My best time in practice for the same size painting is four minutes and eight seconds."

Encyclopedia was shocked, too. *Sailboat in Motion* might be instant art, but it was the worst picture he had ever seen.

"That's one new painting that won't become an old masterpiece," he said.

"Maybe he just slopped paint on the canvas and named it whatever it looked like," Sally suggested.

"No," Pablo replied. "A contestant must describe what he's painting as he goes along. And he can't be a professional artist. Those are the rules."

"John Helmsly sure didn't lie about himself," Sally declared. "He never said he was an artist."

Encyclopedia had seen enough.

"When is your turn, Pablo?" he asked.

"There are twelve artists entered in the speed-painting contest," Pablo answered. "I'm the only kid, and so I paint last."

"I'll come back in an hour," Encyclopedia said bravely. His eyes hurt from watching *Sailboat in Motion* take shape. He staggered off in search of relief.

There was no relief for sore eyes anywhere in the gym. It was filled with works of modern art. The pictures appeared to have been made by throwing cans of paint into a jet engine's exhaust. The sculptures looked like pickings from a train wreck.

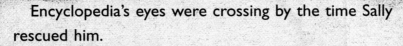

Encyclopedia's eyes were crossing by the time Sally rescued him.

"Come quickly," she urged. "Pablo paints next."

The boy artist was making his first brushstroke when the detectives reached the speed-painting corner.

As he worked, Pablo explained what he was painting. His landscape, *Grass in October,* took four minutes and ten seconds to complete.

Grass in October was judged good. But it was not good enough to overcome Pablo's poor time. He finished second. John Helmsly won.

"You should feel great," Sally told Pablo. "You beat all the other artists."

Pablo refused to be comforted. "Second prize is a bathroom rug," he said dejectedly. "First prize is a weekend trip to the state capital and all you can eat."

"I think John Helmsly cheated," Sally said angrily. "He used a knife."

"That isn't against the rules," Pablo muttered.

Sally wouldn't give up. "Maybe he didn't tell the truth about himself or his picture. The boat could be a whale sneezing. Encyclopedia, if you can prove John Helmsly lied, Pablo would be moved up to first place."

Encyclopedia smiled. "Of course he lied."

How did Encyclopedia know?

Solution to
The Case of the Painting Contest

John Helmsly claimed that he was a sea captain. He believed that a picture of a boat painted by a sea captain would favorably influence the judges.

However, he used no sea captain words would use.

He said, "The boat is moving at about only four knots an hour." A "knot" means a nautical mile per hour. So what he actually said was, "The boat is moving at about only four knots an hour an hour." Nonsense!

He also said "front" instead of "bow," "back" instead of "stern," and "map" instead of "chart."

When Encyclopedia pointed out his mistakes to the judges, John Helmsly confessed. He was really a professional artist.

He withdrew from the contest, and first prize was awarded to Pablo.

ART AND LITERATURE

The characters in the stories in this theme express their feelings through their art. In turn, people respond with feelings of their own. How do the figures in the painting *Three Musicians* express themselves? If you could hear their music, how might it make you feel?

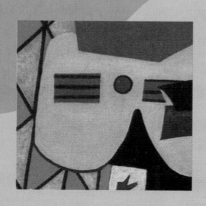

Three Musicians (1921) by Pablo Picasso. Oil on canvas (79" × 87 3/4"). The Museum of Modern Art, New York, Mrs. Simon Guggenheim Fund. Photograph ©1995 The Museum of Modern Art, New York. ©1995 The estate of Pablo Picasso/Artists Rights Society (ARS), NY.

Three Musicians by Pablo Picasso

Like Wang Yani, Spanish artist Pablo Picasso showed unusual
artistic skill at an early age. By the time he was 19 years old, Picasso
was a well-known artist in Paris, where he lived for most of his life.
Picasso's art sometimes shows his sense of humor.
Look carefully for something humorous in *Three Musicians*.

A Girl with the Write Stuff

U·S· kids

Scholarship Racer Blooms at the Fitness Farm

While other kids are reading books, Bonnie-Alise Leggat is writing them. Not only is she writing, but she's also winning awards. At age seven, she won first place in a statewide writing competition.

Alise wanted to enter that competition again, but the next year it was cancelled. While looking for other contests to enter, Alise read about Landmark Editions.

Every year, a publishing company called Landmark Editions holds a writing contest for children. The young writers must write and illustrate their own books. If they win, their books get published.

Alise and several classmates looked at all the other Landmark books written by kids.

"We figured there had to be something the same in all the books," said Alise. "We found that every book had one main character. Every character had to have a problem by the second page. Every book had something in it that kids that age would not normally know."

Soon the students started writing their own books. "I wanted to do something that a girl wouldn't normally do," said Alise. "I wanted it to be something different, original, and boyish. I came up with Amy and couldn't stop writing about her."

In Alise's story, a character named Amy wants to play football. But Amy's mother wants her to be a ballerina. When Amy gets injured in football, her mother finally gets her wish. Some funny situations arise when Amy tries to dance.

Alise was one of 7,000 students who sent stories to Landmark. She was surprised and delighted when she won first place in her age group. Landmark paid for Alise and her mother to visit their offices in Kansas City. They stayed a week. Alise worked on her book, with help from her editor and art director.

"I worked eight and nine hours a day. It wasn't all fun and games. My mom sat in and said, 'Keep going, Alise.'"

When Alise went home, she worked on the illustrations for three more months. Last October the book was finally published. Alise receives royalties (a small amount of money) for books that are sold. She is also paid to speak to schools about her experience.

"My advice to other kids," says Alise, "is to keep on writing. It will pay off some day."

Bonnie-Alise Leggat proudly displays a copy of her book.

PHOTO BY ALAN WOHLLEBEN

Teachers' Choice
Notable
Trade Book
in Social Studies

PUEBLO STORYTELLER

BY DIANE HOYT-GOLDSMITH
PHOTOGRAPHS BY LAWRENCE MIGDALE

April lives with her grandparents in the Cochiti Pueblo[1] near Santa Fe, New Mexico. Although many of the Cochiti people work or go to school outside the pueblo, they still follow the ways of their ancestors in their crafts and celebrations. The older family members pass these traditions on to the younger generation, just as they have for years.

---

[1] *Pueblo* means "village" or "town."

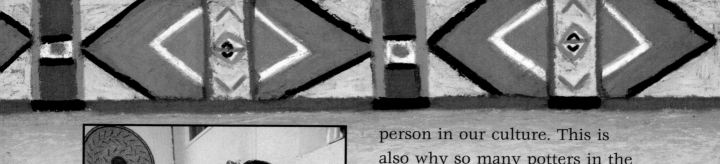

 April's grandfather kneads the fine sand into the clay indoors, where the wind will not blow it away.

Since the early days of pueblo life, our people have learned about the past by listening to storytellers. Until now, we have never had a written language, so many of our stories cannot be found in books. This is why the storyteller is such an important person in our culture. This is also why so many potters in the Cochiti Pueblo make clay figures of the storyteller.

When my grandmother makes a Storyteller, she always thinks about her own grand-father. When she was a young girl, she enjoyed many happy hours in his company. In those days, they didn't have a televi-sion or a gas heater. She would sit on her grandfather's lap near a little fireplace in the corner of the room and listen to him tell stories about his life.

Working on the clay figure, my grandmother creates a face that looks like her grandfather's. She gives him the traditional hairstyle of a pueblo man from the old days. She models the clay to show his long hair pulled back in a loop behind his head with a colorful band to hold it in place.

My grandmother makes arms and legs from smaller cylinders.

She attaches these to the body with bits of moistened clay. Then she models boots or moccasins from the clay.

She always makes his face look very kind. He sits with his mouth open, as if he were singing a song or telling a story. His eyes are closed as he thinks in the backward way, remembering the past.

Each potter who makes a Storyteller figure works in a different style. Some Storytellers are large and some are small. Many potters create the figure of a woman, remembering a favorite aunt or grandmother. Others, like my grandmother, design a figure that reminds them of their grandfather.

 April's grandmother shows her how to join the edges of the slab with a little water to form a cylinder.

A Storyteller is left to dry in the corner of the kitchen. On the shelf above the clay figure, you can see a ladle made from a gourd.

When the Storyteller is complete, my grandmother makes many tiny figures out of the clay. These are shaped like little pueblo children and she attaches them, one by one, to the Storyteller figure. She crowds them all onto his lap, so they can listen carefully to his tales, just as she did so long ago.

My grandmother adds as many children as she can fit. She tells me that on every Storyteller she makes, there is one child

who looks just like me! This makes me feel very special.

After all the modeling is finished, the pottery is left to dry. This takes many days.

When the pottery is hard and dry, it is my grandfather's turn to work on it. He rubs the surfaces of the pottery with sandpaper until they are smooth enough to paint. My grandfather tells me he likes to be in a happy, patient mood when he is sanding the pottery. The work must be done carefully. It cannot be rushed.

Sometimes the pottery will break or crack before it is finished. Instead of throwing the ruined pottery away in the garbage, the pueblo potters give the clay back to the earth where it came from. My grandfather often takes a broken pot down to the river and throws it in the water. Sometimes he will take the broken pieces back up into the hills near the pueblo.

 April's grandmother makes the figure of a little child. Then she attaches the child to the body of the Storyteller with bits of moistened clay.

After the pieces are sanded, my grandmother covers them with a thin layer of white clay that has been mixed with water, called slip *(SLIP)*. When the slip dries, it gives the pottery a clean, white surface that can be polished and painted.

To get a shiny surface, my grandmother polishes her pots with special stones. These polishing stones are very important to the pueblo potters. Each one gives a different patina or shine. Polishing stones are treasured, and the good ones are passed down from one generation to the next.

My grandmother likes to paint her pottery in a very quiet place. She needs to concentrate so that the lines she draws will be straight and the shapes that she makes will be beautiful.

For the red color, my grandmother uses a clay that is mixed with water. For the black, she uses guaco *(GWA-koh)*, an inky liquid made by boiling down a wild plant that grows in the fields near our house. It is called Rocky Mountain beeweed. This same plant is something we pick in the spring and eat as one of our vegetables.

After my grandmother finishes painting the pottery, it is time for the firing. This is the final step. Firing the pottery makes the clay very strong so it will last for a long time.

My grandparents work together to build a kiln *(KILN)* outside in the yard. They go out to the pasture and collect many pieces of dried cow manure. We call these "cow pies" because they are so flat and round. My grandparents lay some wood under a metal grate and put the pottery on top of it. They arrange the cow pies in a single layer on the top and sides of the pottery.

The cow pies are mostly made of grass, and they burn easily. They make the fire all around the

 April's grandmother rubs the bottom of a pot with a polishing stone that came to her from her mother. On her work table are bowls of red clay mixed with water and guaco.

pottery burn evenly at a very high temperature. We burn cow pies instead of wood because they do not contain pitch or sap that could stain the beautifully painted surfaces of the pottery.

After the fire is lit, we can only watch and wait. When the fire burns out and the pottery cools, my grandmother rakes the ashes away. We carefully remove the pottery and clean off any small bits of grit or ash. "Now the work is finished," my grandfather tells me proudly. "It is perfect and beautiful, made by our own hands from the earth's elements of fire, water, and clay."

Making the Cochiti Drum

Sometimes my grandmother likes to make a clay figure that looks like a man playing the Cochiti drum. The Cochiti people are famous for the drums they make. My own uncle is a drum maker.

My uncle makes drums of every size. He makes the tiny ones for my grandmother's clay figures. He also makes small drums for children, large drums for trading, and special ceremonial drums for our pueblo dances.

My uncle begins with the trunk of a large aspen or cottonwood tree. He saws it into drum-size lengths. Then he scrapes the bark off with a drawknife. Using hot coals, he carefully burns a hole down the middle of the log to make it hollow. Then he uses a handmade chisel to cut away more wood. When this is done, he has completed the drum frame.

April's uncle uses a drawknife to remove the bark from an alder log. He reaches out, cuts into the bark, and then pulls the knife back toward his body.

To make the head of the drum, my uncle uses a large piece of cowhide. The hide has been soaked in water so it is soft and easy to bend. He cuts two round pieces that fit over the top and bottom of the drum frame. Then, with a long, thin cord cut from the hide, he sews them together in a zigzag pattern.

My uncle tightens the cords, one by one, until the drum-heads are firm. As the wet hide dries, the drumheads get tighter and tighter.

Every drum my uncle makes has its own special sound, its own voice. Because the drums are made by hand, each one makes a different sound. When they are finished, my uncle plays them. Some are loud and some are soft. Some are high and some are low. Some rumble like thunder and others rat-tat-tat like dry leaves in the wind.

When we play the drums in a pueblo ceremony, the voices of the drums mix with the voices of the singers to make music for the dancers.

My uncle learned to make drums by watching his foster father work. He is proud to know the way to make an instrument with a beautiful, strong voice. He likes to work with his hands and he shares what he knows with me.

Painting the drum is the very last step. April's uncle shows her how the painted designs make each drum special. On this drum, the black shapes represent the sky and the white shapes are clouds.

The Buffalo Dance

In the pueblos along the Rio Grande, children learn to dance almost as soon as they learn to walk. We all have drums in our homes that we play. Our parents and grandparents sing to us and show us the way to move. Dances are performed at our Pueblo Feast Day and for special ceremonies. Everyone takes part. On these occasions, we gather in the plaza. This large open space is the center of pueblo life.

As the singers begin to chant their songs in our ancient Indian language, the drums begin to sound. The singer is the storyteller and the voice of the drum is his music.

The dancers move in patterns passed down from one generation to the next. The dances we do today are very much like the dances our ancestors performed hundreds of years ago.

The Buffalo Dance is one of these. It began a long time ago, when there were large herds of buffalo on the western Plains. Our ancestors crossed the mountains to the north to hunt the buffalo. They often traded the hides to other Indians on the Plains. They always carried the meat back to the pueblo to help their people survive the long winter months.

Sometimes we dance to have a successful hunt or to bring rains to our dry lands. Sometimes we dance to have a fruitful harvest or to cure the sick. And sometimes we dance just for fun!

April joins two Tewa boys from San Juan Pueblo for the Buffalo Dance. They take small steps as they move to the drumbeats. The boys, dressed in buffalo headdresses, carry a lightning bolt in one hand and a gourd rattle in the other. They wear embroidered kilts.

Pueblo Storyteller

For me there is a special time at the end of every day. After the work is finished and I am ready to go to bed, my grandmother and grandfather tell me stories from the past. Sometimes they tell about the legends of the pueblo people. Other times they tell about things that happened in their own lives.

My grandmother likes to tell about when she was a girl. She lived in a Tewa *(TAY-wah)* pueblo to the north called San Juan. She remembers autumn, a time when her whole family worked together to harvest and husk the corn crop. The corn came in many colors—red and orange, yellow and white, blue and purple, and even the deepest black.

Her family would sit in the shade of a ramada *(rah-MAH-dah)* built of cedar branches. Sheltered from the hot sun, the workers would remove the husks from a mountain of colorful corn. All the time they were working, they would laugh at jokes, sing songs, and share stories.

My grandmother tells me there were always lots of children around—her brothers and sisters, their cousins and friends—and they always had fun. My grandfather tells how the boys would use their slingshots to hurl stones at the crows who came too close to the corncobs that were drying in the sun.

As I listen to their stories, I can almost hear the sound of laughter as the children play at their games. I can smell the bread baking as the women prepare to feed their families. I can see the mounds of corn, colored like the rainbow, drying in the sun.

Meet
Diane Hoyt-Goldsmith

To write *Pueblo Storyteller*, Diane Hoyt-Goldsmith spent time with Pueblo Indians in New Mexico, watching and learning about their traditional way of life. While she was there she made many friends who helped with the book. One friend taught her about Pueblo pottery. Others showed her how to make a drum and perform a traditional dance. Her experience with the Pueblo Indians resulted in a fascinating book, and gave her memories she will never forget.

Diane Hoyt-Goldsmith fell in love with the art and traditions of Native Americans while in college. She began to collect examples of the art of the Pacific Northwest tribes. Little by little her collection of masks, bent wood boxes, and totem poles from different tribal groups grew.

Today she has a large collection of Native American art and is considered an expert on the subject. She believes that it is important to keep Native American art and traditions alive, and she helps do this by sharing her knowledge in her books.

RESPONSE CORNER

MEDIA BLITZ

The pueblo storyteller has an important job to do. He or she passes on the history of the tribe. Work in a group to make a chart comparing and contrasting three ways of passing on information: by speaking, in print (books, magazines, newspapers), and on television. When you present your chart to your classmates, tell which way you think works best.

MAIL-ORDER TREASURES

April's family makes many beautiful objects in ways handed down from older to younger generations. Write and illustrate a mail-order catalog that they could send to interested buyers. In your descriptions of the items, explain their traditional use.

SHOW AND TELL

Make your own storyteller out of clay, or bring to class examples of ways your own family passes along information from generation to generation. Examples might include a photo album, old letters, or stories of family happenings. Share the information with your classmates.

WHAT DO YOU THINK?

- What cultural traditions are kept alive by the people in April's family?

- Which of the skills described in the selection would you like to have? Why?

- Do you think the people of the Cochiti Pueblo will be doing many of the same things one hundred years from now? Why or why not?

GARY SOTO

THE SKIRT

illustrated by Eric Velasquez

Award-Winning
Author

Miata always seems to be losing things! She is proud of her mother's skirt, which she is to wear in a dance performance. She takes it to school but soon discovers that she has left it on the school bus. Since she doesn't want to tell her mother, she and her friend Ana sneak into the schoolyard to find it. They manage to squeeze into the bus and get the skirt, but their friend Rodolfo almost gets them caught. Finally, they get home with the skirt, and Miata is ready for the dance.

THE SKIRT

BY GARY SOTO

ILLUSTRATED BY JENNIFER BOLTEN

Sunday morning. The family sat down early to *chorizo con huevos*.[1] They ate happily in silence, pinching up their breakfast with ripped pieces of tortilla. The radio in the kitchen was softly playing Mexican songs.

Miata's mother took a sip of her coffee. Then, getting up, she said, "Miata, I have a surprise for you."

Miata looked up. She had a little stain of ketchup in the corner of her mouth. Her mother went to the hall closet and returned with a crinkled bag.

"You have some stuff on your mouth, Miata," Little Joe said. His cheek was flecked with ketchup and the corners of his mouth stained white with milk.

---

[1] *chorizo con huevos* (chō•rē´sō kōn wā´bōs): sausage with eggs

Miata pressed a napkin to her mouth and ignored her brother. She was curious about the bag in her mother's hand.

"Now close your eyes," her mother said. Her smile was bright.

Miata closed her eyes. Maybe it was a new jacket, she thought. Maybe it was a Nintendo. Maybe it was a pair of new shoes. Her mother had been promising her new shoes.

When her mother patted her hand, she opened her eyes. Her mother was holding up a skirt. A beautiful new *folklórico*[2] skirt. The shiny lace rippled in the light. It smelled new. It was still stiff from not being worn.

"It's pretty, *mi'ja*,[3]" her father remarked. "You'll be the prettiest girl at the dance."

Miata forced a smile. "But I have a skirt, Mom."

"That old thing?" her mother said. "Stand up."

Her mother pressed the skirt to her waist. "It's a little long, but you can wear it just for today."

"It looks neat," Little Joe said. He now had ketchup on his elbows.

"Thanks, Mom," Miata said. She hugged her mother and went to her bedroom.

---

[2] *folklórico* (fōlk•lō´rē•kō): a traditional folk art style

[3] *mi'ja* (mē´hä): my daughter

As Miata dressed for church she thought of all the trouble she went through to rescue her old skirt: slipping through the locked gate, rolling off the hood of the bus, getting scraped up. She remembered how they hid behind the oil barrel, and how Rodolfo just slurped on his soda while they were so scared. *Qué* bother! What a waste of time.

But it *is* pretty, she thought. She admired the new skirt that was fanned out on the bed. She liked the bright new colors and its fresh smell. She liked the rustle that sounded like walking through knee-high weeds. She pictured herself twirling in the middle of her friends.

She felt sorry for her old skirt. It was like a flower dead on its stem. She folded it carefully and put it in her bottom drawer. She brushed her hair and then stopped. She felt sad for her old skirt. It had belonged to her mother when she was a little girl.

She took it out of the bottom drawer. Next to the new skirt it looked faded as an old calendar. A blue stain darkened the hem. A piece of red lace was loose and falling off. The button was cracked. The skirt was smudged from time and wear.

"I'm going to take you both," she said. "I won't play favorites."

She pushed both of the skirts into her backpack. She finished combing her hair and put on her *milagro*[4] earrings.

---

[4] *milagro* (mē•lä´grō): a traditional heart design

"*Andale*,[5]" her mother called from the living room. "We're going to be late."

Miata picked up her backpack and gave it a soft pat. "We're going dancing," she said to the skirts.

Miata's father was outside warming up their car. Little Joe was stomping on an empty soda can. He was trying to hook it onto the bottom of his shoe. His father called Little Joe to get in the car. Miata and her mother came hurrying down the steps. A bloom of perfume and beauty trailed behind them.

Miata went to church with her family. The priest talked and talked, but Miata yawned only three times. Tears of sleepiness came to her eyes. Her mother seemed happy. She kept looking down at Miata and Little Joe.

After church the dancers raced to the rectory, where they changed and practiced.

"Do your best," Mrs. Carranza, the dance teacher, said. "And remember to smile."

"Here we go," Miata said to Ana.

The six girls marched out to the courtyard. Their faces were bright. Their hair was coiled into buns. They stood in a circle with their hands on their hips. As the cassette music played, Miata spun around the courtyard. The grown-ups and kids all ate donuts and watched.

---

[5] *Andale* (än´dä•lā): hurry up

Miata twirled like a pinwheel, the old skirt showing under the new skirt. Miata was wearing both of them. Her mother recognized the old skirt and clapped and smiled proudly at her daughter. And everyone, even the babies, clapped for the spinning colors of Mexico.

Meet the Author

GARY SOTO

Gary Soto is well known for writing stories and poems that reflect his cultural background and personal experiences. Here, interviewer Ilene Cooper asks him how he got started.

Cooper: Was it easy to start your writing career?

Soto: No, becoming a writer was hard for me. I was not a good student. The people around me were not readers.

Cooper: But things turned out fine for you?

Soto: Yes, I went to college and read some poetry, and I said, "Wow, I want to do that." Then I found some teachers who helped me. Later I wrote a book of short stories for young people called *Baseball in April*. Once it was published, it met with a really good response.

Cooper: What do you tell young people who want to become writers?

Soto: Value your experiences. They can all become a part of your storytelling. Find a good teacher to help you—and read. Anyone who wants to become a writer should read as much as possible!

by Alexis De Veaux
illustrated by Tom Feelings

I am the creativity

Award-Winning
Illustrator

I am the dance step
of the paintbrush singing
I am the sculpture
of the song
the flame breath
of words
giving new life to paper
yes, I am the creativity
that never dies
I am the creativity
keeping my people
alive

MAKE A PRESENTATION

SHOW ME

Miata treasured her mother's skirt. With the permission of the owner, bring to class an object or an article of clothing that is important to you for personal or cultural reasons. Explain why it is important in your life or the owner's.

RESPONSE

WRITE A LETTER

DEAR DAUGHTER

Imagine that you are Miata's mother. Write a letter to Miata about the performance. Tell your feelings about Miata's dancing and her decision to wear your old skirt under the new one. You may want to use the idea from the poem "I Am the Creativity" that Miata's dance is "keeping her people alive."

CREATE A FLYER

READ ALL ABOUT IT!

With a group, make a flyer advertising the performance by Miata and her friends. Show symbols of Mexico and pictures of Mexican dance costumes. Be sure to give the date, time, and place. Then post the flyer in your classroom.

CORNER

WHAT DO YOU THINK?

- Why wasn't Miata thrilled when she first saw her mother's gift?

- What did you enjoy about the story and the poem?

- Do you think Miata's solution was a good one? Why or why not?

575

Alvin Ailey

By Andrea Davis Pinkney
Illustrated by Brian Pinkney

ALVIN AILEY became one of the world's most famous dancers. He also formed one of the first integrated dance companies—The Alvin Ailey Dance Theater—which has performed internationally before more than 15 million people. As a boy, Ailey loved clapping his hands and moving to the gospel music at the True Vine Baptist Church of Navasota, Texas. Then when he was eighteen, he and his mother moved to Los Angeles, where he heard a different kind of music—jazz and blues.

1949–1953
Lester Horton's Dance School

More than anything, Alvin wanted to study dance. But when Alvin arrived in Los Angeles not everyone could take dance lessons. In 1949 not many dance schools accepted black students. And almost none taught the fluid moves that Alvin liked so much—almost none but the Lester Horton Dance Theater School, a modern dance school that welcomed students of all races.

Lester's door was open to anyone serious about learning to dance. And, at age eighteen, Alvin Ailey was serious, especially when he saw how Lester's dancers moved. One student, Carmen de Lavallade, danced with a butterfly's grace. Another, James Truitte, made modern dance look easy. But Lester worked his students hard. Sometimes they danced all day.

After hours in the studio, droplets of sweat dotted Alvin's forehead. He tingled inside, ready to try Lester's steps once more. At first, Alvin kept time to Lester's beat and followed Lester's moves. Then Alvin's own rhythm took over, and he started creating his own steps. Alvin's tempo worked from his belly to his elbows, then oozed through his thighs and feet.

"What is Alvin *doing*?" one student asked.

"Whatever he's doing, he's sure doing it fine," two dancers agreed.

Some tried to follow Alvin's moves, but even Alvin didn't know which way his body would reel him next.

Alvin's steps flowed from one to another. His loops and spins just came to him, the way daydreams do.

Alvin danced at Lester Horton's school almost every day. He taught the other students his special moves.

In 1950, Alvin joined Lester Horton's dance company. Soon Alvin performed his own choreography for small audiences who gathered at Lester's studio. Alvin's dances told stories. He flung his arms and shim-shammed his middle to express jubilation. His dips and slides could even show anger and pain. Modern dance let Alvin's imagination whirl.

All the while, Lester watched Alvin grow into a strong dancer and choreographer. Lester told Alvin to study and learn as much as he could about dance. He encouraged Alvin to use his memories and his African-American heritage to make dances that were unforgettable.

1958–1960
Blues Suite–Revelations

Alvin's satchel hung heavy on his shoulder. His shoes rapped a beat on the sidewalk while taxicabs honked their horns. He was glad to be in New York City, where he came to learn ballet from Karel Shook and modern dance techniques from Martha Graham, two of the best teachers in the world.

Alvin took dance classes all over town, and he met dancers who showed him moves he'd never seen before. So many dancers were black. Like Alvin, their dreams soared higher than New York's tallest skyscrapers.

Alvin gathered some of the dancers he'd seen in classes around the city. He chose the men and women who had just the right moves to dance his choreography. Alvin told them he wanted to start a modern dance company that would dance to blues and gospel music—the heritage of African-American people. Nine dancers believed in Alvin's idea. This was the beginning of the Alvin Ailey American Dance Theater.

On March 30, 1958, on an old wooden stage at the 92nd Street Y, Alvin and his friends premiered with *Blues Suite*, dances set in a honky-tonk dance hall. Stage lights cast moody shadows against the glimmer of each dancer's skin. The women flaunted red-hot dresses with shoes and stockings to match; the men wore black hats slouched low on their heads. They danced to the swanky-swank of a jazz rhapsody.

Alvin's choreography depicted the blues, that weepy sadness all folks feel now and then. *Blues Suite* stirred every soul in the room.

Alvin was on his way to making it big. Word spread quickly about him and his dancers. Newspapers hailed Alvin. Radio stations announced his debut.

An even bigger thrill came when the 92nd Street Y asked Alvin to perform again. He knew they hardly ever invited dance companies to come back. Alvin was eager to show off his next work.

On January 31, 1960, gospel harmonies filled the concert hall at the 92nd Street Y.

Rock-rock-rock
Rocka-my-soul
Ohhh, rocka-my-soul

Alvin clapped in time to the music, the same way he did when he was a boy. But now, Alvin rejoiced onstage in *Revelations*, a suite of dances he created to celebrate the traditions of True Vine Baptist Church in Navasota, Texas.

The audience swayed in their seats as Alvin and his company gloried in their dance. High-stepping ladies appeared onstage sweeping their skirts. They danced with grace and haughty attitudes. Alvin and the other men jumped lively to the rhythm, strutting and dipping in sassy revelry.

Revelations honored the heart and the dignity of black people while showing that hope and joy are for everyone. With his sleek moves, Alvin shared his experiences and his dreams in a way no dancer had ever done.

When *Revelations* ended, the audience went wild with applause. They stomped and shouted. "More!" they yelled. "*More!*"

Taking a bow, Alvin let out a breath. He raised his eyes toward heaven, satisfied and proud.

Andrea Davis Pinkney and Brian Pinkney

AUTHOR AND ILLUSTRATOR

When authors and illustrators tell stories about real people, they have to research their subjects. Interviewer Ilene Cooper asked Andrea Davis Pinkney and her husband, illustrator Brian Pinkney, about the work they did to prepare for creating *Alvin Ailey*.

Cooper: Most authors and illustrators do a good deal of research for biographies, but I understand that for this book you two went so far as to take dancing lessons.

Davis Pinkney: That's right. Brian and I studied the Katherine Dunham dance technique, which is what Alvin Ailey's choreography is based on. We took the classes with one of the original members of Alvin Ailey's Dance Theater.

Cooper: In what ways did learning to dance help you?

Davis Pinkney: In Ailey's technique, the hands and feet are positioned in a certain way. We wanted to know how that felt, so there would be no mistakes in either the book's text or the art.

Pinkney: I bought videos of Alvin Ailey dancing. I would watch those, stopping and starting the VCR, so my sketches could capture his movements. I also learned the choreography for several of the dances and then used myself as a model for the pictures of Ailey.

Response Corner

WRITE AN AD

Dancers Wanted

How might Alvin Ailey have found out about the Lester Horton Dance Theater School? One way is through an advertisement in a Los Angeles newspaper. Write an ad for the Lester Horton Dance Theater School. To attract artists like Alvin Ailey, make sure the ad tells about things that interest dancers.

CREATE A DANCE

Acting Up?

The movements in Ailey's dances often tell stories. Choose a folktale or another story that classmates might know, and create dance steps and gestures to go along with it. Perform the dance for your classmates.

World Tour

The American Dance Theater performs all over the world. Plan a schedule for their next world tour. Locate the world's major cities on a map, and choose those that they can reach on a three-month tour. List the cities, and beside each one, write the number of days the dancers should stay. Include other information you think is important as well.

What Do You Think?

- What important decisions did Alvin Ailey make that helped him succeed as a dancer?
- What kind of performing art would you like to participate in? Why?
- How do you think Alvin Ailey's life might be different if he were starting out as a dancer today?

THEME
WRAP-UP

The people in the selections in this theme expressed themselves through the arts. What is one quality each of these people seemed to have?

Suppose that Wang Yani, Bonnie-Alise Leggat, April, and Miata got together and formed their own arts club. How could they combine their talents to create an exciting presentation for their friends and families?

ACTIVITY CORNER

Which of the arts interests you most? Find a picture of a painting or sculpture you really enjoy, a song or poem that has special meaning for you, or a video of a dance that you enjoy. Share your findings with classmates. If possible, tell about the artist. Explain why you like the piece you have chosen.

Glossary

WHAT IS A GLOSSARY?

A glossary is like a small dictionary. It is a list of words used in the book with their pronunciations, meanings, and other useful information. Glossaries appear at the end of many nonfiction books and textbooks to explain how to pronounce a word and what the word means. Being familiar with the words in a book will help you understand what you are reading.

Using the

Like a dictionary, this glossary lists words in alphabetical order. To find a word, look it up by its first letter or letters.

To save time, use the **guide words** at the top of each page. These show you the first and last words on the page. Look at the guide words to see if your word falls between them alphabetically.

Here is an example of a glossary entry.

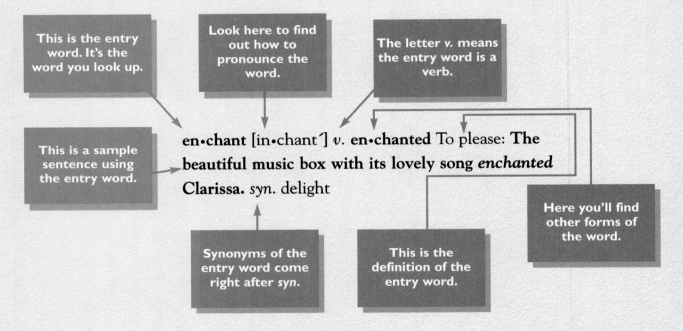

This is the entry word. It's the word you look up.

Look here to find out how to pronounce the word.

The letter *v.* means the entry word is a verb.

This is a sample sentence using the entry word.

en·chant [in·chant´] *v.* **en·chanted** To please: **The beautiful music box with its lovely song** *enchanted* **Clarissa.** *syn.* delight

Synonyms of the entry word come right after *syn.*

This is the definition of the entry word.

Here you'll find other forms of the word.

ETYMOLOGY

Etymology is the study or history of how words are developed. Words often have interesting backgrounds that can help you remember what they mean. Look in the margins of the glossary to find the etymologies of certain words.

Here is an example of an etymology:

pollen Both the words *pollen* and *powder* come from the Latin word *pulvis,* which means "dust."

Glossary

PRONUNCIATION

The pronunciation in brackets is a respelling that shows how the word is pronounced.

The **pronunciation key** explains what the symbols in a respelling mean. A shortened pronunciation key appears on every other page of the glossary.

- separates words into syllables
- ´ indicates light stress on a syllable
- ´ indicates heavier stress on a syllable

PRONUNCIATION KEY*

a	add, map	m	move, seem	u	up, done
ā	ace, rate	n	nice, tin	û(r)	burn, term
â(r)	care, air	ng	ring, song	yo͞o	fuse, few
ä	palm, father	o	odd, hot	v	vain, eve
b	bat, rub	ō	open, so	w	win, away
ch	check, catch	ô	order, jaw	y	yet, yearn
d	dog, rod	oi	oil, boy	z	zest, muse
e	end, pet	ou	pout, now	zh	vision, pleasure
ē	equal, tree	o͝o	took, full	ə	the schwa, an
f	fit, half	o͞o	pool, food		unstressed vowel
g	go, log	p	pit, stop		representing the
h	hope, hate	r	run, poor		sound spelled
i	it, give	s	see, pass		a in *above*
ī	ice, write	sh	sure, rush		e in *sicken*
j	joy, ledge	t	talk, sit		i in *possible*
k	cool, take	th	thin, both		o in *melon*
l	look, rule	t͟h	this, bathe		u in *circus*

Abbreviations: *adj.* adjective, *adv.* adverb, *conj.* conjunction, *interj.* interjection, *n.* noun, *prep.* preposition, *pron.* pronoun, *syn.* synonym, *v.* verb.

*The Pronunciation Key, adapted entries, and the Short Key that appear on the following pages are reprinted from *HBJ School Dictionary* Copyright © 1990 by Harcourt Brace & Company. Reprinted by permission of Harcourt Brace & Company.

acrobats

applause

bridle   This word comes from Old English and is related to the word *braid*, because most bridles long ago were braided to make them stronger. Both words mean "to move or pull."

A

a·ban·don [ə·ban´dən] *v.* **a·ban·doned** To leave behind: **When the car ran out of gas, they** *abandoned* **it and started walking.**

ac·ro·bat [ak´rə·bat´] *n.* **ac·ro·bats** A person who does stunts, often on a trapeze.

a·dapt [ə·dapt´] *v.* To change to fit a new situation: **It was hard for Tran to** *adapt* **to the new school.**

a·gent [ā´jənt] *n.* Someone who has the power to do business for a person or group.

ap·peal [ə·pēl´] *v.* To interest or attract: **Lilly changed the channel because the television show didn't** *appeal* **to her.**

ap·plause [ə·plôz´] *n.* Clapping of hands.

ar·ti·fi·cial [är´tə·fish´əl] *adj.* Not natural; made by people.

as·sure [ə·shŏŏr´] *v.* **as·sured** To make a person sure or certain of something: **Carlos** *assured* **me there was no homework.**

au·di·tion [ô·dish´ən] *v.* To try out for a part: **Julio is going to** *audition* **for the lead role.**

av·a·lanche [av´ə·lanch´] *n.* **av·a·lanch·es** The sliding of a lot of snow, ice, or rock down a hillside.

B

board·ing·house [bôr´ding·hous´] *n.* A house where people pay to get meals and a room to sleep in.

breed [brēd] *n.* **breeds** One special kind of an animal.

bri·dle [brīd´(ə)l] *n.* Leather straps put over the face and mouth of a horse to control it.

C

cau·tious·ly [kô´shəs·lē] *adv.* In a careful way. *syn.* carefully

cen·tu·ry [sen´chə·rē] *n.* A one-hundred-year period that goes from a year ending in 00 to a year ending in 99.

chain re·ac·tion [chān rē·ak´shən] *n.* **chain re·ac·tions** Something that causes another thing that then causes another thing.

chem·i·cal [kem´i·kəl] *n.* **chem·i·cals** Materials used in or made by science.

chis·el [chiz´(ə)l] *n.* A hand tool with a sharp blade that is hit with a hammer to cut or shape wood.

cho·re·og·ra·phy [kôr´ē·og´rə·fē] *n.* A planned set of dance moves.

cit·i·zen·ship [sit´ə·zən·ship´] *n.* Being a member of a country: **Jo's mother passed the test required to get her American *citizenship*.**

coil [koil] *v.* **coiled** To twist into a spiral shape.

com·pan·ion [kəm·pan´yən] *n.* A person or animal that keeps someone company.

com·pose [kəm·pōz´] *v.* **com·posed** To write or make: **Jenny *composed* a song for her mother's birthday.**

con·fi·dent·ly [kon´fə·dənt·lē] *adv.* In a way that shows a person is sure about what he or she is doing.

con·quer [kong´kər] *v.* To win control of by force: **Early explorers tried to *conquer* nature.**

con·scious [kon´shəs] *adj.* Able to hear, see, or feel; awake: **When she became *conscious*, she told the doctor how she had hurt her head.**

con·stant·ly [kon´stənt·lē] *adv.* Without stopping.

con·tent [kən·tent´] *adj.* Happy and satisfied: **Sitting by the quiet pond on a sunny day, Ryan felt *content*.**

con·vince [kən·vins´] *v.* **con·vinced** To make someone believe: **Billy *convinced* me his story was true.**

cul·ture [kul´chər] *n.* The way of life of a people.

cur·rent [kûr´ənt] *n.* The flow of water.

cus·tom [kus´təm] *n.* Something the members of a group do regularly.

cy·cle [sī´kəl] *n.* A set of events that keeps happening over and over.

cy·lin·der [sil´in·dər] *n.* **cy·lin·ders** A shape like a soup can.

chisel

coil

a	add	o͝o	took
ā	ace	o͞o	pool
â	care	u	up
ä	palm	û	burn
e	end	yo͞o	fuse
ē	equal	oi	oil
i	it	ou	pout
ī	ice	ng	ring
o	odd	th	thin
ō	open	t͟h	this
ô	order	zh	vision

ə = {
a in *above*
e in *sicken*
i in *possible*
o in *melon*
u in *circus*
}

debut English takes this word from French, where it means "beginning." It probably started as a sports word describing where players started a game "from a certain point" or *de but.*

disguise

D

de·but [dā·byŏŏ´ or dā´ byŏŏ´] *n.* The first time someone performs in public.

del·i·cate [del´ə·kit] *adj.* Easy to break: **The salesperson would not let us touch the *delicate* glass.**

de·scen·dant [di·sen´dənt] *n.* A person born later into a family or group.

de·spair [di·spâr´] *n.* The feeling that all hope is lost.

de·ter·mi·na·tion [di·tûr´mə·nā´shən] *n.* A strong sense of what you want to do; purpose and courage.

de·vice [di·vīs´] *n.* An instrument or tool.

dig·ni·ty [dig´nə·tē] *n.* Honor or worth; pride and self-respect: **We respect the *dignity* of all people.**

dis·crim·i·na·tion [dis·krim´ə·nā´shən] *n.* Prejudice in actions or attitude: **All kinds of *discrimination* are illegal at work.**

dis·grace [dis·grās´] *v.* **dis·graced** To bring shame; to embarrass.

dis·guise [dis·gīz´] *v.* **dis·guis·ing** To change the way you look: **Jeremy put on glasses and a fake nose, *disguising* himself.**

dis·rupt [dis·rupt´] *v.* **dis·rupt·ed** To disturb or put something out of order: **When the hamster escaped, the math lesson was *disrupted.***

dis·tin·guished [dis·ting´gwisht] *adj.* Famous or well-respected: **The *distinguished* guests sat onstage.**

dis·trict [dis´trikt] *n.* A division of a town or other area.

dread [dred] *v.* **dread·ed** To wait with fear: **Jan *dreaded* going to the dentist.**

E

ef·fect [i·fekt´] *n.* **ef·fects** A special result: **The photographer adjusted the lights to get the right *effects.***

e·merge [i·mûrj´] *v.* **e·merg·es** To come out into the open: **The mouse *emerges* from its hole after the cat leaves.**

em·i·grant [em´ə·grənt] *n.* **em·i·grants** A person who leaves a country to move to another.

en·a·ble [in·ā′bəl] *v.* **en·a·bles** To give the ability to do something: **A telephone** *enables* **people to talk over long distances.**

en·chant [in·chant′] *v.* **en·chant·ed** To please: **The beautiful music box** *enchanted* **Clarissa.** *syn.* delight

en·dan·gered [in·dān′jərd] *adj.* In danger of dying out.

en·gi·neer·ing [en′jə·nir′ing] *n.* Planning and building roads, bridges, buildings, and machines.

e·ra [ir′ə or ē′rə] *n.* A period in history.

ex·hi·bi·tion [ek′sə·bish′ən] *n.* A public show.

ex·pres·sion [ik·spresh′ən] *n.* A look on the face that shows how someone feels.

F

fron·tier [frun·tir′] *n.* A new or unknown land or area, with few people.

G

gal·lop [gal′əp] *n.* The fastest way a horse runs.

gen·er·a·tion [je′nə·rā′shən] *n.* **gen·er·a·tions** All the people born and living at about the same time: **Three** *generations* **of my family have lived in this house.**

grant [grant] *n.* **grants** Something that is given for a special reason, often by the government: **Professor Chan received two $25,000** *grants* **to continue his work.**

H

hab·i·tat [hab′ə·tat′] *n.* A place where an animal lives.

haze [hāz] *n.* A cloud of small drops of water or dust particles in the air, like a fog.

herb [(h)ûrb] *n.* **herbs** Plants used for medicine.

her·i·tage [her′ə·tij] *n.* Beliefs or ways of doing things handed down for many years by a group of people.

exhibition

herb

a	add	o͝o	took
ā	ace	o͞o	pool
â	care	u	up
ä	palm	û	burn
e	end	yo͞o	fuse
ē	equal	oi	oil
i	it	ou	pout
ī	ice	ng	ring
o	odd	th	thin
ō	open	t͟h	this
ô	order	zh	vision

ə = {
  a in *above*
  e in *sicken*
  i in *possible*
  o in *melon*
  u in *circus*
}

jubilation

kiln

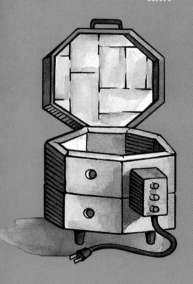

her·o·ine [her´ō·in] *n.* The main female character.

hos·til·i·ty [hos·til´ə·tē] *n.* Hate or dislike.

hu·mil·i·a·tion [hyoo·mil´ē·ā´shən] *n.* **hu·mil·i·a·tions** Something that makes a person feel embarrassed.

I

ig·nore [ig·nôr´] *v.* **ig·nored** To pay no attention to. *syn.* overlook

im·pa·tient [im·pā´shənt] *adj.* Annoyed because things are taking too long.

im·pres·sion [im·presh´ən] *n.* **im·pres·sions** A feeling or image fixed in a person's mind: **I saw the animal for only a moment, but I had *impressions* of teeth and big eyes.**

in·dif·fer·ent [in·dif´rənt or in·dif´ər·ənt] *adj.* Not caring: **Sam was *indifferent* about who won the ball game.**

in·gre·di·ent [in·grē´dē·ənt] *n.* **in·gre·di·ents** One of the items put into a mixture.

in·spi·ra·tion [in´spə·rā´shən] *n.* A good idea that comes to someone.

in·stall [in·stôl´] *v.* **in·stalled** To attach in position: **When the weather got warm, Dad *installed* a window air conditioner.**

in·stinct [in´stingkt] *n.* **in·stincts** A natural feeling that causes a living thing to do something: **When animals face an enemy, their *instincts* tell them to run.**

J

ju·bi·la·tion [joo´ bə·lā´shən] *n.* Gladness.

K

kiln [kil(n)] *n.* An oven for hardening things made from clay.

L

leg·end [lej´ənd] *n.* **leg·ends** A story that comes from early times.

M

man·tle [man´təl] *n.* Something that covers: **A *mantle* of ice covered the stream.**

mead·ow [med´ō] *n.* A large area of land where grass grows.

me·chan·i·cal [mə·kan´i·kəl] *adj.* Run by a machine: **The *mechanical* dog could bark and do back flips.**

mes·quite [mes·kēt´] *n.* A thorny bush found in the southwestern United States, Mexico, and Central America.

mil·len·ni·um [mi·len´ē·əm] *n.* One thousand years: **Every century in this *millennium* has brought many changes.**

mim·ic [mim´ik] *v.* To copy closely: **Tommy can *mimic* exactly the way that a duck walks.**

min·i·a·ture [min´(ē)·ə·chər] *adj.* Very small: **Jill's dollhouse even had *miniature* dishes.** *syn.* tiny

mo·not·o·ny [mə·not´ə·nē] *n.* The condition of things always being the same.

N

nec·tar [nek´tər] *n.* A sweet liquid made by flowers.

no·tice·a·ble [nō´tis·ə·bəl] *adj.* Easily seen. *syn.* conspicuous

nour·ish [nûr´ish] *v.* To help to grow by giving food: **Birds gather insects and worms to *nourish* their young.**

O

oc·cu·pa·tion [ok´yə·pā´shən] *n.* A person's job.

o·mit [ō·mit´] *v.* To leave out: **You can *omit* problem two on the math test.**

op·por·tu·ni·ty [op´ər·t(y)oo´nə·tē] *n.* **op·por·tu·ni·ties** A chance to do something.

op·pres·sion [ə·presh´ən] *n.* The act of forcing people to do what you want: **The people fought against the *oppression* of the evil king.**

o·rig·i·nate [ə·rij´ə·nāt´] *v.* **o·rig·i·nat·ed** To make or create: **The ice-cream cone *originated* in Roman times.**

meadow

a	add	o͝o	took
ā	ace	o͞o	pool
â	care	u	up
ä	palm	û	burn
e	end	yo͞o	fuse
ē	equal	oi	oil
i	it	ou	pout
ī	ice	ng	ring
o	odd	th	thin
ō	open	th	this
ô	order	zh	vision

ə = {
a in *above*
e in *sicken*
i in *possible*
o in *melon*
u in *circus*

pollen

potter

ramble In Latin, *ambulare* means "to walk." Later, *re-* was added to mean "walk back." Today, we use the word to mean "to walk around" or "to wind."

or·phan [ôr´fən] *v.* **or·phaned** To deprive of both parents by death: **Several children were left** *orphaned* **after the accident.**

P

pas·ser·by [pas´ər·bī] *n.* **pas·sers·by** A person who goes by.

pa·trol [pə·trōl´] *v.* To go around and check an area.

pe·ti·tion [pə·tish´ən] *n.* **petitions** A paper asking for something, usually signed by many people to show support.

pol·len [pol´ən] *n.* A powder produced by plants.

pot·ter [pot´ər] *n.* **pot·ters** A person who makes pots from clay.

prej·u·dice [prej´ə·dis] *n.* Hatred or dislike for a group, race, or religion: **When Sarah didn't invite any boys to her party, Justin said she was showing** *prejudice.*

prod·i·gy [prod´ə·jē] *n.* **prod·i·gies** A child with amazing talent.

pro·duc·tion [prə·duk´shən] *n.* The process of producing something.

pros·pect [pros´pekt´] *v.* **pros·pect·ing** To search or look for.

pro·té·gée [prō´tə·zhā´] (refers to a female) *n.* A person who is guided by someone older. (The masculine form of this word is *protégé.*)

Q

qual·i·ty [kwol´ə·tē] *n.* How good something is: **Mom says** *quality* **is more important than price.**

R

ram·ble [ram´bəl] *v.* **ram·bles** To go on and on: **The path** *rambles* **through trees and over a hill.**

ran·sack [ran´sak´] *v.* **ran·sacked** To make a mess in search of something: **The thief** *ransacked* **the house looking for valuables.**

re·cov·er·y [ri·kuv´ər·ē] *n.* A return to being well: **Julie's** *recovery* **from the flu took two weeks.**

re·luc·tant [ri·luk´tənt] *adj.* Not willing to do something: **Pete was *reluctant* to skip dinner.**

rem·e·dy [rem´ə·dē] *n.* **rem·e·dies** Something that heals: **There are many home *remedies* for the common cold.**

res·cue [res´kyōō] *v.* To save from danger.

re·sem·ble [ri·zem´bəl] *v.* To look like.

re·side [ri·zīd´] *v.* To live somewhere.

rhythm [rith´əm] *n.* A sensing of the beat of music: **The group danced with *rhythm* and expression.**

rip·ple [rip´əl] *v.* **rip·pled** To move like small waves of water: **The curtains *rippled* in the gentle wind.**

ro·dent [rōd´(ə)nt] *n.* **ro·dents** Animals such as mice and rats.

ro·de·o [rō´dē·ō or rō·dā´ō] *n.* A contest in which people show off their skills in handling cattle and horses.

rus·tle [rus´(ə)l] *n.* A whispery noise of something moving.

sat·is·fy [sat´is·fī] *v.* **sat·is·fied** To free from doubt or worry: **John's parents were *satisfied* he had done the best he could.** *syn.* convince

scen·er·y [sē´nə·rē] *n.* Stage backgrounds that show different places in a play.

scrub·land [skrub´ land] *n.* Poor land covered with low trees and bushes.

sculpt [skulpt] *v.* **sculpt·ed** To carve and shape: **Mickey *sculpted* a face in the soft wood.** *syn.* form

seg·re·ga·tion [seg´rə·gā´shən] *n.* The condition of being placed apart from others: **Because of *segregation*, blacks and whites couldn't go to the same schools.**

sen·ti·nel [sen´tə·nəl] *n.* A person who watches and guards.

set·tler [set´ lər] *n.* **set·tlers** A pioneer who moves to a new place to live.

si·lo [sī´ lō] *n.* **si·los** A tower in which things are stored.

rescue

a	add	o͝o	took
ā	ace	o͞o	pool
â	care	u	up
ä	palm	û	burn
e	end	yo͞o	fuse
ē	equal	oi	oil
i	it	ou	pout
ī	ice	ng	ring
o	odd	th	thin
ō	open	t͟h	this
ô	order	zh	vision

ə = { a in *above*
e in *sicken*
i in *possible*
o in *melon*
u in *circus*

skillet

skillet

smolder This word is related to the English word *smell*. They both come from the old word *smel* or *smol*. At first this word was used to mean "a bad smell" or "a smoky smell."

skil·let [skil′it] *n.* **skil·lets** A shallow pan usually used for frying.

smol·der·ing [smōl′dər·ing] *adj.* Burning without flame: **A *smoldering* log started a fire.**

splen·did [splen′did] *adj.* Very beautiful and wonderful.

stalk [stôk] *v.* **stalks** To follow quietly and secretly and sneak up on.

stim·u·late [stim′yə·lāt′] *v.* **stim·u·lates** To make something work better and faster: **Exercise *stimulates* the muscles.**

stir·rup [stûr′əp or stir′əp] *n.* **stir·rups** The loop at the end of a strap on each side of a saddle, for the rider's foot.

strad·dle [strad′(ə)l] *v.* To put one leg on each side of.

stun [stun] *v.* **stunned** To shock; to surprise: **The students were *stunned* when a small bird suddenly flew into the room.**

suc·ceed [sək·sēd′] *v.* To finish what is planned: **I know that you will *succeed*, because you have studied hard.**

suf·fo·cate [suf′ə·kāt′] *v.* To die from not being able to breathe.

su·per·vise [sōō′pər·vīz′] *v.* To watch over what other people are doing: **My mom wants to *supervise* the movers when they move our piano.**

sup·ply [sə·plī′] *v.* To give what is needed: **The camping guides will *supply* us with tents and packs.**

sur·round·ings [sə·roun′dingz] *n.* The place and conditions that are around something.

sur·vi·val [sər·vī′vəl] *n.* The act of staying alive.

T

tal·ent [tal′ənt] *n.* Something someone can do well.

tech·nique [tek·nēk′] *n.* A special way to do something.

tem·po [tem′pō] *n.* The speed of the beat: **The sad song was played at a slow *tempo*.**

tra·di·tion·al [trə·dish′ən·əl] *adj.* Matching the way a people have done things for a long time: **At Thanksgiving, the *traditional* meat is turkey.**

trance [trans] *n.* A thoughtful or dreamlike state, such as being half awake and half asleep.

trans·la·tion [trans·lā´shən] *n.* A version in another language.

U

u·ten·sil [yoo·ten´səl] *n.* **u·ten·sils** A tool.

V

vic·tim [vik´tim] *n.* A person who has been hurt.

vol·un·teer [vol´ən·tir´] *n.* **vol·un·teers** A person who freely gives his or her time to do something.

W

wan·der [won´dər] *v.* **wan·der·ing** To travel around with no goal: **There was nothing to do, so we went *wandering* through the stores.**

wa·ver [wā´vər] *v.* **wa·ver·ing** To move unsurely back and forth, with poor balance: **Peggy was *wavering* at the edge of the dock, and we were afraid she would fall into the lake.**

whin·ny [(h)win´ē] *v.* **whin·nies** A gentle noise that a horse makes: **My horse *whinnies* softly when I pet her.**

won·drous [wun´drəs] *adj.* Marvelous: **The play they saw was *wondrous*.** *syn.* excellent

Y

yield [yēld] *n.* Product; result: **Although they worked for two weeks, the *yield* was less than a handful of gold.**

utensil

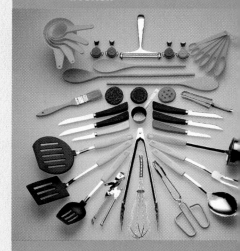

trance From Latin and Old French comes the word *transire*, which means "to go across from life to death." People in *trances* are alive, yet they seem "dead to the world," somewhere between being asleep and being awake.

a	add	o͝o	took
ā	ace	o͞o	pool
â	care	u	up
ä	palm	û	burn
e	end	yo͞o	fuse
ē	equal	oi	oil
i	it	ou	pout
ī	ice	ng	ring
o	odd	th	thin
ō	open	t͟h	this
ô	order	zh	vision

ə = {
a in *above*
e in *sicken*
i in *possible*
o in *melon*
u in *circus*

605

INDEX OF
Titles and Authors

Page numbers in color refer to biographical information.

Printed in the United States of America

Acknowledgments

For permission to reprint copyrighted material, grateful acknowledgment is made to the following sources:

Harry N. Abrams, Inc., New York: "The Ages Flow" by Ikenaga Eri and "Open" by Chikaoka Saori from *Festival in My Heart: Poems by Japanese Children*, selected and translated from the Japanese by Bruno Navasky. Published by Harry N. Abrams, Inc., 1993.

Atheneum Books for Young Readers, an imprint of Simon & Schuster: The Gold Coin by Alma Flor Ada, illustrated by Neil Waldman. Text copyright © 1991 by Alma Flor Ada; illustrations copyright © 1991 by Neil Waldman. Cover illustration by Nancy Oleksa from *The Chickenhouse House* by Ellen Howard. Illustration copyright © 1991 by Nancy Oleksa.

Bantam Doubleday Dell Books for Young Readers, a division of Bantam Doubleday Dell Publishing Group, Inc., New York: Cover illustration by Rick Mujica from *Felita* by Nicholasa Mohr. Illustration copyright © 1990 by Rick Mujica. Cover illustration from *Mop, Moondance, and the Nagasaki Knights* by Walter Dean Myers. Copyright © 1992 by Walter Dean Myers. From *The Skirt* by Gary Soto, cover illustration by Eric Velasquez. Text copyright © 1992 by Gary Soto.

Boyds Mills Press: Cover illustration by Gary Undercuffler from *The Violin Man* by Maureen Brett Hooper. Illustration copyright © 1991 by Boyds Mills Press.

Gwendolyn Brooks: "Computer" from *Very Young Poets* by Gwendolyn Brooks. Text copyright © 1991 by Gwendolyn Brooks. Published by Third World Press, Chicago.

Curtis Brown Ltd.: "All Kinds of Grands" by Lucille Clifton from *Poems for Grandmothers*, selected by Myra Cohn Livingston. Text copyright © 1990 by Lucille Clifton. "Mechanical Menagerie" from *One Winter Night in August and Other Nonsense Jingles* by X. J. Kennedy. Text copyright © 1975 by X. J. Kennedy.

Carolrhoda Books, Inc., Minneapolis, MN: Cover illustration by Amy Johnson from *What Are You Figuring Now? A Story about Benjamin Banneker* by Jeri Ferris. Illustration copyright © 1988 by Carolrhoda Books, Inc. Cover illustration by Lydia M. Anderson from *Mr. Blue Jeans: A Story about Levi Strauss* by Maryann N. Weidt. Illustration copyright © 1990 by Carolrhoda Books, Inc.

Children's Better Health Institute, Indianapolis, IN: "A Girl with the Write Stuff" from *U.S. Kids, A Weekly Reader* Magazine, March 1993. Text copyright © 1993 by Children's Better Health Institute, Benjamin Franklin Literary & Medical Society, Inc.

Children's Book Press, San Francisco, CA: Cover illustration by Fernando Olivera from *The Woman Who Outshone the Sun* by Rosalma Zubizarreta, Harriet Rohmer, and David Schecter. Illustration copyright © 1991 by Fernando Olivera.

Children's Press, Inc: From *Extraordinary Black Americans* by Susan Altman. Text copyright © 1989 by Regensteiner Publishing Enterprises, Inc.

Clarion Books, a Houghton Mifflin Company imprint: Mandy Sue Day by Roberta Karim, illustrated by Karen Ritz. Text copyright © 1994 by Roberta Karim; illustrations copyright © 1994 by Karen Ritz. Cover illustration from *June 29, 1999* by David Wiesner. Copyright © 1992 by David Wiesner.

Cobblehill Books, an affiliate of Dutton Children's Books, a division of Penguin Books USA Inc.: Cover illustration by Leslie W. Bowman from *The Canada Geese Quilt* by Natalie Kinsey-Warnock. Illustration copyright © 1989 by Leslie W. Bowman. *Hugger to the Rescue* by Dorothy Hinshaw Patent, photographs by William Muñoz. Text copyright © 1994 by Dorothy Hinshaw Patent; photographs copyright © 1994 by William Muñoz.

Cobblestone Publishing, Inc., 7 School St., Peterborough, NH 03458: "Time on the Road" by Vicki Burton from *Cobblestone: The National Road*, June 1991. Text © 1991 by Cobblestone Publishing, Inc.

Crown Publishers, Inc.: Hiding Out: Camouflage in the Wild by James Martin, photographs by Art Wolfe. Text copyright © 1993 by James Martin; photographs copyright © 1993 by Art Wolfe. Cover photograph by Art Wolfe from *Chameleons: Dragons in the Trees* by James Martin. Photograph copyright © 1991 by Art Wolfe.

Dell Books, a division of Bantam Doubleday Dell Publishing Group, Inc.: From *The Story of Annie Sullivan* by Bernice Selden. Text copyright © 1987 by Parachute Press.

Dial Books for Young Readers, a division of Penguin Books USA Inc.: "I am the creativity" by Alexis De Veaux, illustrated by Tom Feelings from *Soul Looks Back In Wonder* by Tom Feelings. Text copyright © 1993 by Alexis De Veaux; illustrations copyright © 1993 by Tom Feelings. From *Felita* by Nicholasa Mohr. Text copyright © 1979 by Nicholasa Mohr.

Dillon Press, an imprint of Silver Burdett Press, Simon & Schuster Elementary: Cover illustration from *Pure Gold: Kristi Yamaguchi* by Jeff Savage. Copyright ©1993 by Jeff Savage.

Gallimard Jeunesse: Cover illustration from *Paint and Painting*. Copyright © 1993 by Éditions Gallimard Jeunesse; English translation copyright © by Scholastic Inc.

Greenwillow Books, a division of William Morrow & Company, Inc.: "Michael Built a Bicycle" from *The New Kid on the Block* by Jack Prelutsky. Text copyright © 1984 by Jack Prelutsky.

Hampton-Brown Books: "Teachers" from *A Chorus of Cultures: Developing Literacy Through Multicultural Poetry* by Alma Flor Ada, Violet J. Harris, and Lee Bennett Hopkins. Text copyright © 1993 by Hampton-Brown Books.

Harcourt Brace & Company: The Nightingale by Hans Christian Andersen, adaptation and illustrations by Demi. Copyright © 1985 by Demi. Cover photograph by Richard Hewett from *A Guide Dog Puppy Grows Up* by Caroline Arnold. Photograph copyright © 1991 by Richard Hewett. *A River Ran Wild* by Lynne Cherry. Copyright © 1992 by Lynne Cherry. *The Great Kapok Tree: A Tale of the Amazon Rain Forest* by Lynne Cherry. Copyright © 1990 by Lynne Cherry. Cover illustration from *The Dragon and the Unicorn* by Lynne Cherry. Copyright © 1995 by Lynne Cherry. *Teammates* by Peter Golenbock, illustrated by Paul Bacon. Text copyright © 1990 by Golenbock Communications, Inc.; illustrations copyright © 1990 by Paul Bacon. *Bonesy and Isabel* by Michael J. Rosen, illustrated by James Ransome. Text copyright © 1995 by Michael J. Rosen; illustrations copyright © 1995 by James E. Ransome. From "The People, Yes" by Carl Sandburg. Text copyright 1936 by Harcourt Brace & Company, renewed 1964 by Carl Sandburg. Cover illustration by Catherine Deeter from *Finding the Green Stone* by Alice Walker. Illustration copyright © 1991 by Catherine Deeter.

HarperCollins Publishers: "We Have Our Moments" from *Sports Pages* by Arnold Adoff. Text copyright © 1986 by Arnold Adoff. "Moving to Salem" from *Long Ago in Oregon* by Claudia Lewis. Text copyright © 1987 by Claudia Lewis. "The Young Rooster" and cover illustration from *Fables* by Arnold Lobel. Copyright © 1980 by Arnold Lobel. From *Be Kind to Your Mother (Earth)* in *Be Kind to Your Mother (Earth) and Blame It on the Wolf: Two Original Plays* by Douglas Love. Text and cover illustration copyright © 1993 by Douglas Love. Cover illustration by Vladimir Vagin from *The King's Equal* by Katherine Paterson. Illustration copyright © 1992 by Vladimir Vagin. From *Pioneers: A Library of Congress Book* by Martin W. Sandler. Text copyright © 1994 by Eagle Productions, Inc. *Sierra* by Diane Siebert, illustrated by Wendell Minor. Text copyright © 1991 by Diane Siebert; illustrations copyright © 1991 by Wendell Minor. Cover illustration by Pat Cummings from *Stealing Home* by Mary Stolz. Illustration copyright © 1992 by Pat Cummings. Cover illustration by Garth Williams from *Charlotte's Web* by E. B. White. Copyright 1952 by E. B. White; illustration copyright renewed © 1980 by Garth Williams. From *Little House on the Prairie* by Laura Ingalls Wilder, illustrated by Garth Williams. Text copyright 1935 by Laura Ingalls Wilder, text copyright renewed © 1963, 1991 by Roger Lea MacBride; illustrations copyright 1953 by Garth Williams, illustrations copyright renewed © 1981 by Garth Williams. "Little House"® is a registered trademark of HarperCollins Publishers, Inc.

Ruth Heller: "Jellies" by Ruth Heller. Copyright © 1993 by Ruth Heller Trust of 1987.

Holiday House, Inc.: From *Pueblo Storyteller* by Diane Hoyt-Goldsmith, photographs by Lawrence Migdale. Text copyright © 1991 by Diane Hoyt-Goldsmith; photographs copyright © 1991 by Lawrence Migdale. Cover photograph by Lawrence Migdale from *Totem Pole* by Diane Hoyt-Goldsmith. Photograph copyright © 1990 by Lawrence Migdale.

Houghton Mifflin Company: Cover illustration from *Just a Dream* by Chris Van Allsburg. Copyright © 1990 by Chris Van Allsburg.

Hyperion Books for Children: From *Alvin Ailey* by Andrea Davis Pinkney, illustrated by Brian Pinkney. Text © 1993 by Andrea Davis Pinkney; illustrations © 1993 by Brian Pinkney.

Lee & Low Books, Inc.: Cover illustration by Cornelius Van Wright and Ying-Hwa Hu from *Zora Hurston and the Chinaberry Tree* by William Miller. Illustration copyright © 1994 by Cornelius Van Wright and Ying-Hwa Hu.

Libraries Unlimited, Inc. (800-237-6124): "Why Birds Are Never Hungry" and cover photograph from *Folk Songs of the Hmong* by Norma J. Livo and Dia Cha. Text and cover photograph copyright © 1991 by Libraries Unlimited, Inc.

Little, Brown and Company: From *By the Great Horn Spoon!* by Sid Fleischman. Text and cover illustration copyright © 1963 by Sid Fleischman, Inc.; renewed © by Sid Fleischman, Inc.

Lothrop, Lee & Shepard Books, a division of William Morrow & Company, Inc.: From *Justin and the Best Biscuits in the World* by Mildred Pitts Walter, cover illustration by Catherine Stock. Text copyright © 1986 by Mildred Pitts Walter; cover illustration © 1986 by Catherine Stock.

Macmillan Publishing Company: Cover illustration by Diane deGroat from *Jace the Ace* by Joanne Rocklin. Illustration copyright © 1990 by Diane deGroat.

Viqui Maggio: Cover illustration by Viqui Maggio from *Ellis Island* by William Jay Jacobs. Illustration copyright © 1990 by Viqui Maggio.

The Millbrook Press, Inc.: Cover photograph courtesy of the Miami *Herald* from *Marjory Stoneman Douglas: Friend of the Everglades* by Tricia Andryszewski.

Morrow Junior Books, a division of William Morrow and Company, Inc.: Cover illustration by Mark Graham from *A Llama in the Family* by Johanna Hurwitz. Illustration copyright © 1994 by Mark Graham. Cover illustration by Sheila Hamanaka from *Class President* by Johanna Hurwitz. Illustration copyright © 1990 by Sheila Hamanaka. "The Case of the Painting Contest" from *Encyclopedia Brown and the Case of the Treasure Hunt* by Donald J. Sobol. Text copyright © 1988 by Donald J. Sobol; cover illustration copyright © 1988 by Gail Owens.

Philomel Books: Cover illustration by Mike Wimmer from *Flight: The Journey of Charles Lindbergh* by Robert Burleigh. Illustration copyright © 1991 by Mike Wimmer.

G. P. Putnam's Sons: Mirette on the High Wire by Emily Arnold McCully. Copyright © 1992 by Emily Arnold McCully.

Scholastic Inc.: Jaguarundi by Virginia Hamilton, illustrated by Floyd Cooper. Text copyright © 1995 by Virginia Hamilton; illustrations copyright © 1995 by Floyd Cooper. From *A Young Painter: The Life and Paintings of Wang Yani-China's Extraordinary Young Artist* by Zheng Zhensun and Alice Low. Text copyright © 1991 by New China Pictures Company and Byron Preiss Visual Communications Inc. Cover illustration from *Scholastic Encyclopedia of Transportation*. Copyright © 1995 by Scholastic Inc.

Sierra Club Books for Children: Cover photograph by Sidnee Wheelwright from *Come Back, Salmon* by Molly Cone. Photograph © by Sidnee Wheelwright.

Simon & Schuster Books for Young Readers, a division of Simon & Schuster: The Almond Orchard by Laura Jane Coats. Copyright © 1991 by Laura Jane Coats.

Gareth Stevens Publishing, Milwaukee, WI: Cover photograph by Simon Shepheard/IMPACT photos from *Garbage and Recycling* by Judith Woodburn. Photo © by Simon Shepheard/IMPACT Photos.

Carmen Tafolla: "Much to Learn" from *A Chorus of Cultures* by Alma Flor Ada, Violet J. Harris, and Lee Bennett Hopkins. Text © by Carmen Tafolla.

Chris Van Allsburg: Cover illustration by Chris Van Allsburg from *The Big Book for Our Planet*, edited by Ann Durell, Jean Craighead George, and Katherine Paterson. Illustration © 1993 by Chris Van Allsburg.

Viking Penguin, a division of Penguin Books USA Inc.: From *Blue Willow* by Doris Gates. Text copyright 1940 by Doris Gates; text copyright renewed © 1968 by Doris Gates.

Walker and Company, 435 Hudson Street, New York, NY 10014: Cover illustration by Barbara Lavallee from *This Place is Wet* by Vicki Cobb. Illustration copyright © 1989 by Barbara Lavallee.

Franklin Watts, Inc.: From *The California Gold Rush* by Elizabeth Van Steenwyk. Copyright © 1991 by Elizabeth Van Steenwyk.

World Book Publishing: From "Tropical Rain Forest" in *The World Book Encyclopedia*, Volume 19. Text © 1992 by World Book, Inc.

Photo Credits

Key: (t) top, (b) bottom, (c) center, (l) left, (r) right, (bg) background, (i) inset.

R. Mastrioanni/Black Star/Harcourt Brace & Company, 39; John Lei/OPC, 70, 108(l), 109, 326, 376, 420(t), 435; UPI/Mettmann, 80; Brown Brothers, 81-82; Michael Greenlar/Black Star/Harcourt Brace & Company, 107; Picture Perfect USA, 108(r); William Muñoz, 142-159; Courtesy of Erich Lessing/Art Resource, 160-161; David Herman/Devaney Stock Photo, 162-163; National Baseball Library, 186-187(i), 206; Joe Devenney/The Image Bank, 186-187, 206(i); Courtesy of Herb Ross, 186-187(bg), 203, 207(l); AP/Wide World Photos. 207(r); Patricia J. Wynne/National Geographic Society, 235; Jeff Rycus/Black Star/Harcourt Brace & Company, 261; Norbert Wu/Masterfile, 262(l); Loren McIntyre/Woodfin Camp & Associates, 262(r); Gregory Dimijian/Photo Researchers, 263; Art Wolfe, 268-287; Robert Siebert, 301; Library of Congress, 31-321, 324-325; Bo Zaunders/The Stock Market, 326-331(bg); H. D. Thoreau/WestLight, 370-371; Lois Gervais/WestLight, 372-373; Courtesy of Alma Flor Ada, 397; Dale Higgins/Harcourt Brace & Company, 417; Stock Montage, 420(b/l), 421(t/l), 421(b); The Walker Collection of A'Lelia Bundels, 421(t/r); Minnesoata Historical Society, 420(b/r); M. Angelo/WestLight, 420-433, 438-439; 571; Zheng Zhensun, 522-537; Tom Sobolik/Black Star/Harcourt Brace & Company, 519, 589; Courtesy of Scholastic, 535; The Museum of Modern Art, New York/The Estate of Pablo Picasso/Artists Rights Society (ARS), NY, 545; Lawrence Migdale, 548-563

Illustration Credits

Francis Livingston, Cover Art; Kristen Funkhouser, 4-5; Terry Widener, 6-7; Dale Varzaal, 8-9; Martha Ann Booth, 10-11; Heidi Younger, 12-13; Jose Ortega, 14-15; Kristen Funkhouser, 17-21; Karen Ritz, 22-38,42-43; William Low, 40-41; Byron Gin, 44-69, 72; Robert Steele, 70-71; Arnold Lobel, 74-76; Winslow Homer, 78-79; Emily Arnold McCully, 84-107, 110-111; Terry Widener, 113-117, 208; James Ransome, 118-141, Sofonisba Anguissola, 160-161, Mike Reed, 162-185; Paul Bacon, 186-203, 206-207; Don Mahoney, 204-205; Dale Varzaal, 209-213, 304; Lynne Cherry, 214-231, 234-235; Patricia Wynne, 232-233; Margaret Cusack, 236-237; Floyd Cooper, 238-261, 264-265; Gabriele Munter, 266-267; Martha Ann Booth, 305-309, 400; Al Van Nil, 322-323; Garth Williams, 326-331; Jacqui Morgan, 332-347; William Henry Jackson, 348-349, Historical Pictures Services, 351-352, 355, 357, 365; The Bettmann Archive, 359, 361-363; Museum of the City of New York, 364; Gary Head, 366-375; Niel Waldman, 376-399; Heidi Younger, 401-405, 496; Laura Jane Coats, 406-419; Colin Bootman, 420-433, 438-439; Daniel Moreton, 434; Dave Joly, 436-437; Mark Reidy 440-441; Jacob Lawrence, 442-443; Lynne Cherry, 444-471; Obadinah Heavner, 472-491, 494-495; Ruth Heller, 492-493; Jose Ortega, 495-501, 592; Demi, 502-521, Wang Yani, 522-537; Mary Beth Schwark, 538-543; Pablo Picasso, 545; Donna Perrone, 548-563; Jennifer Bolton, 564-571, 574-575; Tom Feelings, 572-573; Brian Pinkney, 576-591; Mark Reidy, 1-2; Mary Beth Schwark, 1-6; Jose Ortega, 2-3, 497-501, 592; Lambert Davis, 4-5, 7, 18-21, 112; Terry Widener, 6-7, 113-117, 208; Dale Verzaal, 8-9, 209-213, 304; Martha Ann Booth, 10-11, 305-400; Tracy Sabin, 12-13, 401-405, 496; William Low, 40-41; Byron Gin, 42-67; Donna Perrone, 55, 548-561; Robert Steele, 70-71; Mike Reed, 150-171, Ron Mahoney, 204-205; Margaret Cusack, 256-257; Al Van Nil, 322-323; Jacqui Morgan, 332-345; Gary Head, 366-375; Colin Bootman, 420-421, 423, 425, 427, 429, 430, 432; Daniel Moreton, 434-435; Dave Joly, 436-437; Obadinah Heavner, 472-491; Jennifer Bolton, 564-571